MW01028129

# Banking
## *on the*
# People

DEMOCRATIZING MONEY
IN THE DIGITAL AGE

**ELLEN BROWN**

DEMOCRACY
COLLABORATIVE

*Banking on the People: Democratizing Money in the Digital Age*
©2019 Ellen Brown & The Democracy Collaborative

ISBN: 978-09-984719-1-4

Published by The Democracy Collaborative
The Ring Building
1200 18th Street NW
Suite 1225
Washington, D.C. 20036
www.democracycollaborative.org
www.thenextsystem.org

Interior typography by Kate Khatib / Owl Grammar Press.
Typeset in Adobe Caslon Pro, and Gotham.
Cover graphics by Bob Lanphear
Printed by LightningSource.

# CONTENTS

## INTRODUCTION
## AN AUSPICIOUS TIME FOR A BANKING REVOLUTION

*"All experience has shown that mankind is more disposed to suffer—while evils are sufferable—than to right themselves by abolishing the forms to which they are accustomed."*
—*American Declaration of Independence*

**So wrote Thomas Jefferson in 1776,** but the evils to which we are accustomed may no longer be sufferable. The "wealth gap" has gotten so wide that six men now own as much wealth as half the global population.[1] The US government is $22 trillion in debt and governments globally are nearly $250 trillion in debt. Households and businesses also have higher total debt than ever before. The banking crises of 2008-09 wiped out over $19 trillion in household wealth, turned some 10 million families out of their homes, and cost almost 9 million jobs in the United States alone.[2] Yet the culpable banks got off scot-free, bailed out at the expense of local economies and the people, who paid for it with cuts in government spending, lost jobs and lost homes.

Ever-widening inequality followed, along with the Occupy Wall Street movement and an increasing popular distrust of both big banks and governments. Public sentiment in the United States has turned against not just Wall Street but the Federal Reserve (the "Fed"), with calls to audit it and to end its decades-long independence from government oversight and control. At the other extreme, "crypto-anarchists" are promoting the use of private cryptocurrencies that would bypass governments and banks altogether.

We are living in revolutionary times, with voters rejecting business as usual in favor of the wrecking ball. The surprise 2016 Brexit referendum, in which UK voters rejected EU membership, was followed by the surprise election of Donald Trump, in which US voters rejected establishment politics. Brexit was followed by threats of Frexit (France), Italexit (Italy), and Catalonia's attempted secession from Spain. As the European Union threatens to break apart, Asia is consolidating through its massive Belt and Road Initiative and is attempting to dethrone the dollar. It is out with the old and in with the new everywhere. The time is ripe for change.

All of which makes this an auspicious time for a revolution against an international banking oligopoly that has long held the world captive. Bankers are the gatekeepers controlling who gets credit and on what terms, extracting massive profits that they can invest for their own speculative purposes, while people and governments are crippled by debts they cannot possibly repay. Fixing the banking problem requires more than regulation that merely tweaks an obsolete system. We need a radical overhaul of the monetary system itself, and that means rethinking what money is and how it enters the economy. We went off the gold standard nearly a century ago, yet we still perceive money to be a physical thing that must be dug from the earth or acquired from someone else. In fact, money today is simply credit, as

Benjamin Franklin declared; and credit is abundant, arising with the trade, limited only by the availability of workers and materials to supply the demand.

We need a new economic model, one designed to elicit the abundance of which the economy is capable. Implementing that sort of systemic change is not as radical as it sounds. Money is just a contractual agreement among participating community members, and in the United States that contract has been changed every 20 or 30 years going back to colonial times. Those changes are detailed in the Appendix, which contains a summary of America's trial-and-error monetary evolution drawn from my earlier books *Web of Debt* and *The Public Bank Solution* along with a glossary of unfamiliar terms.

Over the course of three centuries, US money has evolved from government-issued scrip in the American colonies to government-minted coins when the colonies became a nation, to nearly all privately issued money today. Dissatisfaction with an extractive and outdated banking system, along with revolutionary developments in software technology, have prompted a wave of proposals for redesigning the monetary system and the currencies it uses. Some pundits talk of a "currency reset" after an anticipated dollar crash. What would replace the dollar? Bitcoin? The Chinese yuan? Gold and silver coins? An assortment of national central bank digital currencies, or local community currencies, or cryptocurrencies? The time is ripe with possibilities.

Part I of this book looks at where we are now: how our banking system really works, the inherent contradictions in the model, and why regulation has not worked to fix them. Part II explores some new developments and proposes a model that bypasses exploitation for private profit, turning banking into a public utility that serves the people and the economy.

*Ellen Brown*
*Los Angeles, California*
*February 2019*

# PART I
# MODERN BANKING: HOW IT WORKS, WHY IT HAS FAILED, AND WHY REGULATION HASN'T FIXED IT

*"We are completely dependent on the commercial banks. Someone has to borrow every dollar we have in circulation, cash or credit. If the banks create ample synthetic money we are prosperous; if not, we starve."*

—**Robert Hemphill, Credit Manager of the Federal Reserve Bank of Atlanta, 1934**[3]

# CHAPTER 1
## THE END OF THE DEBT-GROWTH MODEL

*"Anyone who believes exponential growth can go on forever in a
finite world is either a madman or an economist."*
—*Attributed to American economist Kenneth E Boulding*

**"We really didn't see that coming,"** said Federal
Reserve Chair Janet Yellen in 2016 of the banking collapse
that proved to be the most devastating economic crisis of
our era.[4] Her predecessors Ben Bernanke and Alan Greenspan acknowledged the same thing.[5] These highly creden-
tialed economists sat at the apex of the international banking
pyramid and had a mandate to provide the nation with a safe
and stable monetary system. How could they not see the on-
coming steamroller that would collapse the global economy
and turn 10 million American families out of their homes?

The answer seems to be that they were looking in the
wrong place, working from an obsolete model. The traditional banking system was carefully circumscribed with regulations; but the collapse was not in the traditional banking
system. It was in the shadow banking system, where derivatives, repos and securitized financial products hide behind
a curtain of obscurity. "Shadow banks" are financial intermediaries that facilitate the creation of credit without being

subjected to regulatory oversight.[6] This unregulated system is highly unstable and vulnerable to bank runs, creating phantom credit that can be vacuumed up as quickly as it is created. The run on the shadow banks in September 2008 forced massive asset sales at fire sale prices, shrinking the value of assets on the balance sheets of banks, resulting in their technical insolvency. Credit shrank across markets globally, causing the system to collapse in domino fashion.

The Dodd-Frank Wall Street Reform and Consumer Protection Act of 2010 was one of the largest, most complicated, and most regulatorily burdensome pieces of legislation ever implemented. Yet it too did little to rein in the shadow banking system. The problem is that commercial banks need the shadow banks' dark pools of liquidity to stay afloat. They are where the rabbits are hidden that banks pull out of their hats when depositors and borrowers come for their money at the same time. But the rabbits are skittish and will run at the first sign of trouble. We need a new source of liquidity (cash-like liquid assets), one that can be relied on to be there on demand.

The conventional economic model overlooks not only the shadow banks but the banking alchemy that makes them necessary. It assumes that banks are merely intermediaries, taking in the money of depositors and lending it out again. But banks *create* deposits when they make loans, as detailed in Chapter 3. Through the accepted practice of double-entry bookkeeping, banks turn our promises to pay into new money in the form of deposits that did not exist before; and the biggest banks create most of this debt-turned-money. The shadow banks then provide the liquidity needed to balance the banks' books.

Money created as credit by banks is not actually a bad system. What the banks are really doing is guaranteeing the borrowers' own credit, turning it into a form of "money" acceptable in the marketplace. But the banks are privately owned and controlled, mandated to serve shareholder profits rather than the broader economy. They are not transparent or accountable to the public. They can speculate and take disruptive risks that can threaten economic stability, while bypassing local businesses and socially beneficial investments.

The bankers' private privilege of creating the national money supply is also a major factor in the widening gap between rich and poor. According to a January 2017 report by the New Economics Foundation titled "Making Money from Money," 73 percent of the burgeoning profits of banks arise from the unique right to create money on their books.[7] The result is a government-supported monopoly that drains resources from the productive economy and gives a megalithic international banking empire enormous power over people and governments.

## Marching to the Drums of Wall Street

Much of the problem with the current system can be traced to the US Federal Reserve. Ever since the 1970s, the Fed and other central banks have declared their independence from political control; but independence has really come to mean a central bank that has been captured by very large banking interests. The Fed might be independent of oversight by politicians, but it is not a neutral arbiter. This has not always been the case. According to Timothy Canova, Professor of Law and Public Finance at Nova Southeastern University, during the Great Depression and coming out of it the Fed as a practical matter was not independent but took its marching orders from the White House and the Treasury; and that decade, he says, was the most successful in American economic history.[8]

Today, however, Wall Street largely calls the shots. Commercial banks actually own the stock of the twelve Federal Reserve Banks, which are organized as private corporations. This stock does not carry the control given to holders of common stock in for-profit organizations and may not be sold or pledged as collateral, but it does pay a yearly dividend and carries voting rights. Member banks appoint six of the nine members of each Bank's board of directors and have a vote in the election of the Reserve Bank presidents.[9]

These privately elected presidents, in turn, serve on the Federal Open Market Committee (FOMC), which sets national monetary policy. The FOMC includes the seven-member Federal Reserve Board of Governors, the president of the New York Fed, and four other Reserve Bank presidents on a rotating basis. As of October 2018, three positions on the Federal Reserve Board were vacant, leaving the Reserve Bank presidents in majority control of the FOMC's policy decisions. (One position was filled on a temporary basis in late November.) The FOMC's decisions have major implications for the public, yet the public is completely shut out of the process of choosing the decision-makers.[10]

The Federal Reserve Board in Washington, D.C. is appointed by the president and is considered "federal," including being subject to Freedom of Information Act requests as are other federal agencies. But the regional Federal Reserve Banks claim exemption from the Act as private institutions. Their daily operations and transactions are thus largely shielded from good faith disclosure and public oversight. Unlike for other agencies, the Fed's Inspector General is not independent but is an appointee of the Federal Reserve Chair, and the Government Accountability Office is prohibited from reviewing many important aspects of the Fed's work.[11]

In 2008, under the leadership of the New York Federal Reserve Bank, the central bank pursued interventions that blatantly benefited the very institutions it was charged with regulating, at the expense of the public it should have been serving. The financial crisis highlighted the failure of US regulatory bodies, and in particular of the regional New York Federal Reserve Bank, to identify systemic risk and to properly supervise the banks; and the unprecedented use of emergency lending to bail out failing Wall Street banks raised serious concerns about transparency and pervasive conflicts of interest. Many regional Fed board members were affiliated with banks and companies that received a combined $4 trillion in emergency low-interest loans from the Federal Reserve during the financial crisis. The banks recovered, but many Americans are still struggling 10 years later.[12]

## Faith-based Monetary Policy

Corruption shielded from public oversight is one problem; faulty economic models are another. The FOMC sets monetary policy based on the controversial "Phillips curve," an obsolete economic model purporting to demonstrate that as the economy nears full employment, prices rise. The Phillips curve has been shown to be virtually useless in predicting inflation, as Janet Yellen has admitted and the Fed's own data shows.[13] Minneapolis Fed President Neel Kashkari calls the continued reliance on the Phillips curve "faith-based" monetary policy.[14] But monetary policy is controlled by the secretive, Wall Street-dominated FOMC, which has evidently ignored those concerns.

The Federal Reserve must balance two statutory mandates that are said to be in conflict: it must maintain price stability while at the same time promoting maximum employment.[15] The theory is that when the economy hits full employment, workers will demand higher wages, driving prices up and reducing the value of the currency. "Full employment" in a healthy economy is considered to be 4.7 percent unemployment, taking into account the "natural rate of unemployment" of people between jobs or voluntarily out of work. When unemployment drops below that, alarm bells sound and the Fed jumps into action to tighten the money supply by raising interest rates.

As of April 2018, the official unemployment rate had dropped to a "risky" 4.3 percent, prompting the Fed to take aggressive steps to tighten the money supply. According to official figures, the economy was at full employment; yet neither wages nor consumer prices had shot up. One reason is that in today's globalized economy, cheaper labor is available abroad, so wage earners dare not demand more.[16] The official unemployment figure also ignores the great mass of discouraged unemployed who are no longer looking for work, and it includes people as employed who are working only part-time or well below capacity. It also overlooks the untapped potential of machines, as well as the fact that jobs both skilled and unskilled can readily be outsourced abroad. There is now a glut not only of manual laborers but of college graduates.

In fact, the economy's ability to generate supply in response to demand, keeping prices stable, is far from being at full capacity today, as the trend lines for gross domestic product (GDP) over the last decade show. According to a July 2017 paper from the Roosevelt Institute called "What Recovery? The Case for Continued Expansionary Policy at the Fed":

> GDP remains well below both the long-run trend and the level predicted by forecasters a decade ago. In 2016, real per capita GDP was 10 percent below the Congressional Budget Office's (CBO) 2006 forecast, and shows no signs of returning to the predicted level.[17]

The report showed that the most likely explanation for this lackluster growth was weak demand. Wages have remained stagnant and have not kept up with productivity, so consumers do not have money to spend; and before producers will produce, they need customers knocking on their doors. In 2017, US gross domestic product was $19.4 trillion. If it was 10 percent below capacity, the money circulating in the economy ("demand") would need to be increased by another $2 trillion to generate enough supply to bring the economy to full productive capacity.

The push to shrink the money supply is based on another controversial model, the monetarist dictum that "inflation is always and everywhere a monetary phenomenon"—prices go up from "too much money chasing too few goods." That is called "demand-pull" inflation, and it does happen; but much more common historically is "cost-push" inflation. Prices go up because producers' costs go up, and *a major producer cost is the cost of borrowing money.* In an environment in which consumers are not spending because they are heavily in debt, raising interest rates is more likely to drive consumer prices up than down, by driving producers' costs up. The predictable result will be slowing markets, increasing unemployment, and another Great Recession.

But the Fed obeys hypothetical models, which say it is time to throw cold water on the "irrational exuberance" of the markets. Acting through the FOMC, the Fed has been following the same playbook it followed in the decade leading up to the 2008 crisis, when it created a housing bubble by sharply lowering interest rates, then popped the bubble by sharply raising rates. In an attempt to avoid a recession after the dot. com bubble burst, the Fed lowered the fed funds rate 11 times in 1-½ years, from 6.5 percent in May 2000 to 1.75 percent in December 2001. The resulting flood of cheap money, combined with lax lending standards, then attracted subprime borrowers. Housing prices went up but the Consumer Price Index remained low, emboldening the Fed to slash interest rates to 1 percent by June 2003. Housing prices then shot up; and in June 2004, the Fed began raising interest rates. Two years later, the fed funds rate had reached 5.25 percent. Predictably, home prices fell, and subprime borrowers who could not afford the higher rates began defaulting on their loans.[18]

Defaults of the lenders followed. In September 2008, the Federal National Mortgage Association (Fannie Mae) and the Federal Home Loan Mortgage Corporation (Freddie Mac)—two private corporations that are part of the shadow banking system—were put into conservatorship, effectively nationalizing them. The surprise move was actually a bailout of the financial derivatives industry, avoiding a $1.4 trillion "event of default" that could have bankrupted Wall Street and much of the rest of the financial world.

The same month, the government rescued the financial derivatives industry again when it bailed out American International Group (AIG), an insurance company. When Lehman Brothers went bankrupt in September 2008, the government finally closed the bailout window, and the collapse of the economy followed.

## The Derivatives Time Bomb and "Peak Debt"

Derivatives are not all bad. They have been traded for centuries, originally to protect farmers from the vagaries of the weather and agricultural markets. Derivatives are financial instruments that have no intrinsic value but derive their value from something else. They are sold as "insurance," but they are basically just bets. You can "hedge your bet" that something you own will go up by placing a side bet that it will go down. "Hedge funds" hedge bets in the derivatives market. Bets can be placed on anything, from the price of tea in China to the movements of specific markets. Derivative instruments can be traded either on an exchange or over-the-counter (OTC), with the latter accounting for around 90 percent of derivatives trading.

Derivatives can serve a useful purpose for businesses and governments in the management of various financial risks; but in terms of volume, that sort of legitimate "end-user" risk management is thought to account for no more than 5 percent of all OTC derivatives traded.[19] The rest are just traded for speculation in a giant financial casino. Derivatives have become such a popular form of gambling that the notional value of the global derivatives market has grown to many times the GDP of the world.

The Bank for International Settlements reported that total derivatives trades in 2008 exceeded one quadrillion dollars—that's *1,000 trillion dollars.*[20] How is that figure even possible? The answer is that gamblers can bet as much as they want. They can bet money they don't have, and that is where the huge increase in risk comes in. If losing counterparties can't pay up, players who have hedged their bets by betting both ways cannot collect on their winning bets; and that means they cannot afford to pay their losing bets, causing other players to also default on their bets. The dominos can go down in a cascade of cross-defaults that infects the whole banking industry and jeopardizes the global pyramid scheme. Governments have continually had to prop up the financial economy and its risky derivatives scheme to prevent them from taking down the physical economy. Huge liabilities have been transferred from big banks to governments, plunging them into a debt trap from which escape no longer appears possible as a matter of simple math.

But debt is the business of bankers, and the Fed has dutifully played its role in propping the system back up. Following the collapse of Lehman Brothers, it ran the same script it had run after the dot-com collapse, feverishly trying to breathe life back into the insolvent megabanks by re-creating the debt bubbles that had collapsed and taken the banks down with them. Again the Fed dropped the fed funds rate, this time nearly to zero. At the same time, it generated $3.7 trillion through "quantitative easing" to free up the banks' balance sheets. But the "wealth effect" this was supposed to create created wealth only for the already-rich, leaving Main Street and the businesses on which productivity depends straddled with a debt bubble of unprecedented proportions.

In December 2016, the Fed thought it had revived the system enough to "normalize" interest rates by raising them again. By December 2018 it had raised rates nine times. But the economy has reached what economist Roger Arnold calls "peak debt." Nearly all net future income globally is required to service existing debt, precluding new productivity and GDP growth. Raising rates now will only precipitate a new wave of defaults.[21] The predictable result will be another recession, and this one could be worse than the last, since debt levels are substantially higher everywhere.[22] Since 1950, the Fed has embarked on 13 rate-hiking cycles, and 10 of these have resulted in recessions.[23]

Much of the debt with which the world is encumbered is at variable interest rates. These rates will rise in tandem with either the interbank lending rate or the London Interbank Offered Rate (LIBOR) set by private agreement of the biggest banks. The interest on $3.5 trillion globally is linked to LIBOR, including $1.2 trillion in consumer mortgages.[24] By March 2018, the LIBOR rate had risen to an alarming 2.3 percent, up from just 0.3 percent 2½ years earlier. Raising rates further will not put a lid on prices. It will force prices up. Manufacturers will have to raise their prices to cover their own costs of financing, to pay for labor and materials before their products are sold as well as to build factories, buy equipment and expand. Governments will also have to pay more to borrow, driving taxes up.[25]

The US federal debt has more than doubled since the 2008 financial crisis, shooting up from $9.4 trillion in mid-2008 to over $21 trillion in mid-2018.[26] This debt is never paid off. The government just keeps paying the interest on it, and interest rates are rising. The Fed has announced plans to raise rates by 2020 to "normal" levels—a fed funds target of 3.5 percent—and to *sell* about $1.5 trillion in federal securities at the rate of $50 billion monthly.[27] This will further grow the mountain of federal debt on the market; and unlike the Fed, which rebates the interest to the government after deducting its costs, the new buyers of these securities will be pocketing the interest, adding to the taxpayers' bill.

If the Fed follows through with its plans, projections are that by 2027, US taxpayers will owe *$1 trillion annually just in interest on the federal debt*.[28] That is enough to fund President Donald Trump's trillion-dollar infrastructure plan *every year*, and it is a direct transfer of wealth from the middle class to the wealthy investors holding most of the bonds. Where will this money come from? Crippling taxes, wholesale privatization of public assets, and elimination of social services will not be sufficient to cover the bill.

## The FOMC and the "Power Revolution"

The irony is that the United States does not need to carry a debt to bondholders at all. It has been financially sovereign ever since President Franklin D. Roosevelt took the dollar off the gold standard domestically in 1933. This was recognized by Beardsley Ruml, Chairman of the Federal Reserve Bank of New York, in a 1945 presentation before the American Bar Association titled "Taxes for Revenue Are Obsolete."

"The necessity for government to tax in order to maintain both its independence and its solvency is true for state and local governments," he said, "but it is not true for a national government." The government was now at liberty to spend as needed to meet its budget, drawing on credit issued by its own central bank. It could do this until price inflation indicated a weakened purchasing power of the currency. Then, and only then, would the government need to levy taxes—not to fund the budget but to counteract inflation by contracting the money supply. The principal purpose of taxes, said Ruml, was "the maintenance of a dollar which has stable purchasing power over the years. Sometimes this purpose is stated as 'the avoidance of inflation.'"[29]

The government could be funded without taxes by drawing on credit from its own central bank; and since there was no longer a need for gold to cover the loan, the central bank would not have to borrow. It could just create the money on its books. This insight is a basic tenet of Modern Monetary Theory: the government does not need to borrow or tax, at least until prices shoot up. It can just create the money it needs by writing an overdraft on its account at the Fed.[30]

It could do that in theory, but some laws would need to be changed. Currently the federal government is required to have the money in its account before spending it.[31] After the dollar went off the gold standard in 1933, Congress could have had the Fed just print money and lend it to the government, cutting the banks out. But Wall Street lobbied for an amendment to the Federal Reserve Act, forbidding the Fed to buy bonds directly from the Treasury as it had done in the past.[32]

The Treasury can borrow from itself by transferring money from "intragovernmental accounts"—Social Security and other trust funds that are under the auspices of the Treasury and have a surplus. But these funds do not include the Federal Reserve, which can lend to the government only by buying federal securities from bond dealers. The Fed's website states, "The Federal Reserve's holdings of Treasury securities are categorized as 'held by the public,' because they are not in government accounts," further evidence that the Fed is considered independent of the government.[33]

According to Marriner Eccles, chairman of the Federal Reserve from 1934 to 1948, the prohibition against allowing the government to borrow from its own central bank was written into the Banking Act of 1935 at the behest of the securities dealers. A historical review on the website of the New York Federal Reserve quotes Eccles as stating, "I think the real reasons for writing the prohibition into the [Banking Act] ... can be traced to certain Government bond dealers who quite naturally had their eyes on business that might be lost to them if direct purchasing were permitted."[34]

The government was required to sell bonds through Wall Street middlemen, which the Fed could buy only through "open market operations" conducted by the Open Market Committee. Wright Patman, Chairman of the House Committee on Banking and Currency from 1963 to 1975, called the official sanctioning of the Federal Open Market Committee in the banking laws of 1933 and 1935 "the power revolution"– the transfer of the "money power" to the banks. The FOMC established a mechanism by which money was created through bond sales in what was essentially a rigged market. Patman said, "The 'open market' is in reality a tightly closed market." Only a selected few bond dealers were entitled to bid on the bonds the Treasury made available for auction each week. The practical effect, he said, was to take money from the taxpayer and give it to these dealers.[35]

That massive Wall Street subsidy was the subject of testimony by Eccles to the House Committee on Banking and Currency on March 3-5, 1947. Patman asked Eccles, "Now, since 1935, in order for the Federal Reserve banks to buy Government bonds, they had to go through a middleman, is that correct?" Eccles replied in the affirmative. Patman then launched into a prophetic warning, stating:

> I am opposed to the United States Government, which possesses the sovereign and exclusive privilege of creating money, paying private bankers for the use of its own money. These private bankers do not hire their own money to the Government; they hire only the Government's money to the Government, and collect an interest charge annually.

> ... I insist it is absolutely wrong for this committee to permit this condition to continue and saddle the taxpayers of this Nation with a burden of debt that they will not be able to liquidate in a hundred years or two hundred years. Do you know that we are carrying a million dollars' worth of bonds that were issued during the War between the States and we have paid 4 [dollars] in interest for every 1 dollar that was borrowed? We are still paying on them and still owe them. Do you know that on the Panama Canal convertible 3's, we have already paid more than $50,000,000 in interest and we will soon have paid $75,000,000 in interest and still owe the $50,000,000 principal on those bonds? If you judge the future by the past, the people will be compelled to pay a dollar, $2, and $5 in interest for every $1 they borrow.[36]

The truth of that statement is painfully evident today, when we have a $21 trillion debt that cannot possibly be repaid. The government just keeps rolling it over and paying the interest to banks and bondholders, feeding the "financialized" economy in which money makes money without producing new goods and services. The financialized economy has become a parasite feeding off the real economy, driving producers and workers further and further into debt.

In the 1960s, Patman attempted to have the Fed nationalized. The effort failed, but his committee did succeed in forcing the central bank to rebate its profits to the Treasury after deducting its costs.[37] The prohibition against direct lending by the central bank to the government, however, remains in force. The money power is still with the FOMC and the banks.

Today the debt-growth model has reached its limits, as even the Bank for International Settlements, the "central bankers' bank" in Switzerland, acknowledges. In its June 2016 annual report, the BIS said that debt levels were too high, productivity growth was too low, and the room for policy maneuver was too narrow. "The global economy cannot afford to rely any longer on the debt-fueled growth model that has brought it to the current juncture," the BIS warned.[38] But the solutions it proposed would continue the austerity policies long imposed on countries that cannot pay their debts. It prescribed "prudential, fiscal and, above all, structural policies"—"structural readjustment." That means privatizing public assets, slashing services, and raising taxes, choking off the very productivity needed to pay the nations' debts. That approach has repeatedly been tried and has failed, as witnessed most recently in the devastated economy of Greece.

Meanwhile, according to Minneapolis Fed president Neel Kashkari, financial regulation since 2008 has reduced the chances of another government bailout only modestly, from 84 percent to 67 percent.[39] That means there is still a 67 percent chance of another major systemwide crisis, and this one could be worse than the last.[40] The biggest banks are bigger, local banks are fewer, and global debt levels are higher. The economy has farther to fall. The regulators' models are obsolete, aimed at a form of "old-fashioned banking" that has long since been abandoned. How that simple system evolved into one dependent on complex "financial products" that even regulators have trouble understanding is the subject of the next chapter.

*Takeaway: Federal Reserve policy is made behind closed doors, by bankers and academics chiefly serving the interests of bankers. Asset bubbles are created when money is "loose," followed by busts when the money supply is "tightened," driving up the debt on which banks collect interest and fees. But we have reached "peak debt," and regulation has failed to curb the excesses in the system. We need a new model, one designed to serve the needs of the public and the economy rather than to maximize shareholder profits at their expense.*

## CHAPTER 2

# THE NEW FACE OF BANKING: FROM GEORGE BAILEY'S SAVINGS AND LOAN TO PROPRIETARY TRADING AND DERIVATIVES

*"Regarding the Great Depression. You're right, we did it. We're very sorry ... we won't do it again."*

—*Then-Federal Reserve Governor Ben Bernanke to economist Milton Friedman in a 2002 speech in Friedman's honor[41]*

**Banking isn't what it used to be,** or what most people think it is. The common perception is that bankers recycle the deposits of "savers," providing credit for families, small businesses, corporations, and state and local governments. The classic prototype is the small-town banker played by Jimmy Stewart in the 1946 movie "It's a Wonderful Life." But George Bailey (Stewart) soon discovered that in the early 1930s, lending depositors' money to their neighbors was very risky; and the savings and loan crisis half a century later showed that this model was still very risky despite the banking reforms and protections passed during Roosevelt's New Deal. Progressive attempts to eliminate risk have simply shifted it to an unsuspecting public, hidden behind a curtain of obscurity that is impenetrable not only to consumers but often to the regulators and politicians who make the rules.

The failure of monetary policy to fix a systemically flawed banking model was evident soon after the Federal Reserve was born in 1913. In the "Roaring Twenties," the young central bank triggered a credit bubble with low interest rates, then "took away the punch bowl" by tightening the money supply, a policy it has repeated several times since. Higher interest rates increased margin calls on the over-leveraged stock market, triggering its collapse in 1929.[42] Brokers called in their loans, and gold was withdrawn from the banks in a banking panic. At a 40 percent gold reserve requirement, two dollars withdrawn in gold meant that three dollars in loans had to be called in. But the Fed did not intervene to halt the bleeding, and by 1933 the money supply had shrunk by a third. It stopped only when Roosevelt declared a bank holiday, closed the banks, and took the dollar off the gold standard domestically.[43]

In a Public Broadcasting Service interview in October 2000, economist Milton Friedman blamed the Fed for causing the Great Depression. He said:

> The Federal Reserve System had been established to prevent what actually happened. It was set up to avoid a situation in which you would have to close down banks, in which you would have a banking crisis. And yet, under the Federal Reserve System, you had the worst banking crisis in the history of the United States. There's no other example I can think of, of a government measure which produced so clearly the opposite of the results that were intended.[44]

Then as now, rescuing the banks required radical government intervention. In 1933, the Glass-Steagall Act was passed, separating depository banking from investment banking and authorizing federal insurance on deposits up to $100,000 (now $250,000) through the Federal Deposit Insurance Corporation.

Those interventions stabilized the banking system for several decades; but they were not sufficient to prevent another crisis in the 1980s, when Fed Chairman Paul Volcker raised interest rates to unprecedented levels in an effort to stem inflation.[45] The commercial banks' prime rate (the rate at which banks borrowed) reached 20 percent at a time when the savings and loan associations (S&Ls) were averaging 7.5 percent on long-term mortgage loans. The S&Ls had to pay more to attract depositors or to borrow on the interbank market than they earned, causing huge losses.[46] The crisis was worsened by deregulation of the S&L industry and fraud. Rather than admit to insolvency, some S&Ls, aided by lax regulatory oversight, invested in highly speculative strategies. The result was to substantially increase the S&Ls' economic losses by the time their insolvency was discovered.[47] The underlying problem, however, was a mismatch between variable short-term borrowing rates and fixed long-term mortgage rates. Thirty-year mortgages were being funded with volatile short-term loans.

The industry response to this problem was *securitization*: mortgages were bundled as "securities" and offloaded by selling them to investors. Securitization not only allowed the banks to avoid the risks that came with volatile interest rates but gave them the power to lend again and again.

*Credit derivatives* were also devised, which transferred the risk of default to yet other parties. In congressional hearings in the early 1990s, derivatives trading was challenged as being an illegal form of gambling. But the practice was legitimized by Fed Chairman Alan Greenspan, who not only lent legal and regulatory support to the trade but actively promoted derivatives as a way to improve "risk management." He had worked for the savings and loan industry and had seen the S&Ls get crushed, and he was bent on pushing risk off the banks onto someone else. But the cost was an increase in risk to the financial system as a whole.[48]

Although not all officials agreed, the Clinton administration and Congress decided that regulation of financial services would benefit the economy, and that the derivatives market should be largely unregulated. This position was codified in the Commodities Futures Modernization Act of 2000 and the Gramm-Leach-Bliley Act, also known as the Financial Services Modernization Act of 1999.[49] For depository banks to bet in the derivatives casino, that portion of the Glass-Steagall Act separating depository banking from investment banking had to be repealed, and this was achieved through the Gramm-Leach-Bliley Act.

Turning mortgages into securities and selling them to investors seemed virtually risk-free for the lenders—so risk-free that underwriting standards were dropped. Commentators said wryly that "anyone with a pulse" could get a loan. The result was a massive housing bubble, which crashed after the Fed subsequently raised interest rates. When Lehman Brothers went bankrupt, alarmed investors rejected the banks' mispriced "structured financial products," forcing the banks to keep their bad loans on their books. Many banks then became insolvent. Smaller banks were liquidated or sold to larger banks, while the largest banks were bailed out by the government.

## From Deregulation to Overregulation

A new round of reforms and bank workarounds followed, creating a system in which "old-fashioned banking" was increasingly unprofitable. The result was to drive the biggest banks largely out of that business. They are no longer doing much of what most people think of as banking—taking deposits, issuing checks, and making consumer and small business loans. As observed in a February 2014 article titled "Banks Don't Do Much Banking Anymore—And That's a Serious Problem":

> The "big six" Wall Street mega-banks—Bank of America, JPMorgan Chase, Wells Fargo, and Citi, along with investment banks Goldman Sachs and Morgan Stanley—take deposits these days almost as an afterthought. It gets them into communities (you can view bank branches as little more than building-sized billboards for more profitable financial services), and, more important, it unlocks federal safety net programs like Federal Deposit Insurance Corporation (FDIC) insurance and the "discount window," the Federal Reserve's program of low-interest loans. Mega-banks assert that they actually lose money on small deposits, and while we shouldn't take this claim too seriously, it's clear that deposits are not their primary concern.[50]

A blatant example of banks serving as building-sized billboards for more profitable financial services hit the news in September 2016, when Wells Fargo was fined $185 million for fraudulently generating over 1.5 million accounts just to get the fees.[51] More fines followed as new abuses were discovered.

Propped up with over $20 trillion in government aid, Wall Street has pulled through the banking crisis and is now thriving. However, Main Street businesses and the local governments that depend on them for taxes are struggling to survive. While major corporations can turn to the stock market, small businesses depend on bank loans for working capital and funds to expand; but banks tightened their underwriting of small business loans at the beginning of the recession and have been slow to loosen them.[52]

Local business lending comes largely from local banks; and the number of US banks with assets under $100 million dropped by 90 percent between 1984 and 2018, from about 12,000 to 1,200.[53] This was due in large part to the crushing effect of regulations aimed at "fighting the last war." The regulatory burden imposed by the 2010 Dodd-Frank Act exacerbated the trend toward bank "consolidation" (big banks buying local banks), but the number had already dropped to only 2,625 by 2010. What occurred between those dates was the World Trade Center attack on September 11, 2001. Six weeks later, the 1,100 page Patriot Act was dropped on congressional legislators, who were required to vote on it the next day.[54] The Patriot Act not only expanded the federal government's wiretapping and surveillance powers but outlawed the funding of "terrorism," imposing greater scrutiny on banks and stiff criminal penalties for noncompliance.

Banks must now collect and verify customer-provided information, check names of customers against lists of known or suspected terrorists, determine risk levels posed by customers, and report suspicious persons, organizations and transactions. One small banker complained that banks have been turned into spies secretly reporting to the federal government.[55] If they fail to comply, they can face very expensive enforcement actions, whether or not actual money-laundering crimes are alleged. In 2010, a small New Jersey bank pleaded guilty to conspiracy to violate the Bank Secrecy Act and was fined *$5 million* for failure to file suspicious-activity and cash-transaction reports. The bank was acquired a few months later by another bank. Another small New Jersey bank was ordered to shut down a large international wire transfer business because of deficiencies in monitoring for suspicious transactions. It closed its doors after it was hit with *$8 million* in fines over its inadequate monitoring policies.[56]

Avoiding massive fines requires hiring specialized staff and purchasing anti-laundering software, and the regulatory burden is getting worse. In February 2017, the Financial Crimes Enforcement Network proposed a new rule that would add a new category requiring the flagging of suspicious "cyberevents," requiring institutions to detect and report all kinds of digital mischief, whether directed at a customer's account or at the bank itself. One large bank estimated that the proposed change would cost it an additional $9.6 million every year.[57] Banks have also been hit with increased capital requirements under Basel III, a regulatory framework imposed by the Financial Stability Board housed in the Bank for International Settlements in Switzerland. The result has been to largely eliminate the smaller banks' profit margins.[58] The upshot of all these regulations is that small banks have little recourse but to sell out to the larger banks, which have large compliance departments and can skirt the capital requirements by parking assets in off-balance-sheet vehicles.[59]

Critics have suggested that this bank consolidation was actually the intent of the new rules. In a September

2014 article titled "The FDIC's New Capital Rules and Their Expected Impact on Community Banks," Richard Morris et al. noted that "a full discussion of the rules would resemble an advanced course in calculus," and that the regulators had ignored protests that the rules would have a devastating impact on community banks. The authors suggested that the rules reflected "the new vision of bank regulation—that there should be bigger and fewer banks in the industry."[60]

In a speech in July 2015, House Financial Services Committee Chairman Jeb Hensarling, sponsor of the Financial CHOICE Act downsizing Dodd-Frank, echoed that thought. He said:

> Since the passage of Dodd-Frank, the big banks are bigger and the small banks are fewer. But because Washington can control a handful of big established firms much easier than many small and zealous competitors, this is likely an intended consequence of the Act. Dodd-Frank concentrates greater assets in fewer institutions. It codifies into law 'Too Big to Fail'. ...[61]

A congressional bill passed in May 2018 rolled back parts of Dodd-Frank, easing reporting requirements on all but the largest banks.[62] But the damage had already been done. Bank consolidation has created banking oligopolies with massive political power and the ability to suppress competition. In fact, the May 2018 rollback is expected to increase that trend, since it raised the threshold for "systemically important" banks with stringent reporting requirements from $50 billion to $250 billion in assets. That means me-

dium-sized banks can now absorb smaller banks and grow
without worrying about hitting the threshold.

By 2017, the six largest US banks had increased their
assets by around 40 percent since the crisis and controlled
almost 70 percent of the assets in the US financial system.
J.P. Morgan Chase, the largest US bank, had more than $2.4
trillion in assets — larger than most countries.[63] Between
2007 and 2017, the three largest US banks—J.P. Morgan,
Bank of America and Wells Fargo—added more than $2.4
trillion in domestic deposits, a 180 percent increase. At the
end of 2007, those three banks held 20 percent of the country's deposits. By the end of 2017, they held 32 percent, or
$3.8 trillion.[64] Sucking up local deposits has given them a
cheap source of liquidity, but they are not returning that
liquidity to local communities to meet lending needs. They
are required by their business model to maximize profits for
their shareholders, which means they will always go for the
big hedge fund loan over the small local business loan, even
if the local loan is not inherently risky or unprofitable but is
just less profitable than other options.

## Where the Money Is: From Credit Lines to Credit Cards

By 2014, loans to businesses had shrunk to just 11.5 percent
of bank balance sheets.[65] Big banks have also retreated from
the residential mortgage market.[66] Government-owned Fannie Mae and Freddie Mac, along with other federal agencies
now own or guarantee 90 percent of all new mortgages.[67]
Banks are not even lending much to each other these days.
Deposit-taking banks went from issuing 60 percent of all

interbank loans in 2006 to issuing only 26 percent of them by the end of 2012.[68] Today, the interbank lending market is largely controlled by the Federal Home Loan Bank system, a GSE (government-sponsored enterprise) created in 1932 to provide financing for housing.

If the biggest banks are not doing much in the way of residential mortgages, small business loans, or interbank loans, what are they doing? Six monopolistic megabanks now control two-thirds of total financial assets.[69] At investment banks such as Morgan Stanley and Goldman Sachs, trading for their own profit generates a far higher proportion of revenues than traditional investment bank activities such as raising money for new businesses.[70]

Meanwhile, the credit lines once depended on by local businesses for their cash flow are being replaced with credit cards. In recent years, according to the Federal Reserve, credit card earnings have almost always been higher than returns on all other commercial bank activities.[71] And the largest banks reap the lion's share of these earnings. In 2015, the average return on assets for big card-issuing banks was more than triple that for all commercial banks.[72] In 2016, JPMorgan Chase set a record by crossing the $1 trillion mark in merchant processing volume.[73]

Besides carrying higher interest rates than other commercial loans, credit card debt comes with lucrative fees. There are late payment fees, fees for exceeding the credit limit, balance transfer fees, cash withdrawal fees, annual fees and, most lucrative of all, the merchant fees that accrue at the point of sale. In a typical $100 credit card purchase, only $97.25 goes to the seller. Of the rest, $2.20 goes to the issuing bank, $0.23 goes to the payment processor, $0.19

goes to the acquiring bank, and $0.13 goes to the card network. Although Visa and MasterCard set the rates, it is their member banks—the issuers of the credit cards—that actually receive the interchange fees. Issuing credit cards has become a highly concentrated industry, with the top four card issuers—Citigroup, Bank of America, JP Morgan Chase, and Capital One—accounting for more than 70 percent of all cards in circulation.[74]

Note that this merchant fee is not just 2.75 percent annually. It is 2.75 percent on *every transaction*, on a loan that is for only about 30 days. Loans to credit card borrowers who pay on time range from 1 to 60 days, depending on when in the billing cycle the bill is issued and paid; but assuming 30 days on average, that is *33 percent annually* just for merchant fees (12 months times 2.75 percent), in addition to interest and other fees. Little wonder banks are favoring credit card loans over the riskier and less lucrative commercial and business loans that were once their bread-and-butter business.

A merchants' fee is equivalent to a private sales tax, and merchants must pay it whether or not their customers pay the bill. To recoup the cost, they wind up raising their prices, which go up for all customers whether or not they use credit cards. The effect on trade is actually worse than from a public sales tax, which would be spent by the local government on services and infrastructure, returning the money to the people and the local economy. A private tax imposed by banks typically winds up in the financialized economy of money-making-money, removing purchasing power from the local economy. The whole business is so lucrative that not just banks but companies like General Electric, which once put their resources into product innovation and development, are now becoming credit card companies because that is where the money is. Financialization is killing the economy, productivity, innovation, and consumer demand.[75]

Meanwhile wage stagnation, along with skyrocketing educational, medical and housing costs, have left families seriously short of funds, throwing them into the arms of lenders. By 2016, US credit card debt had reached $1 trillion; and at an average annual rate of 18.76 percent, consumers who carried a balance on their credit cards were paying about $1,292 annually in interest on it.[76] Worse yet are the "payday" loans resorted to by the unbanked and underbanked, which average 400 percent interest annually or more. In 2015, according to the Campaign for Postal Banking, nearly 28 percent of US households were underserved by traditional banks. They included over four million workers without a bank account, who received pay on a payroll card and spent $40-$50 per month on ATM fees just to access their pay. The average underserved household spent $2,412 annually—nearly 10 percent of gross income—in fees and interest for nonbank financial services.[77]

Today the commercial lending business has largely migrated to unregulated intermediaries belonging to the shadow banking system, a sector that includes mutual funds, private equity funds, hedge funds and the asset management divisions of insurance companies and banks. By 2013, business loans as a percentage of bank balance sheets had dropped to just 11.5 percent.[78] Unregulated "peer-to-peer" lending platforms have also gotten into the game. The shadow banks provide services for businesses that cannot get traditional loans, but they generally charge more than traditional banks, and borrowers must put up substantial collateral.[79]

Shadow lenders, too, go for maximum profit, causing capital to rush from one speculative bubble to the next, and since there are virtually no limits on their unregulated borrowing, they can leverage loans to very risky levels. These hidden risks can spread to the traditional banks, with which the shadow banks are closely intertwined. Stringent regulations aimed at harnessing the traditional banking system have done little to eliminate these shadow bank risks. By 2013, the shadow banking sector controlled about *$53 trillion* in assets, up 60 percent since the 2008-09 financial crisis. Ten firms each individually controlled over $1 trillion, with BlackRock, the largest, managing $4.1 trillion in assets.[80] By 2018, BlackRock was up to *$6 trillion* under management, making it larger than the world's largest conventional bank (which is in China). Yet BlackRock escaped the regulations imposed on traditional banks under the Dodd-Frank Wall Street Reform and Consumer Protection Act of 2010.

## Concealing the Risks of an Inherently Risky Business Model

Not just the shadow banks but the conventional banking giants remain quite risky, despite the attempts of the Dodd-Frank Act to harness them. The act requires these "systemically important" financial institutions to come up with "living wills" showing they can fail without having to be bailed out by the government.[81] But in a review in April 2016, a full six years after the act was passed, five of eight too-big-to-fail banks still failed to satisfy the requirement. In a 19-page letter that month to the CEO of JPMorgan Chase, the Federal Reserve said that a deficiency had been identified in Chase's wind-down plan that was so grave that it could "pose serious adverse effects to the financial stability of the United States."[82]

In June 2017, for the first time in seven years, the Federal Reserve passed all 34 of the country's biggest banks on their stress tests, paving the way for the largest dividend payments in almost a decade. But the New York Times editorial board was skeptical, stating, "It's entirely possible that the system is more fragile than the Fed's stress tests indicate." The authors said international accounting rules would have valued the banks' capital less generously. This was due to the regulators' differing assessment of the risks posed by the derivatives that collapsed the economy in 2008-09.[83]

The risks baked into the banks' exotic derivatives scheme are evident in the numbers. In the first quarter of 2016, US banks held derivatives with a notional (or hypothetical) value totaling $193 trillion, more than twice the gross domestic product of all the countries of the world combined. The vast majority of these derivatives were held by just four giant banks.[84] JPMorgan Chase, which topped the list at $52.9 trillion, has a deposit base of only about $1.4 trillion.[85] Increasing capital or collateral requirements is not likely to contain the damage in a major crisis, because the money simply is not there.

Commentators who play down this derivative risk argue that "notional" exposure grossly overstates real exposure, since the players typically bet both ways, netting their claims out. But as pointed out on *Zero Hedge,* a popular financial blog, "net immediately becomes gross when just one counterparty in the collateral chains fails—case in point, the Lehman and AIG failures and the resulting scramble to bail out the entire world which cost trillions in taxpayer funds."[86]

The potential for this sort of nuclear reaction was what prompted billionaire investor Warren Buffett to call derivatives "weapons of financial mass destruction."[87] It is also why major derivatives players cannot be allowed to go down.

Today the fragility of the system is still there, but it is hidden behind so many layers of financial complexity that the players themselves cannot determine the degree of risk to which they are exposed. Multiple parties think they own the same collateral, until the music stops and they find themselves without chairs. That includes not just individual and institutional investors but state and local governments, which often share "pooled" collateral subject to multiple claims.[88] As software developer Caitlin Long explained in an April 2016 article titled "Why Financial Regulators Are Warming to Blockchains":

> ... [T]he issue is that market players re-use the same collateral over, and over, and over again, multiple times a day, to create credit. The process is called "rehypothecation."
>
> Multiple parties' financial statements therefore report that they own the very same asset at the same time. They have IOUs from each other to pay back that asset — hence, a chain of counterparty exposure that's hard to track.[89]

The reuse of collateral in the shadow banking system allows credit to expand to meet the needs of borrowers, a feature considered vital to vibrant markets. The risk is that multiple parties will rush to claim the collateral at the same time, only to find that their "security" is an illusion. Avoiding risk requires transparency; but as shown in the next chapter, illusion is actually necessary to keep the banking game going.

*Takeaway: Banks are no longer serving the credit and deposit needs of the public and the economy. As private profit-oriented institutions, they serve the short-term profit goals of their shareholders; and old-fashioned banking is no longer profitable. What is profitable for banks, however, is highly risky for the economy. This contradictory tension in the system has not been resolved by regulation, which has often just made it worse.*

## CHAPTER 3
# SLEIGHT OF HAND IS ESSENTIAL TO MODERN FINANCE

*"The process by which banks create money is so simple that the mind is repelled."*

— *John Kenneth Galbraith,* Money: Whence It Came, Where It Went *(1975)*

**To restore honesty to banking,** we first need transparency. The problem is that sleight of hand is an essential element of the current banking scheme. Opacity is "a feature, not a bug." Modern banking must be opaque because it is inherently risky, and depositors and investors would not entrust their money to it if they knew what those risks were. Yet their money and their trust are necessary to generate the bank credit that now composes the vast majority of the money supply, the credit that supports not only the speculative, financialized economy but the real economy where goods and services are produced. If we want honesty and transparency, we need to design a new banking model, one that is not dependent on deception to work.

In a 2011 blog post titled "Why Is Finance So Complex?", computer programmer Steve Randy Waldman explained the problem like this:

Opacity is absolutely essential to modern finance. ... The core purpose of *status quo* finance is to coax people into accepting risks that they would not, if fully informed, consent to bear. ...

Like so many good con-men, bankers make themselves believed by persuading each and every investor individually that, although *someone* might lose if stuff happens, it will be someone else. You're in on the con. If something goes wrong, each and every investor is assured, there will be a bagholder, but it won't be you. Bankers assure us of this in a bunch of different ways. First and foremost, they offer an ironclad, moneyback guarantee. You can have your money back any time you want, on demand. At the first hint of a problem, you'll be able to get out. They tell that to everyone, without blushing at all. Second, they point to all the other people standing in front of you to take the hit if anything goes wrong. ...

If the trail of tears were truly clear, if it were as obvious as it is in textbooks who takes what losses, banking systems would simply fail in their core task of attracting risk-averse investment to deploy in risky projects. Almost everyone who invests in a major bank believes themselves to be investing in a safe enterprise. ... Banks innovate and interconnect, swap and reinsure, guarantee and hedge, precisely so that it is not clear where losses will fall, so that each and every stakeholder of each and every entity can hold an image in their minds of some guarantor or affiliate or patsy who will take a hit before they do.

The system has benefits, says Waldman. Societies that lack opaque, "faintly fraudulent" financial systems fail to develop and prosper. Insufficient economic risks are taken to sustain growth and development. But the benefits are outweighed by the costs; and one of those costs, he says, is that "it enables a great deal of theft by those placed at the center of the shell game."[90]

## Sleight of Hand with Phantom Money

The bankers' shell game actually goes back several centuries, to when money consisted officially of gold and silver coins. In the 18th century, goldsmiths-turned-bankers discovered they could print and lend multiple promissory notes (or "banknotes") for the same gold, since people came for their gold only about 10 percent of the time. The trick for the banker was to come up with the necessary gold on demand. Called "fractional reserve" lending, it was a shell game in which the peas were moved back and forth under the shells so they appeared to be in two places at once. It was a risky venture that led to repeated bank failures, bank runs, and bank panics when the lenders could not come up with the gold.

In the 1860s, the federal government attempted to move all banks into the national banking system by heavily taxing these private banknotes. But many banks avoided the tax by simply writing the loan money into their borrowers' checking accounts. Rather than paper banknotes with the bank's name on them, the borrowers got paper checks they could write themselves. In the 20th century, checks were largely replaced with plastic cards; and in the 21st century, cell phones and computers trade in cyberspace without paper or plastic. But what is being traded is still simply the bank's promise to pay on demand, something the bank has traded for the borrower's promise, turning the borrower's promise into "money."

This banking alchemy, once relegated to "conspiracy theory," was acknowledged by economists at the Bank of England (BOE) in March 2014 and confirmed by researchers at the Bundesbank (the German central bank) in April 2017.[91] The BOE report, titled "Money Creation in the Modern Economy," said that many common assumptions about how banking works are simply wrong. The researchers wrote:

> The reality of how money is created today differs from the description found in some economics textbooks: Rather than banks receiving deposits when households save and then lending them out, bank lending creates deposits.
>
> ... Whenever a bank makes a loan, it simultaneously creates a matching deposit in the borrower's bank account, *thereby creating new money.*[92] [Emphasis added.]

The authors said that nearly 97 percent of the UK money supply consists of bank deposits created in this way.

The significance of these revelations was explored in a later Bank of England paper published in May 2015, titled "Banks Are Not Intermediaries of Loanable Funds—And Why This Matters." Economists Zoltan Jakab and Michael Kumhof argued that the reason central bank monetary policy has not responded well to the bank-induced Great Recession after the 2008 crisis was that central bankers were operating from the wrong model. In a summary in *Vox*, the authors explained:

[V]irtually all of the newly developed models are based on the highly misleading "intermediation of loanable funds" theory of banking (Jakab and Kumhof 2015). We argue instead that the correct framework is "money creation" theory.

In the intermediation of loanable funds model, ... lending starts with banks collecting deposits of real resources from savers and ends with the lending of those resources to borrowers. The problem with this view is that, in the real world, *there are no pre-existing loanable funds* . ...

The bank ... creates its own funding, deposits, through lending. It does so through a pure bookkeeping transaction that involves no real resources, and that acquires its economic significance through the fact that bank deposits are any modern economy's generally accepted medium of exchange.[93] [Emphasis added.]

*Deposits created by banks are the medium of exchange of modern economies.* Our money is created by banks, not governments. Deposits are just the banks' IOUs, their promises to pay "on demand." When the borrower takes out a bank loan, what he gets in return is not sovereign money, the official currency of the realm. It is the bank's promise to pay in sovereign money on demand. And these bank obligations are the economy's accepted medium of exchange.

David Graeber, writing in *The Guardian*, underscored the dramatic implications:

... [M]oney is really just an IOU. The role of the central bank is to preside over a legal order that effectively grants banks the exclusive right to create IOUs of a certain kind, ones that the government will recognise as legal tender by its willingness to accept them in payment of taxes. There's really no limit on how much banks could create, provided they can find someone willing to borrow it.[94]

The result of these revelations, wrote Graeber, is to throw the entire theoretical basis for austerity out the window. Among other politically explosive implications, "Just consider what might happen if mortgage holders realised the money the bank lent them is not, really, the life savings of some thrifty pensioner, but something the bank just whisked into existence through its possession of a magic wand which we, the public, handed over to it."

If banks just whisk money into existence, governments can do the same, and often have done it historically. If money is just a bank's IOU, governments do not need to sell off public assets and slash public services in order to pay their debts. Governments can create money the same way commercial banks do, simply with accounting entries on their books.

## "Monetizing" Debt: The Key Function of Banks

People individually can also create money. As economist Hyman Minsky put it, "Anyone can create money. The challenge is to have it accepted." The true role of the bank is not to act as an intermediary transferring existing funds from depositor to borrower but to "monetize" the borrower's own promise to pay, turning it into a form of money that can be spent in the marketplace. The borrower's credit is traded for bank credit, which today is our most common form of money.

This contrasts with the prevailing neoclassical monetarist view that money is a commodity in fixed supply that must be borrowed before it can be lent.[95]

The accounting magic that allows this alchemy to happen also traces back centuries, to the invention of double-entry bookkeeping. Jakab and Kumhof explain:

> Specifically, whenever a bank makes a new loan to a non-bank ('customer X'), it creates a new loan entry in the name of customer X on the asset side of its balance sheet, and it simultaneously creates a new and equal-sized deposit entry, also in the name of customer X, on the liability side of its balance sheet.

> ... [T]he key insight is that banks are not intermediaries of real loanable funds. Instead they provide financing through the creation of new monetary purchasing power for their borrowers. This involves the expansion or contraction of gross bookkeeping positions on bank balance sheets, rather than the channelling of real resources through banks.

Official acknowledgment of this process may be new, but the concept of credit as money actually predates gold used as money. As David Graeber shows in *Debt: The First 5,000 Years*, drawing on the research of Prof. Michael Hudson, the earliest money systems in recorded history date back to the Sumerians, who used a simple accounting system for keeping track of trades and obligations 5,000 years ago.[96]

Rather than a commodity in fixed supply, money today is "elastic." New purchasing power (money) is created when

loans are made and extinguished when they are paid off. The
bank deposits that are our accepted medium of exchange are
created and destroyed by banks every day in response to the
demand for credit. The implications for monetary and economic reform are huge. We have been held captive by banks
that control the money taps of a currency created from our
own IOUs.

As Perry Mehrling, professor of economics at Bernard
College, explains this process:

> [E]ach of us, in our interface with the essentially financial
> system that is modern capitalism, operates essentially as a
> bank, meaning a cash inflow, cash outflow entity. ... [T]he
> elasticity of credit ... allows us to spend today and put off
> payment to the future.[97]

*Each of us operates as a bank.* We extend our own credit, which the bank trades for "bank credit," turning it
into fungible paper or digits that sellers will accept in the
marketplace. The IOU created between our spending the
money and paying it back becomes "currency" in the hands
of the creditor, a promise to pay that he can spend in the
market.

Currency today is not a "thing" but a "flow." The word
itself comes from the Latin *currentia*, meaning to run or
flow. Currency facilitates the flow of goods and services from
producers to consumers. Money is simply debits and credits, pluses and minuses, zeros and ones, and it is continually
being created and destroyed by banks across the country. It
is created as an advance against future repayment and extinguished when payment is made.

## Check Kiting by Another Name

Advocates of the banks-as-intermediaries theory protest that banks actually do borrow the money they lend rather than simply creating it as bank credit on their books. Deposits may be created initially with accounting entries, but this money will soon be spent, typically by a check that finds its way into another bank; and this check will have to be cleared through the Federal Reserve or another clearinghouse. The receiving bank's reserve account will be credited and the issuing bank's reserve account will be debited by the amount of the check, leaving a deficit in the issuing bank's account at the central bank. Money will then have to be borrowed to balance the bank's books.[98] As the process is explained in a May 2013 article in *Forbes*:

> [B]anks settle their books at the end of the day. They might have lent out more than they took in deposits: or the other way around. But at 4 pm, 4:30 pm or so every bank's books must balance. So, those with excess funds lend to those with too little just overnight. The money's paid back in the morning and then the whole rigmarole is done again the next afternoon. OK, maybe this all sounds a bit silly but if they didn't do this then the system just wouldn't work as it does. Without it if you wanted to take your money out of the bank you would have to wait until someone had put some in: by being able to borrow from other banks this can be avoided.[99]

More than a bit silly, it sounds fraudulent. Banks lend money they don't have, simply by writing it into the accounts of borrowers; and to balance their books when this checkbook money leaves the bank, they borrow the money back. When individuals write a check on an account with no money in it, deposit the check in another bank, and withdraw the funds, it is called "check kiting" and carries criminal penalties. But banks can get away with writing nonexistent funds into customer accounts because few people can follow the trick. The bank can borrow the money later from another bank, money newly deposited in its own bank, or the money market. Banks usually just borrow overnight to balance their books, returning the funds the next morning. But borrow it from where? Somewhere in the system, the money will have been created as the deposit of another bank.

Consider this scenario: Bank A creates a $50,000 loan simply by writing that figure into the borrower's deposit account. The borrower writes a check on the account which is deposited in Bank B. Meanwhile, Bank B creates a $50,000 loan as a deposit which becomes a check that is deposited in Bank A. Both banks' books have incoming $50,000 deposits, so they balance; but both deposits were simply created in another bank with accounting entries. One hundred thousand dollars have been added to "M2," the circulating money supply, which includes deposits. When the loans are paid back, the process is reversed: the money disappears and the money supply shrinks.

Banks are able to create money as deposits by maintaining the fiction that they are merely acting as intermediaries that take in deposits and lend them out again; and what allows them to maintain that fiction is that they are chartered as "depository banks." So says Richard Werner, Chair of International Banking at the University of Southampton in the UK, in an illuminating series of academic papers published in 2014. He notes that not just banks but nonbank financial institutions (such as stockbrokers) maintain deposit accounts for their customers. But nonbanks are required to hold client deposits in segregated accounts with a bank or money market fund, leaving legal ownership with the depositor. Institutions with banking licenses are exempted from these rules, allowing them to keep customer deposits on their own balance sheets.[100]

Werner is a professor in the UK, but this is also true in the United States: when you deposit money in the bank, it is no longer your money. It becomes the property of the bank, and you become an unsecured creditor. The bank's obligation is simply to come up with the money on demand. As explained in a December 2016 article in the *University of Chicago Law Review* titled "Safe Banking: Finance and Democracy":

> A general deposit is a loan made to a bank. This means that the bank is the general depositor's debtor, but that the bank has legal title to the funds deposited; these funds may be commingled with the bank's other funds. All the general depositor has is a general, unsecured claim against the bank …. [T]he bank is free to use the deposit as it sees fit.[101]

Werner notes that the bank is also able to access the records of its customers and invent new deposits that were not actually paid in. The casual observer cannot tell the difference between money coming from outside the bank and a new deposit written into a borrower's account. Even the loan officers are probably unaware of this accounting gimmick. They are given parameters within which they can issue loans and they follow those guidelines.

To prove his case, Werner did something he says had never been done before—he conducted an empirical test at an actual bank. The test involved a loan of €200,000 to Werner, executed by the bank's credit manager while its directors watched. The entire process was filmed and the transactions were photographed. The result: €200,000 appeared immediately as a new asset on the bank's books and in the borrower's account. No one from the bank checked to see if the bank had deposits or assets sufficient to make the loan; no money was taken from any other account or drawn down from the central bank; and no other accounts at the bank were affected by the transaction. The "creation of new money" theory was thus confirmed, he says, and the "intermediation" and "fractional reserve" theories of loan creation were disproved.[102]

## The Controversial Debt Virus Theory

The failure to acknowledge that banks create new money, says Werner, has contributed to false economic models, and financial and economic policies that have not worked and have caused serious harm to countries and economies across the world. But the flaw in the system is not that banks turn their borrowers' credit into money. In fact, this credit-generating feature is essential to keeping the wheels of industry turning. The corruption comes with manipulation by human gatekeepers. The acceptance of our credit-turned-currency requires validation by a third-party middleman, which today takes the form of a bank; and privately owned banks have a mandate to maximize profits for their shareholders. Having control of the money spigots gives them massive power to divert funds away from the public interest toward their own. Banks sell credit for profit, and they are out to sell as much as they can. The result is booms and then busts when these credit bubbles can no longer be sustained.

That is one problem with the current model, but there is a more fundamental flaw. Credit bubbles *must* eventually burst, because the circulating money supply is never sufficient to repay the collective debt. One obvious problem is that banks create the principal but not the interest necessary to pay off their loans. As Bernard Lietaer, a former Belgian central banker, explained it in 1997:

> Money is created when banks lend it into existence. When a bank provides you with a $100,000 mortgage, it creates only the principal, which you spend and which then circulates in the economy. The bank expects you to pay back $200,000 over the next 20 years, but it doesn't create the second $100,000—the interest. Instead, the bank sends you out into the tough world to battle against everybody else to bring back the second $100,000. ...
>
> I have come to the conclusion that greed and fear of scarcity are in fact being continuously created and amplified as a direct result of the kind of money we are using. ... [W]e can produce more than enough food to feed everybody, and there is definitely enough work for everybody in the world, but there is clearly not enough money to pay for it all. The scarcity is in our national currencies. In fact, the job of central banks is to create and maintain that currency scarcity. The direct consequence is that we have to fight with each other in order to survive.[103]

Debunkers of this "debt virus theory" argue that the interest paid to banks goes into their profits, which do circulate back into the economy via bank salaries and expenditures, increasing economic activity and helping to pay off the interest. That is the argument, but most bank profits do not end up in the productive economy as wages or commercial purchases. They go into the financialized economy—money making more money in the form of speculative assets, additional loans at interest, or investments reaping dividends. The productive economy ends up supporting two economies, one where goods and services are produced in return for the wages that buy them, the other a speculative parasite that feeds off the productive economy, forcing it further and further into debt. The unsustainable result is that incomes collectively are insufficient to buy all the gross domestic product that the nation produces.

Even without the interest factor, there would be insufficient money in the economy to repay the collective debt. This is because not just banks but "savers" in general withhold money from the circulating money supply. They hold it as cash or in savings accounts or brokerage accounts or the bond market or abroad. An estimated $21 trillion is now sequestered away in offshore tax havens.[104] All of this money was created as a debt to a bank, which must be repaid to balance the books.[105]

In a 2018 book called *The Road to Debt Bondage: How Banks Create Unpayable Debt*, political economist Derryl Hermanutz estimates that only 20 percent of the money supply is actually available for loan repayment. This is the money held in deposit accounts—the money we expect to spend on our everyday purchases and expenses, including paying down loans. The money that we don't need for expenditures we save or invest in some way. When we do need the money, we liquidate a portion of those assets and move the proceeds into our deposit accounts, from which we can spend it via check or bank card. So the collective total held in deposit accounts—or about 20 percent of the total money supply today—is all that is actually available for the repayment of loans at any one time, although the entire bank-created money supply originated as a loan requiring repayment.[106]

For the system to be sustainable, the gap between debt and the money available to repay it needs to be closed in some way. Ancient rulers did it with periodic "debt jubilees"—debt forgiveness.[107] Some other possibilities for closing the gap are explored in Part II of this book.

## The Two-tiered Banking System: "Reserves" vs. "Bank Money"

There is another little-known feature of today's monetary system that needs to be understood in order to follow the proposals in Part II. This is that banks and the public trade in different forms of money. Individuals and other "non-banks" trade in the bank money created as deposits on the banks' books. Banks trade with each other and with the central bank using central bank "reserves." These are two completely separate monetary systems, which cannot be commingled with each other. That explains why the Fed's massive quantitative easing programs have not created the hyperinflation that was widely predicted. The assets the Fed bought were acquired by crediting bank reserve accounts, which cannot jump the divide to inflate the supply of "bank money" circulating in the real economy.[108]

In order to understand how that system evolved, we need to go back to 1913, when the Federal Reserve system was set up as a mechanism for clearing payments between banks. In times of panic before that, banks did not trust each other's banknotes or their checks and would refuse to take them, contributing to bank runs. The Federal Reserve was established not only as a reserve for the gold used to pay depositors but to stabilize the system by eliminating the unstable banknotes issued privately by banks, replacing them with Federal Reserve Notes. Banks were required to clear their checks through the central bank and to accept each other's checks once cleared, restoring confidence in the system. Early in the 20th century, when the dollar was still on the gold standard, payments were cleared with gold or cash or electronically by telegraph. Today, however, the central bank clears payments with reserves that it creates itself. Reserves are cleared through "open market operations," in which the central bank buys securities from banks simply by crediting their accounts at the Fed with newly created reserves.

In a June 2017 research paper, Prof. Joseph Huber, chair of economic and environmental sociology at Martin Luther University of Halle-Wittenberg, Germany, explained the two different money circuits like this:

> One is the public circulation of bankmoney among non-banks. Bankmoney is another term for demand deposits. ... Except for some government bodies, nonbanks are not admitted to central bank accounts.

> The other circuit is the interbank circulation of reserves among banks. ... [T]he reserves referred to here are pay-

ment reserves, i.e. liquid excess reserves for making interbank payments, in contrast to basically illiquid minimum
reserve requirements.

The two circuits are separate and never mingle . ... Reserves
and bankmoney represent two distinct classes of money
that cannot be exchanged for one another. Customers never
obtain reserves in their current accounts, and bankmoney
cannot be transferred into a bank's central bank account.[109]

Cash, says Huber, represents a third money circuit:

[R]ather than circulating between central bank accounts
(reserves) or between bank accounts (bankmoney), traditional solid cash circulates from hand to hand in public
circulation, without needing banks, or central banks
respectively, as a trusted third party.

Cash is the currency issued by governments through
their central banks. At one time, "cash was king." But in
today's economy, privately issued bank money has usurped
the field. Commercial banks create bank money in the same
way that the central bank creates central bank reserves, but
commercial banks credit private accounts while the central
bank credits bank reserve accounts. Another difference is
that when commercial banks do it, they do not just respond
to demand. Huber writes:

The banks supply bankmoney very selectively according to
their own preferences. Ever more frequently they initiate
business opportunities themselves, especially in investment

banking. By contrast, the central banks today deliver the reserves as demanded by the banking sector; or, as needed in a banking and debt crisis to avoid pending bank insolvencies.

Contrary to popular belief, the central bank thus has very little control over the money tap. It plays a reactive rather than a proactive role. Huber explains:

> Within the present frame of split-circuit reserve banking, credit extension and money creation is bank-led. *The initiative of money creation is with the banks, not with the central banks, as is most often assumed.* ... Central banks do not pre-finance the system by setting reserve positions first. The causation runs in the opposite direction. Central banks accommodate the banks' defining demand for central bank money (reserves and cash). ...
>
> Through their pro-active lead in primary credit creation (bankmoney creation), *banks determine the entire money supply, including the accommodating creation of reserves and cash by the central banks.* Bankmoney is not the result of some sort of multiplication of central bank money. Quite to the contrary, the stock of central bank money is a follow-up quantity, a kind of sub-set of the stock of bankmoney. [Emphasis added.]

The model of the "money multiplier," in which central banks control the money supply by controlling bank reserves, is another central bank tool that is now obsolete. Central banks focus instead on manipulating interest rates; but in today's highly indebted economy, raising interest rates will wreak other havoc, as detailed in Chapter 1, and it is a weak tool for controlling the money supply at best. When Fed Chairman Paul Volcker raised the fed funds rate to 20 percent in 1980, the effects were dramatic, since the fed funds market was where banks then turned for liquidity. But today banks have cheaper, unregulated sources of liquidity in the shadow banking system, a system they largely devised themselves to get around the rules. (More on this shortly.)

If the central bank wants to manage the circulating money supply, it needs new tools. Huber's proposal is to eliminate the two-tiered system, make the central bank accessible to everyone, and authorize it to create digital central bank money that can be traded like cash between individuals and other nonbanks without the need for banker middlemen. It is an interesting proposal, which will also be explored in Part II of this book.

*Takeaway: Banking has so far diverged from what most people think it is that it is hard to get our heads around it. Banks don't lend other people's money. What they lend is simply bank credit created on their books, and it is this "bank money" that makes up the vast majority of the money supply today. Only banks are allowed to trade in the "sovereign money" created by the central bank, and they can trade it only with each other. Individuals, businesses and local governments have access only to the bank money created by commercial banks as credit on their books. Covering withdrawals of this accounting-entry money requires the banks to engage in sleight of hand, a risky business.*

## CHAPTER 4
# THE ELEPHANT IN THE ROOM: THE SHADOW BANKING SYSTEM

*The world banking system has evolved into a wildly anarchistic form in which it can only create liquidity—and thus power production—through a highly volatile, permanent speculative frenzy. This means what is conventionally written off as "mere speculation" is actually at the core of "real" or productive national economies, which could not exist without international capital flows powered by market speculation.*

*—Jamie Merchant, "We Don't Need to Break Up The Big Banks. We Need to Put Them Under Democratic Control," February 2016*[110]

**There is another system that creates money** in the form of credit, one that is outside the purview of regulators. In the 19th century, unregulated banks were called "wildcat" banks. In the 21st century, they are called "shadow banks." Shadow banks are financial companies that borrow short-term and lend long-term outside the safety nets of FDIC insurance and the Federal Reserve discount window. They include money market funds, securities broker-dealers, investment and commercial banks and their holding companies, finance companies and mortgage brokers, issuers of asset-backed securities and asset-backed commercial paper, derivative product companies, hedge funds, off-the-books businesses variously known as trusts, special purpose entities, variable interest entities, conduits and structured investment vehicles. Commercial banks also conduct much of their business in the shadow banking system, although most are not classed as shadow banks themselves.[111] According to at least one regulatory expert, regulated banking organizations are actually the largest shadow banks.[112]

The shadow banking system is a black hole of invisible landmines, largely due to a practice called "rehypothecation"—the relending of collateral for multiple loans. How this process contributed to the 2008-09 financial crisis was colorfully described by Gillian Tett in *The Financial Times* like this:

> [B]ankers had become so adept at slicing and dicing debt instruments, and then re-using these in numerous deals, they had in effect spun a great web of leverage and trading activity—in much the same way that sugar is spun in a bowl to create candy floss. ... [W]hen banks receive collateral from hedge funds, they often act as if they owned that collateral outright—and post that as collateral to support their own deals. Thus one piece of collateral can be churned several times to support several deals; hence that great financial candy floss cloud.[113]

The fragility of the shadow system was also graphically described in a May 2013 article on *Zero Hedge* titled "Desperately Seeking $11.2 Trillion in Collateral, or How 'Modern Money' Really Works." The author wrote:

[T]he money held in the shadow banking system ... is literally created in a limbo where "confidence" is really the only collateral. ...

"[H]igh quality collateral" [backstops] trillions of rehypothecated shadow liabilities all of which have negligible margin requirements (and thus provide virtually unlimited leverage) until times turn rough and there is a scramble for collateral . ...

[R]ehypothecation, which is nothing but the paper shuffling of a security from point A to point B to point C and back to point A again, provides up to $7.6 trillion in Schrodinger collateral: or securities which are there but aren't, and certainly not there if and when everybody demands delivery at the same time!

Remember rehypothecation does not mean the collateral is there. It is merely representing a counterparty can have access to said collateral ... eventually ... maybe ... possibly ... in an ideal world in which no other counterparty has claims to the same collateral.

Putting it all together, it means that should the system finally wise up and remove the black box gimmick of rehypothecation which is literally "accounting magic" (and also financial fraud), **the Fed and its peer central banks would need to fill a hole as large as $10 trillion!**[114]

Attempts have been made to regulate this risky practice, addressed in Chapter 6. The problem is that the shadow banking system actually needs to counterfeit collateral, just as the conventional banking system needed to counterfeit banknotes in the fractional reserve system. Collateral is the "gold" of the shadow banks and there is not enough of it to go around. When the rehypothecation of collateral is curtailed by regulation, market liquidity dries up.[115]

## Skirting the Rules with Repo

Shadow banking comes in many forms, but repos and derivatives are where the big money is today.[116] Although the repo market is little known to most people, it is considered the main financing tool of the shadow banking system and a key player in the modern financial scheme.[117]

"Repo" in this case is short for "repurchase." In repo borrowing, the borrower sells the collateral to the lender and promises to repurchase it the next day. Repo operates on the pawnshop model: the borrower gets the money and the investor gets the collateral. If the investor doesn't get his money back, he can recover by foreclosing on the securities. Repos are one-day or short-term deals, continually rolled over or renewed until the money is repaid. They are really a form of securitized loan; but legally, ownership transfers to the lender, who can treat it as his own. The repo lender holds the collateral during the life of the loan and can reuse it as he will. He can short it, use it for another repo loan, or sell it quickly and get his money back without getting tied up in bankruptcy if the borrower defaults or goes bankrupt. Usually the institutional lender rolls over or renews the loan until the funds are needed, just as if the money had been deposited in a bank.

How the repo market evolved was explained in 2010 by Yale professor Gary Gorton in written testimony before the Financial Crisis Inquiry Commission exploring the causes of the financial crisis. He said that large institutional investors (pension funds, mutual funds, hedge funds, sovereign wealth funds) have millions of dollars to park somewhere between investments; but depositing this money in the traditional banking system is risky, since anything over $250,000 is uninsured. The large institutions needed a place to put their funds that was secure, provided them with some interest, and was liquid like a traditional deposit account, allowing quick withdrawal. They wanted the same "ironclad money back guarantee" provided by FDIC deposit insurance, with the ability to get their money back on demand; and the repo market responded to that growing need.[118] Repo replaces the security of deposit insurance with sales and repurchases of highly liquid collateral, typically Treasury debt or mortgage-backed securities. Although it evolved chiefly to satisfy the needs of large investors, it also served the interests of the banks, since it allowed them to get around the capital requirements imposed by regulators on the conventional banking system.[119]

Borrowing from the repo market became so popular that by 2008, it provided half the credit in the country. Securitized mortgage packages could be held on the banks' own books, to be used as collateral for overnight loans in the repo market. One risk for the borrower was that the repo lender could call for more collateral at any time. That meant that even a borrower capable of repaying the loan when due could be ruined by margin calls in the meantime; and that is what happened to Lehman Brothers.[120]

Most repo lenders are money market funds, but they also include states, municipalities, pension funds, mutual funds, foundations, insurers, asset managers and businesses needing a quick, safe place to deposit large pools of cash. According to business reporter Mary Fricker, editor of *RepoWatch.org*, it is not unusual for giant global finance firms to have $100 billion in repo outstanding daily. She warns:

> Repo reeks of systemic risk. Although thousands of financial institutions borrow and lend via repo, 21 companies—the so-called Primary Dealers approved to repo with the New York Fed—are thought to do about 90 percent of the business . ... They also make most of the nation's home loans, do most of the derivative trading and hold much of the country's savings. Plus, they borrow from each other, lend to each other, invest in each other, bet on each other, insure each other, trade with each other, clear for each other, buy from each other and broker for each other.[121]

It is these dangerous features of the repo market that are now thought to have triggered the financial crisis in 2008.[122] But repos managed to escape regulation under Dodd-Frank, and in 2011 about $7 trillion was still being borrowed nightly in this massive market by US and European financial institutions. By 2015 that figure had dropped to $4 trillion, due to tougher regulations that cut profit margins; but the market still remained highly popular, with foreign banks taking up the slack.[123]

## The Money Market and the Money Center Banks

The Primary Dealers that are thought to do 90 percent of the repo business are also those Wall Street firms authorized to transact directly with the Fed and the Treasury Department. They are the government's counterparties, required to submit meaningful bids when new Treasury securities are auctioned. Most are "money market banks" or "money center banks," a different species of banking animal from the more familiar retail banks that take in deposits, write checks, and make consumer and small business loans.

Money center banks have assets in excess of $20 billion. They are usually headquartered in large cities and earn a substantial portion of their revenue from transactions with governments, big businesses, and other banks. The list includes JP Morgan Chase, Bank of America, Citibank, Wells Fargo, HSBC (London), Deutsche Bank (Frankfurt), and Credit Suisse (Zurich). The activities of these megabanks include *portfolio business* (funding assets, securities or loans), *corporate finance* (arranging loans or public offerings for corporate clients), *trading* (including aggressively making loans intended for sale to investors), and *distribution* (selling commercial paper and securities, including US Treasuries, agencies, municipal bonds and other money market paper).[124]

A large share of the deposits in money center banks comes from foreign investors and foreign companies. This access to very large institutions gives the banks essentially unlimited access to capital.[125] The money center banks are also middlemen for the massive money market. In an informative blog called "Money: What It Is, How It Works," William F. Hummel explains:

The U.S. money market is a huge and major part of the
nation's financial system in which banks and other participants trade hundreds of billions of dollars every working
day. It is a wholesale market for low-risk, highly liquid,
short-term debt instruments. ...

Borrowers in the market include domestic and foreign banks,
the Treasury, corporations of all types, the Federal Home
Loan Banks and other federal agencies, dealers in money
market instruments, and many states and municipalities. The
lenders include most of the above plus insurance companies,
pension funds, and various other financial institutions.

... The money market is where the U.S. Treasury can sell
huge quantities of debt with ease. It is also where the
Fed carries out its open market operations to control
interest rates and provide for growth of the money supply.
... It has also become an international short-term capital
market where much of the dollar denominated trade by
foreign entities is financed.[126]

The money market serves vital market functions, including shifting vast sums of money between banks and
providing a means by which funds of cash-rich corporations
and other institutions can be funneled to banks that need
short-term money; and lending in the money market is done
chiefly with repo financing. According to Prof. Gorton, the
repo market is of critical importance to the economy because
it is the funding basis for the traditional banking system.
Without it, traditional banks will not lend and the credit
essential for job creation will not be available.[127]

## Rehypothecation: A Ponzi Scheme of Debt Built on Debt

Commercial banks have customer deposits from which to draw, and if they run out they can borrow the excess deposits of other banks in the fed funds market. So why borrow in the repo market? The short answer is that it is more profitable. Repo borrowing avoids the need to hold reserves against deposits, meet capital requirements, and pay for FDIC insurance. Repo is secured, so the overnight repurchase rate is often lower than the fed funds rate charged by other banks. A repo loan is typically rolled over when it comes due, so a one-day loan can last for months; and the lender can reuse the securities as collateral for its own repo loan, getting its cash back in the meantime. A financial institution can, for example, make or buy home loans, sell them to a trust that turns them into securities, buy the securities with the proceeds, and use the securities as collateral for a repo loan. Or a bank that wants to buy some securities without spending any of its own money can buy them with a repo loan collateralized by the securities it plans to buy. The repo loan finances the bank's purchase of the collateral used to back the loan.[128]

Through this relending or rehypothecation of collateral for multiple loans, the shadow banking system can manufacture credit "out of thin air" just as the traditional banking system does. How a limited supply of home loans can generate an unlimited supply of collateral was illustrated by Fricker with this extreme example of a repo credit chain:

Home loans got pooled with thousands more home loans. That pool got pooled with other pools. Then credit default swaps were issued on the pools of pools, and those credit default swaps themselves got pooled and turned into a security. A financial institution bought that CDS-backed security and repoed it out to another financial institution that re-repoed it to someone else. And all of that happened on the back of the original home loans.

Although the number of home loans might be limited by the number of people wanting a loan, the number of credit default swaps had no such limit. Eureka. *An unlimited supply of repo collateral.*

It was a lucrative business, spawning legions of middlemen all taking their cut. Fricker writes:

Hundreds of service firms—many of them affiliated with giant financial institutions and each other—sprung up to make, service and insure the home loans; to create and manage the loan pools; to create, sell and insure the securities; to broker, trade, match, enforce, document, guarantee, net and clear the repo transactions; to broker, hold, manage, value, insure, invest and adjust the repo collateral; and to lawyer and audit it all.[129]

All of this activity generated a huge demand for collateral. Although the burgeoning mortgage securitization market has been blamed on reckless subprime borrowing, the push came largely from the voracious demand for collateral in an exploding repo market. Traditionally, repos used US Treasuries, quality mortgage securities and other high-grade bonds. But there was quickly a shortage of high-grade collateral.

According to Fricker:

> Financial institutions began turning to their mortgage machines for ever and ever weaker collateral. They sold the loans to off-the-books businesses, or trusts, that they or others had set up. The off-the-books businesses pooled the loans and created asset-backed securities (ABS) that were backed by the cash flow of the loans. Credit rating agencies gave many of these securities high marks—higher than if the financial institutions themselves had created them, because the securities were protected by the off-the-books businesses from any trouble that might develop at the original financial institution. ...
>
> Increasingly, some institutions used these securities as collateral for repo loans. The higher the securities were rated, the more cash they could get from a repo lender. With that cash, some of the firms then made or bought more consumer and business loans, to pool and produce more securities, to use as collateral for more repo loans.[130]

It was a bubble built on a Ponzi scheme of debt; and when the bubble contracted after 2007, so did the credit available for trade, shrinking the money supply. Shadow banks cannot create money as deposits, but they can create "near-money" in the form of short-term debt that is quickly convertible to deposits at a bank.[131] Near-money is often traded as if it were money, even without converting it at a bank. Thus shrinking the near-money supply shrinks the available credit pool.

In a July 2010 study, Manmohan Singh, senior economist at the International Monetary Fund, linked rehypothecation both to the rapid growth of the shadow banking system and to its even faster deflation after the financial crisis. Specifics are hard to come by, since many financial institutions do not report their reuse of collateral and often operate internationally; but he estimated that at its peak in late 2007, the re-use of collateral had increased the size of the shadow banking system by at least 50 percent, or by $3 trillion to $4 trillion. After the banking crisis, this bubble rapidly contracted, dropping from about $4.5 trillion to $2.1 trillion at the largest seven US broker-dealers.[132] According to the St. Louis Federal Reserve, the size of the shadow banking sector was close to $20 trillion at its peak in 2007 and had shrunk to about $15 trillion in 2010, making it at least as big as, if not bigger than, the traditional banking system.[133]

## The Derivatives Casino: Weapons of Mass Destruction

As much as half of the US banking system is thus in the unregulated shadow banking system, and that half is a ticking time bomb waiting for a match. The match that is likely to set it off is the mushrooming derivatives casino, which is also played in the shadows and is dependent on the fragile repo system for financing.[134] Some estimates put the derivatives market as high as $1.2 quadrillion—about sixteen times global GDP.[135]

In a July 2012 opinion piece in *US News & World Report* titled "Derivatives Should Be Banned from Financial Markets," hedge fund manager Jim Rickards explained how this casino works:

Derivatives are bets between two parties that are made today with a payoff in the future based on the value of some
stock, bond, or index. One party will profit if the reference
security or index goes up in value and the other party will
profit if it goes down. These bets usually settle up every
three months based on value at that time, and then a new
calculation period begins. There are many variations on
this basic pattern, but almost all derivatives involve some
form of a bet in which gains and losses are calculated and
settled-up periodically.

The problem, said Rickards, is that "most derivatives do
not derive from an original loan or investment, but are created exclusively to make new bets. Instead of moving risk into
strong hands, *derivatives actually create risk out of thin air.*
*Risk is not being reduced by derivatives; it is growing exponen-*
*tially.*"[136] [Emphasis added.] He argued that the justification
for derivatives is a myth and that the whole business should
be banned.

Of particular concern in the 2008 crisis were the derivatives called "credit default swaps," the most widely traded
form of credit derivative. Credit default swaps turned "insurance" into speculative bets on whether issuers would default
on their bonds. In a typical swap, the "protection buyer" gets
a large payoff from the "protection seller" if the company defaults within a certain period of time, while the "protection
seller" collects periodic payments from the "protection buyer"
for assuming the risk of default.

Traditionally, a purchaser had to have an insurable
interest in order to buy insurance. He could not buy insurance on his neighbor's house, since he would have an in-

centive to burn it down to collect on the policy. But multiple speculators are allowed to buy credit default swaps on a bank or corporation that appears to be in financial trouble. Swaps are widely used just to increase profits by gambling on market changes.

The problem in 2008 was that few if any counterparties guaranteeing these contracts had enough capital to make good on their obligations. Since speculators could pile in without owning the asset, the derivative "insurer" risked owing many times what might have been paid on an ordinary insurance claim.[137] In one blogger's example, a hedge fund could sit back and collect $320,000 a year in premiums just for selling "protection" on a risky BBB junk bond. The premiums were "free" money—free until the bond actually went into default, when the hedge fund could be on the hook for $100 million in claims. That explains the federal government's $182 billion rescue of the giant insurance company AIG (American International Group) in September 2008. Regulators feared that the insurer could not honor its $527 billion in credit default swaps, and no one knew who would be affected.[138] On September 16, 2008, the Federal Reserve agreed to bail out AIG in return for 80 percent of its stock. According to Pam and Russ Martens in *Wall Street on Parade*:

> The bailout money went in the front door of AIG and was then funneled out the back door to the big Wall Street banks that had used AIG as their counterparty to guarantee their bets on Credit Default Swaps. The AIG bailout was effectively a backdoor bailout of the biggest banks on Wall Street.[139]

The AIG bailout occurred two days *after* the bailout
window was closed to Lehman Brothers, a 158-year-old
Wall Street investment firm and major derivatives player.
Why was Lehman not saved? Perhaps because the government had already bailed out mortgage giants Fannie Mae
and Freddie Mac, creating a furor of protest. The taxpayers
could not afford to underwrite the whole quadrillion-dollar
derivatives bubble. The line had to be drawn somewhere, and
Lehman was apparently it. Or was the Fed just saving its
ammunition for AIG?

Whatever the Fed's reasoning, the effect of the Lehman collapse was dramatic, triggering a domino effect that
sent shockwaves around the world. Spooked money market
investors pulled their money out *en masse*, causing a rapid
contraction of the repo market. That in turn collapsed the
securitization market, which fell a full 44 percent in one year,
vaporizing $1 trillion annually in loans for mortgages, cars,
commercial real estate, credit cards, large and small businesses, and other consumer and business needs. Credit financing
was also cut off abroad, strangling housing, consumer and
business lending worldwide.[140]

## The Perverse Incentives Created by "Safe Harbor" in Bankruptcy

Normally, bankruptcy protections save assets from this sort
of fire-sale liquidation. But in 2005, Congress had stipulated
that the collateral posted by bankrupt borrowers for both
repo loans and derivatives had "safe harbor" status, exempt-
ing them from bankruptcy. It was an extraordinary concession to a wildcat banking system that was largely outside

government regulation, but it was pushed through by the banking lobby with little debate.[141]

David Skeel, Professor of Corporate Law at the University of Pennsylvania Law School, argues that safe harbor was the real trigger of the Lehman Brothers collapse. In *The New Financial Deal: Understanding the Dodd-Frank Act and Its (Unintended) Consequences*, he refutes what he calls the "Lehman myth"—the widespread belief that the collapse resulted from the decision to allow Lehman to fail. He says bankruptcy works. The Lehman bankruptcy was orderly, and the derivatives were unwound relatively quickly. What triggered the fall was not the government's failure to intervene but its earlier interventions, when Congress passed the 2005 safe harbor amendment that allowed repo and derivatives to escape the discipline of bankruptcy. When Lehman appeared to be in trouble, the repo and derivatives traders all rushed to claim the collateral before it ran out, and the bankruptcy court had no power to stop them.[142]

The obvious solution would be to repeal the safe harbor amendment. The problem is that this would collapse the repo market, which provides the liquidity considered essential to the banking system. As explained by Professor Enrico Perotti of the University of Amsterdam in a December 2013 article titled "The Roots of Shadow Banking," the safe harbor exemption is actually a critical feature of the shadow banking system, a feature it needs in order to function.

Shadow banks create credit in the form of loans just as the traditional banking system does. Both systems are funding long-term loans with "demandable debt"—short-term loans that can be recalled on demand. In the traditional banking system, the promise that the depositor can get his money back on demand is made credible by government backing in the form of government-backed deposit insurance and access to central bank funding. The shadow banks needed their own variant of "demandable debt," and they got it through the privilege of "super-priority" in bankruptcy. Perotti wrote:

> Safe harbor status grants the privilege of being excluded from mandatory stay, and basically all other restrictions. Safe harbor lenders, which at present include repos and derivative margins, can immediately repossess and resell pledged collateral.

> This gives repos and derivatives extraordinary super-priority over all other claims, including tax and wage claims, deposits, real secured credit and insurance claims. Critically, it ensures immediacy (liquidity) for their holders. Unfortunately, it does so by undermining orderly liquidation.[143]

By undermining the orderly liquidation provided by the bankruptcy system, safe harbor encourages "disorderly liquidation." When a debtor appears to be on shaky ground, there will be a predictable stampede by favored creditors to grab the collateral, in a rush for the exits that can propel an otherwise-viable debtor into bankruptcy. The dilemma of our current banking system is that lenders won't advance the short-term liquidity needed to fund it without an ironclad guarantee; but the guarantee that makes the lender's money safe makes the system itself very risky.

## The Looting of Nations

In a December 2011 article titled "Plan B—How to Loot
Nations and Their Banks Legally," documentary filmmaker
David Malone asserts that the safe harbor amendment that
was supposed to reduce systemic risk actually increases risk
by allowing a whole range of far riskier assets to be used.
These assets are willingly accepted as collateral because if
the borrowers default, the traders can get their money back
before anyone else and no one can stop them. Safe harbor
allows the equivalent of burning down the barn to collect
the insurance. As a result, the repo market has ballooned.
Malone wrote:

> All other creditors—bond holders—risk losing some of
> their money in a bankruptcy. So they have a reason to
> want to avoid bankruptcy of a trading partner. Not so the
> repo and derivatives partners. They would now be best
> served by looting the company—perfectly legally—as
> soon as trouble seemed likely. In fact the repo and deriv-
> atives traders could push a bank that owed them money
> over into bankruptcy when it most suited them as credi-
> tors. When, for example, they might be in need of a bit of
> cash themselves to meet a few pressing creditors of their
> own.

> The collapse of ... Bear Stearns, Lehman Brothers and
> AIG were all directly because repo and derivatives part-
> ners of those institutions suddenly stopped trading and
> "looted" them instead.[144]

It was through "safe harbor" that repo and derivatives became weapons of mass destruction. In Malone's vivid imagery:

> The bankruptcy laws allow a mechanism for banks to disembowel each other. The strongest lend to the weaker and loot them when the moment of crisis approaches. The plan allows the biggest banks, those who happen to be burdened with massive holdings of dodgy euro area bonds, to leap out of the bond crisis and instead profit from a bankruptcy which might otherwise have killed them. All that is required is to know the import of the bankruptcy law and do as much repo, hypothecation and derivative trading with the weaker banks as you can.
>
> ... [S]ome of the biggest banks, themselves, have already constructed and greatly enlarged a now truly massive trip wired auto-destruct on the banking system. ...
>
> ... [T]he banks have created a financial Armageddon looting machine. Their Plan B is a mechanism to loot not just the more vulnerable banks in weaker nations, but those nations themselves. And the looting will not take months, not even days. It could happen in hours if not minutes.[145]

## Derivatives Preempt National Interests

Fear of a major collapse in the shadow banking system has in fact resulted in the looting of whole nations, as Malone predicted. Governments cannot be allowed to default for the same reason AIG could not be allowed to default: the financial institutions ostensibly insuring their bonds with derivatives do not have the funds to cover the bets.

This was dramatically illustrated in the case of Greece in 2010, when hedge funds colluded to short sovereign Greek debt.[146] At its height, the interest rate on the debt reached 30 percent. Coerced by the European Central Bank (ECB), the Greek government wound up forcing brutal austerity measures on the Greek people to try to pay the bill, despite a decisive vote in a national referendum against repayment. Yet Greece represents less than 2 percent of EU GDP. Why was it not allowed to default or renegotiate its debt? According to Graham Summers, chief market strategist for Phoenix Capital Research:

> ... EVERY move the Central Banks have made post-2009 has been aimed at avoiding debt restructuring or defaults in the bond markets.

> ... [G]lobal leverage has exploded to record highs, with the sovereign bond bubble now a staggering $100 trillion in size. ... Globally, over $500 trillion in derivatives trade [is] based on bond yields.[147]

This is what the ECB and other central banks fear: the threat posed by $500 trillion in derivatives bets on $100 trillion in government bonds. If the banks are allowed to collapse, the entire inter-meshed financial system could go down with them. The giant derivative banks thus have a gun to the heads of governments and taxpayers. Public assets must be privatized, public services cut, workers laid off and taxes raised, all to prevent the collapse of a derivative house of cards ostensibly created to protect investors against "risk." The risk is obviously still there. It has just been offloaded by wealthy private players onto governments and their citizens. The next two chapters look at attempts to regulate both the traditional banking system and the shadow banking system, and at why they have largely failed.

*Takeaway: The bank credit composing most of our money today relies for liquidity on a shadow banking system that is highly vulnerable to runs and systemic collapse. The shadow banks, in turn, rely for their liquidity on the risky practice of "rehypothecating" collateral, using the same collateral for multiple transactions. Lacking the protection of deposit insurance, they lobbied for and got super-priority in bankruptcy, a practice that jeopardizes other creditors. The shadow banks are largely unregulated, but regulating them poses other problems.*

## CHAPTER 5

# FIXES THAT FELL SHORT: TARP, QE AND DODD-FRANK

*"The banks—hard to believe in a time when we're facing a banking crisis that many of the banks created—are still the most powerful lobby on Capitol Hill. And they frankly own the place."*

*— US Sen. Dick Durbin, May 2009*[148]

**The massive collapse of global markets** in 2008-09 took regulators and politicians by surprise. Depositors were protected with deposit insurance, and investors have often suffered major losses without triggering government bailouts. The government has sometimes stepped in when jobs were on the line, but in the *dot-com* and *telecom* busts, investors lost almost twice what was lost on subprime mortgages in 2008, yet the government did not feel compelled to rescue them. In the 2008 crisis, however, all financial markets seized up, including business loans, car loans, and money market funds. Why? The seizure was actually in the shadow banking system, something few people had even heard of. As Professor Nouriel Roubini summed up the crisis in a September 14, 2008 newsletter:

What we are facing now is the beginning of the unravelling and collapse of the entire shadow financial system, a system of institutions (broker dealers, hedge funds, private equity funds, SIVs, conduits, etc.) that look like banks (as they borrow short, are highly leveraged and lend and invest long and in illiquid ways) and thus are highly vulnerable to bank-like runs; but unlike banks they are not properly regulated and supervised, they don't have access to deposit insurance and don't have access to the lender of last resort support of the central bank.

As the shadow banking system collapsed, so did the money supply. Fortunately, said Ben Bernanke in a 2002 speech, it was easy to reverse a deflation: just add money to the system. He used Milton Friedman's analogy: money could be "dropped from helicopters."[149] As Fed chairman six years later, Bernanke had his chance to prove his case. But contrary to his own hypothetical example, he did not drop money from helicopters onto the people and the economy. Rather, in the radical policy called "quantitative easing," the Fed selectively targeted the banks.

## Quantitative Easing: Making the World Safe for Bankers

The Fed's first round of QE began in late 2008, when it bought $600 billion in mortgage-backed securities off the books of Wall Street banks. QE1 mirrored TARP, the government's Troubled Asset Relief Program, which removed "troubled" or "toxic" assets from the banks' books. TARP was funded by the Treasury with $700 billion in taxpayer money, but that was as far as Congress was prepared to go. The Fed's QE1 carried on with these purchases simply by crediting the banks' reserve accounts at the Fed. The central bank could do this indefinitely, since the money was just entered with computer key strokes on its books.

The Federal Reserve System held between $700 billion and $800 billion of Treasury notes on its balance sheet before the recession. By June 2010, it held $2.1 trillion of bank debt, mortgage-backed securities, and Treasury notes.[150] When the QE program was officially halted in October 2014, the US central bank had accumulated $4.5 trillion in assets, including $2.7 trillion in federal securities.[151]

Bernanke said the Fed was not "printing money." QE was just an asset swap. The Fed took away something on the asset side of the bank's balance sheet (government securities or mortgage-backed securities) and replaced it with electronically generated dollars. These dollars were held in the banks' reserve accounts at the Fed as "excess reserves" and could not be spent or lent into the economy by the banks. They could only be lent to other banks that needed reserves or used to obtain other reserve assets. As Australian/UK economist Steve Keen explained:

> [R]eserves are there for settlement of accounts between banks, and for the government's interface with the private banking sector, but not for lending from. Banks themselves may ... swap those assets for other forms of assets that are income-yielding, but they are not able to lend from them.[152]

That explains why QE did not generate the hyperinflation that was widely predicted by critics. However, it did not help the real economy either. QE saved the banks from bankruptcy but did not put money in the pockets of consumers, generate credit for local businesses, compensate state and local governments for massive tax losses, or put foreclosed homeowners back in their homes.

Catherine Austin Fitts, former assistant secretary of Housing and Urban Development, said that the real purpose of this exercise was to unwind the toxic mortgage debacle in a way that would not bankrupt pensioners or start another war. She wrote:

> The challenge for Ben Bernanke and the Fed governors since the 2008 bailouts has been how to deal with the backlog of fraud—not just fraudulent mortgages and fraudulent mortgage securities but the derivatives piled on top and the politics of who owns them, such as sovereign nations with nuclear arsenals, and how they feel about taking massive losses on AAA paper purchased in good faith.
>
> On one hand, you could let them all default. The problem is the criminal liabilities would drive the global and national leadership into factionalism that could turn violent, not to mention what such defaults would do to liquidity in the financial system. Then there is the fact that a great deal of the fraudulent paper has been purchased by pension funds. So the mark down would hit the retirement savings of the people who have now also lost their homes or equity in their homes. The politics of this in an election year are terrifying for the Administration to contemplate.[153]

## Interest on Excess Reserves: More Welfare for Banks

QE was politically expedient, and it prevented the sort of Great Depression seen in the 1930s when the banks completely collapsed. But rather than getting money where it was needed in the real, productive economy, QE just flooded the banks with "excess reserves"—over $2 trillion of them. That created other problems, and one of them was that the Fed could no longer manipulate its target fed funds rate by making reserves more scarce, pushing up their price.

In a controversial attempt at controlling interest rates, in October 2008 the Fed therefore began paying interest on excess reserves (IOER).[154] The intent was to put a floor on the federal funds rate, since banks would not have an incentive to lend to other banks below this rate if they could do better at the Fed. What happened instead was that they largely quit lending to each other. They discovered that they could make risk-free profits by borrowing cheaply from the repo market or the Federal Home Loan Banks, which are not traditional depository banks and are therefore not eligible for IOER. The big banks could borrow from the Federal Home Loan Banks while collecting a higher rate of interest on their excess reserves from the Fed or by purchasing US Treasury bonds.[155]

Banks have now largely abandoned the fed funds market, making the Federal Reserve's much-anticipated quarter-percentage-point hikes largely meaningless except as psychological tools for manipulating markets through the mass media.[156] By 2012, the fed funds market was down to a mere $60 billion, versus a repo market estimated in 2014 to be around $4.5 trillion.[157]

To set a floor on the rate at which banks borrow, the Fed has therefore had to resort to another controversial maneuver. It began selling a portion of the massive purchases acquired through QE in the "reverse repo" market (where repos are lent rather than borrowed). The central bank establishes a floor by making its securities available at an overnight rate that is 0.25 percent below IOER. (The floor is established because why lend for less if you can lend risk-free to the central bank?) That increases the banks' borrowing costs on the repo market, which they recoup by raising the rates they charge for loans. But the policy has been criticized as destabilizing the repo market, and the result of paying IOER is another massive windfall for the banks.[158]

As of November 2018, 2.2 percent was being paid in interest on $2 trillion in excess reserves. If rates go to 3.5 percent, as the Fed says it is targeting by 2020, the windfall will be $77 billion annually, most of it going to Wall Street megabanks.[159] This tab is ultimately picked up by the taxpayers, since the Fed returns its profits to the government after deducting its costs, and IOER is included in its costs. IOER has thus become another form of welfare for the banks.

## ZIRP Creates Asset Bubbles

In December 2008, the Fed followed QE and IOER with ZIRP—its Zero Interest Rate Policy: the nominal interest rate (the real rate after factoring in inflation) was set for the fed funds market at zero.[160] ZIRP lowered the cost of borrowing, helped to recapitalize the insolvent banking system, and allowed the government to refinance its burgeoning debt at very low interest. But the policy also had unwanted side effects.

One was that people of retirement age, who normally would have kept their retirement savings in fixed-income high-grade bonds to protect their savings, moved their money into higher-risk higher-return stocks or kept it in cash. Lacking bond income, they spent more of their capital to live, leaving a smaller amount available in credit markets for productive investment. They also spent less, reducing overall demand and economic activity.

Seeing no increase in demand, companies used their earnings to pay down debt rather than reinvesting in their businesses, and they used the low interest rates to buy back their own stock. The result was to inflate a stock market bubble, while productivity, employment and wages stagnated. Stagnant wages meant less spending, further reducing demand and economic activity, while low interest rates encouraged borrowing to buy real estate, re-inflating a real estate bubble.[161]

## Dodd-Frank

Federal bailouts and QE saved the banks from criminal liability for misdeeds that cost over $22 trillion to the United States alone. Some called it the greatest bank heist in history, and the perpetrators had gotten away with it scot-free.[162] Wall Street clearly needed to be reined in, but how?

The response of Congress was the Dodd-Frank Wall Street Reform and Consumer Protection Act of 2010, which was promoted as eliminating "too big to fail." Like the Fed's quantitative easing programs, however, what it ensured was that the biggest banks could not fail, while leaving the repo market largely untouched. Rules focused on mortgages and capital adequacy will not stop the next run on repo.[163]

Title VII of the Dodd-Frank Act did regulate derivatives, but the results were controversial. Uncleared over-the-counter derivatives (also called "swaps") were required to substitute a central clearinghouse for the former bilateral relationship between the parties, and trading and reporting requirements were imposed. But critics complained that the new rules were destabilizing the markets.[164]

It was the conundrum highlighted by Steve Randy Waldman: derivatives encourage investors to invest by passing risk on to someone else; and without them, the investors won't play. But someone else is left holding the bag, and in the end it is likely to be the taxpayers and the global financial system as a whole.

The Volcker Rule, proposed by former Fed Chair Paul Volcker, was added to the congressional proposal for financial overhaul in January 2010 and approved in December 2013. Volcker hoped to reestablish the divide between commercial and investment banking that had been dissolved by a partial repeal of the Glass-Steagall Act in 1999. But the rule has been widely criticized as diminishing liquidity, and the Treasury Department under President Trump has recommended significant changes to it.[165] The market evidently needs the liquidity, even at the risk of blowing up the system.

In other cases, powerful lobbyists managed to bypass the regulations faster than legislators could understand what was going on. A continuing problem with financial regulation is that the slow and cumbersome legislative process cannot keep up with the "financial innovation" that gets around the rules.

The Lincoln Amendment to the Dodd-Frank Act, also called the "swaps push-out rule," required banks to remove some types of risky derivative trades into nonbank affiliates not insured by the FDIC. But in November 2014, language slipped into the congressional spending bill eviscerated that rule. A *Mother Jones* article titled "Citigroup Wrote the Wall Street Giveaway the House Just Approved" warned:

> The Citi-drafted legislation will benefit five of the largest banks in the country—Citigroup, JPMorgan Chase, Goldman Sachs, Bank of America, and Wells Fargo. ... If this measure becomes law, these banks will be able to use FDIC-insured money to bet on nearly anything they want. And if there's another economic downturn, they can count on a taxpayer bailout of their derivatives trading business.[166]

In 2008, Citigroup had collapsed under the weight of its own risk-taking and spread contagion across Wall Street. The result was a government bailout to the tune of $45 billion in equity infusions, over $300 billion in asset guarantees, and more than $2 trillion in cumulative below-market-rate loans from the Federal Reserve. Also as a result of that rescue, Citigroup later managed to eclipse even JPMorgan in total derivatives at the bank holding company level. By 2016, it held $55.6 trillion in notional derivatives versus JPMorgan's $52.3 trillion. Citigroup has also become one of the top three market makers in credit default swaps, which played a major role in its implosion in 2008. It continues to hold insured savings deposits while at the same time engaging in high-risk trading at both its investment bank and its commercial bank.[167]

Citigroup is playing a dangerous game and needs the FDIC to back its bets, even if that means triggering another bank bailout. Its success in watering down the push-out rule was one of many examples of the ability of high-powered banking lobbyists to harness the regulators charged with harnessing the banks.

## Turning Bankruptcy on Its Head: New "Bail-In" Rules Legalize the Confiscation of Creditors' Money

The stated purpose of the Dodd-Frank Act was to solve the problem of giant insolvent institutions that are "highly leveraged and complex, with numerous and dispersed financial operations, extensive off-balance-sheet activities, and opaque financial statements." But rather than eliminating this complex, opaque, highly leveraged financial edifice, the Act sacrifices depositors and other creditors in order to maintain it.[168]

The Dodd-Frank Act states in its preamble that it will "protect the American taxpayer by ending bailouts." But it does this under Title II by imposing the losses of insolvent financial companies on their common and preferred stockholders, debtholders, and other unsecured creditors, through a resolution plan known as a "bail-in." The point of an orderly resolution under the Act is not to make depositors and creditors whole. It is to prevent a systemwide *disorderly* resolution of the sort that followed the Lehman Brothers bankruptcy. Under the old liquidation rules, an insolvent bank was actually "liquidated"—its assets were sold off to repay depositors and creditors. In an "orderly resolution," the accounts of depositors and creditors are emptied to keep the insolvent bank in business.

The template for the Dodd-Frank bail-in protocol was
laid out in 2010 by the Financial Stability Board (FSB) in
Basel, Switzerland. The FSB is a regulatory body that began
as a group of G7 finance ministers and central bank governors organized in a merely advisory capacity following the
Asian crisis of the late 1990s, when its mandates were not
official. But they effectively acquired the force of law when
the G20 leaders gathered to endorse the FSB's rules after the
2008 crisis.

In a 2012 International Monetary Fund paper titled
"From Bail-out to Bail-in: Mandatory Debt Restructuring
of Systemic Financial Institutions," "bail-in" is obscurely
defined as "a statutory power of a resolution authority (as
opposed to contractual arrangements, such as contingent
capital requirements) to restructure the liabilities of a distressed financial institution by writing down its unsecured
debt and/or converting it to equity. The statutory bail-in
power is intended to achieve a prompt recapitalization and
restructuring of the distressed institution."[169] In plainer English, here are some points to note:

- Rather than being put through "bankruptcy," the
  bank's insolvency is "resolved" by the alchemy of
  turning its liabilities (or debts to others) into equity
  (the bank's own money). Insolvent too-big-to-fail
  banks are to be "promptly recapitalized" with this
  "unsecured debt" so they can go on with business as
  usual.
- The insolvent bank is to be made solvent by turning
  its depositors' and creditors' money into bank stock,
  which bears the risk of becoming worthless on the

market or being tied up for years in resolution proceedings. The largest class of unsecured debt of any
bank is its deposits.[170] The bail-in power is statutory,
legalizing the confiscation of creditor funds.

- Unlike with lesser bankrupt businesses in a capitalist
economy, insolvent "systemically important" banks
are not to have their assets sold off for the benefit
of creditors. They are to be kept alive and open for
business at all costs, such costs to be borne by the
creditors.

In 2013, a trial run of the bail-in scheme was executed
in Cyprus. Before they would agree to a Cypriot bailout, the
"troika"–the European Commission, the European Central
Bank and the International Monetary Fund—required the
Cyprus government to agree to the closing of Laiki Bank,
the country's second-largest bank, along with the confiscation of all of the bank's uninsured deposits (all deposits over
€100,000) and 48 percent of the uninsured deposits of the
Bank of Cyprus, the country's largest commercial bank. The
unanticipated raid was characterized in the media as mainly
targeting big foreign depositors, but its primary victims were
local businesses that needed to keep large amounts of money
liquid in order to meet their payroll and business expenses.[171]
Andreas Theophanous, professor of political economy at the
University of Nicosia, said in a January 2018 interview, "The
EU used Cyprus as an experiment, a guinea pig. They wanted
to see how to do the bail-in in a small country like Cyprus,
and whether they could repeat this in bigger countries."[172]

Following that "successful" trial run, similar bail-in tem-
plates made a coordinated appearance worldwide. The lead-

ers of the G20 nations formally rubber-stamped the bail-in
scheme when they met in Brisbane, Australia, in November
2014.[173] New rules required too-big-to-fail banks to keep a
buffer equal to 16 to 20 percent of their risk-weighted assets
in the form of equity (the banks' own capital) or of bonds
that could be converted to equity in the event of insolvency.[174] These securities were called "contingent capital convertible instruments" (CoCos), "bail-inable bonds," or "bail-in
bonds." They said in the fine print that the bondholders
agreed contractually (rather than being forced statutorily)
that if certain conditions occurred, the lender's money would
be turned into bank capital. What this meant was that a
bankrupt bank could confiscate the bondholders' money to
recapitalize itself. Again it was largely the public that would
bear the risk, since the CoCo bonds' target market was the
pension funds.[175] Banks and "shadow" banks were specifically
excluded as buyers of bail-in bonds due to the "fear of contagion": if they held each other's bonds, they could all go down
together. Whether the pensioners went down was apparently
not of concern.

Kept inviolate and untouched in all this were the banks'
liabilities on their repo and derivative bets, which represent-
ed by far the largest exposure of the too-big-to-fail banks.
The over-the-counter derivative market is composed of
banks, hedge funds and other highly sophisticated players
that bet against each other, driving each other's asset prices
up.[176] Derivatives and repo trades are considered "secured"
because collateral is posted by the parties. For some reason,
the wages and other deposits entrusted to banks by their
customers are not considered "security" or "collateral" but
are just loans to the bank. To recover their funds, depositors

must stand in line behind the repo and derivatives investors along with the other unsecured creditors.

State and local governments must also stand in line, although their deposits are considered "secured," because they remain junior to the secured claims with "super-priority." It is an underappreciated risk for local governments, which keep a significant portion of their revenues in Wall Street banks. They do this because smaller local banks lack the capacity to handle their complex business. Local government officials assume they are protected, because banks taking deposits of public funds are required to pledge collateral against any funds exceeding the deposit insurance limit of $250,000. But in a serious crisis, the derivative and repo claims with super-priority may have emptied the vault by the time government officials get to the teller's window. There are also other security issues involved in the pledging of collateral which make that alternative less secure than it appears.[177]

The end result is that the bail-in scheme has turned bankruptcy on its head. Rather than protecting the creditors, it protects the banks. As explained by economist Nathan Lewis in a May 2013 article:

> At first glance, the "bail-in" resembles the normal capitalist process of liabilities restructuring that should occur when a bank becomes insolvent. ...

> The difference with the "bail-in" is that the order of creditor seniority is changed. In the end, it amounts to the cronies (other banks and government) and non-cronies. The cronies get 100 percent or more; the non-cronies,

including non-interest-bearing depositors who should be super-senior, get a kick in the guts instead. ...

In principle, depositors are the most senior creditors in a bank. However, that was changed in the 2005 bankruptcy law, which made derivatives liabilities most senior. Considering the extreme levels of derivatives liabilities that many large banks have, and the opportunity to stuff any bank with derivatives liabilities in the last moment, other creditors could easily find there is nothing left for them at all.[178]

Even in the worst of the bank bankruptcies of the Great Depression, notes Lewis, creditors eventually recovered nearly all of their money. He concluded, "When super-senior depositors have huge losses of 50 percent or more, after a 'bail-in' restructuring, you know that a crime was committed."

## What About Deposit Insurance?

In theory, deposits up to $250,000 are protected by FDIC insurance. But the FDIC fund had only $93 billion in it at the end of 2017.[179] Total US bank deposits were close to $17 trillion, of which about half were covered by FDIC insurance. In a May 2013 article in *USA Today* titled "Can FDIC Handle the Failure of a Megabank?", financial analyst Darrell Delamaide warned:

[T]he biggest failure the FDIC has handled was Washington Mutual in 2008. And while that was plenty big with $307 billion in assets, it was a small fry compared with the $2.5 trillion in assets today at JPMorgan Chase, the $2.2 trillion at Bank of America or the $1.9 trillion at Citigroup.

... There was no possibility that the FDIC could take on the rescue of a Citigroup or Bank of America when the full-fledged financial crisis broke in the fall of that year and threatened the solvency of even the biggest banks.[180]

It was because the FDIC wasn't up to the task that the US Treasury and the Federal Reserve had to step in and bail out the banks in 2008. The 2010 Dodd-Frank Act was supposed to ensure that this never happened again. But skeptics question whether the FDIC or any regulator could actually manage a Dodd-Frank style bail-in, especially in the heat of a crisis when many banks are threatened at once. When a bail-in was tested in 2017 in Italy, the EU-mandated rule was so onerous on unsuspecting small investors that the government resorted to a bailout of its failed banks instead.[181]

The US government's potential exposure to a derivatives collapse was explored in a study involving the cost of the Dodd-Frank rollback in the December 2014 congressional spending bill. It found that the rule reversal allowed banks to keep $10 trillion in swaps trades on their books.[182] In a bailout, these are speculative bets for which taxpayers could be on the hook; and in a bail-in under Dodd-Frank, they are bets for which creditors and depositors could be on the hook.

The FDIC has a credit line with the Treasury up to $500 billion, but who would pay that massive loan back? In theory, it would be the member banks; but a major crisis could render the whole banking industry insolvent, as effectively happened in 2008.[183] The FDIC fund, too, must stand in line behind the bottomless black hole of derivative liabilities. As observed on the blog *Naked Capitalism* by financial analyst Yves Smith (a pen name), this puts depositors at big US banks in a worse position even than Cyprus deposit-holders, since their deposits are now subject to being wiped out by a major derivatives loss.[184]

The next chapter looks at why newer regulations are also inadequate for protecting the public and the economy.

---

*Takeaway: Measures aimed at reining in the biggest banks after the 2008 credit crisis—including QE, ZIRP, IOER and Dodd-Frank—have instead made the megabanks bigger and more powerful at the expense of the public. FDIC insurance and collateralization are inadequate protection for private and public deposits. The regulations have been criticized as destabilizing markets while failing to eliminate "the black box gimmick of rehypothecation and financial fraud."*

## CHAPTER 6
# TEN YEARS AFTER THE CRISIS: STILL FIGHT-ING THE LAST WAR

*Professional forecasters have missed every recession since such records were first kept in 1968. ... [T]hey are, in effect, preparing to fight the last war. To have any chance of anticipating and preventing the next downturn, regulators must look for the threats that have emerged since 2008. They need to recognize that the markets now play an outsized role in the economy, and their attempts to micromanage this vast sea of money have only pushed the risks away from big American banks and toward new lenders outside the banking system . ...*

— *Ruchir Sharma, "How the Next Downturn Will Surprise Us," New York Times, September 18, 2018*[185]

**Congress and industry regulators** continue to debate how to rein in the megabanks and stabilize the system. Proposals include restoring Glass-Steagall, raising capital requirements, heavily taxing the banks, and breaking up the biggest banks into smaller ones. But as Ruchir Sharma observed in *The New York Times* on the tenth anniversary of the Lehman crisis, these proposals are "fighting the last war." Regulations imposed on the traditional banks have driven borrowers into the shadow banks, which are difficult to regulate and are needed for the liquidity demanded by the market. To get a different result, we need a system based on a different economic model.

Yalman Onaran wrote in *Bloomberg* on the same anniversary that reform measures have made the banks safer in some ways. Capital requirements and buffers against losses have increased; the largest firms have been forced to simplify their legal structures; and regulations, including the Volcker Rule, have prompted big broker-dealer banks to get less of their revenue from trading risky structured products. But risk has largely migrated to the shadow banks, and exposure to that unregulated system by the country's largest banks has actually grown. Lending by the eight biggest US banks to nonbank financial firms has quadrupled since 2010, and these banks could be on the hook if the smaller shadow lenders should fail.[186]

Meanwhile, the economy is in a dangerous debt bubble that could bring it crashing down again. Quantitative easing and very low interest rates have boosted stock markets globally, but wages and salaries have stagnated, exacerbating income equality and fueling populist discontent. The Ponzi-like conditions that created the giant subprime lending industry that crashed after 2008 have been transferred from consumers to businesses, which are heavily in debt today. Risky forms of corporate debt have surged, with leveraged loans and junk bonds more than doubling in the past 10 years. The big banks' share in this risky business has shifted to smaller rivals and nonbanks, including hedge funds, smaller banks, and broker-dealers with no banking units.

Other new players that are taking on risk once carried by big banks are the central clearinghouses for derivatives.

Dodd-Frank required financial firms to clear derivative transactions centrally rather than over-the-counter where possible, relieving the big banks in the middle of these transactions from the risk of one side not paying. As a result, almost 90 percent of interest rate swaps, the biggest segment of the market, have now been moved to clearinghouses owned by major exchanges. The problem is that the clearinghouses themselves can have losses from shadow players, and these losses would be imposed on the big banks that compose the clearinghouse membership.

There is also still the problem of the opaque derivatives market, in which the biggest banks remain the largest players. The top six US banks still account for about 35 percent of all derivative contracts worldwide (down from 45 percent in 2010); and the value of derivatives that tie big banks to shadow banks is still seven times global GDP.

Onaran notes that some shadow lenders, including money market funds investing in nongovernment debt, have shrunk since the 2008 crisis, partly due to new regulations and low interest rates. But credit extended by shadow banks overall has grown; and as interest rates rise, money in search of greater profit could again flow back to those funds and away from bank deposits. The banks would then have to go back to borrowing from the shadow lenders, increasing their vulnerability.[187]

## Glass-Steagall: Closing the Barn Door Too Late

New regulations continue to be proposed by politicians and regulators—a tacit sign that the old ones are inadequate. But critics say the newer proposals also miss the mark. The most popular of those currently on the table is to restore the Glass-Steagall Act separating depository from investment banking. The objection of critics is that it is too late: Glass-Steagall is obsolete and will not work in today's economies.

When it was passed in 1933, the only short-term IOUs subject to runs were bank deposits. Glass-Steagall successfully eliminated that risk by creating FDIC deposit insurance and by separating depository banking from risky investment banking. But the 1980s and 1990s introduced new, unregulated forms of short-term funds, including money-market instruments that are as vulnerable to runs as traditional deposits; and separating depository from investment banking would not prevent those contagious panics.

Reimposing Glass-Steagall would not have prevented the domino effect from the 2008 collapse of Bear Stearns, Lehman Brothers and AIG. AIG was an insurance company, not a bank subject to Glass-Steagall; and Bear Stearns and Lehman were independent investment banks that were not gambling with depositors' money. In fact, independent broker/dealers are now considered more prone to collapse than commercial banks specifically because they lack stable deposit bases. They rely on short-term liquidity that can dry up suddenly.[188]

That is what happened to Bear Stearns, which was "saved" only when it was acquired for pennies on the dollar by JPMorgan Chase in June 2008. It is also what happened to Merrill Lynch, which agreed to be acquired by Bank of America after facing a major liquidity crisis; and to Lehman Brothers, which could not find a buyer and went down, taking the market with it. Investment banks Goldman Sachs and Morgan Stanley escaped similar fates only because they did not remain independent investment banks but converted to bank holding companies at the height of the crisis. This reduced pressures on liquidity, partly because they were able to acquire some retail deposits, but mainly because they were granted access to the Fed's discount window.[189] Ultimately, only the government can backstop the banks and prevent bank runs—a strong argument for turning them into public utilities.

In a June 2017 article posted on *The Hill* titled "Glass-Steagall Never Saved Our Financial System, So Why Revive It?," Alex Pollock points out that even when Glass-Steagall was in force, it did not prevent the huge multiple financial busts of 1982 to 1992 that caused more than 2,800 US financial institution failures, or the series of international financial crises of the 1990s.[190] In fact, the shadow banking system evolved in response to those crises, encouraged by the regulators themselves. Banks replaced the "hold to maturity" model with the "originate to distribute" model.[191] Rather than keeping long-term loans on their books, the loans were bundled up, chopped into securities, "insured" with derivatives, and sold to investors. But this scheme proved to be even riskier and more unstable than "old-fashioned banking," as the 2008 crisis showed. Pollock concludes:

> The fundamental problem of banking is always, in the memorable phrase of great banking theorist Walter Bagehot, "smallness of capital." Or, to put the same concept in other words, the problem is "bigness of leverage." So-called "traditional" commercial banking is, in fact, a very

risky business, because making loans on a highly leveraged basis is very risky, especially real estate loans. All of financial history is witness to this.

Moreover, making investments in securities — that is, buying securities, as opposed to being in the securities business — has always been a part of traditional commercial banking. Indeed, it needs to be, for a highly leveraged balance sheet with all loans and no securities would be extremely risky and entirely unacceptable to any prudent banker or regulator.[192]

In a June 2009 speech, Adair Turner, then chairman of the UK Financial Services Authority, echoed that sentiment, stating:

Much of what went wrong went wrong in activities which a commercial bank was free to perform even before Glass Steagall was dismantled. It is, I think, difficult to imagine applying a law which says that a commercial bank cannot hold fixed income securities in its Treasury portfolio, turn loans into securities for distribution but hold them until distribution is achieved, or use credit derivatives to manage credit risks. And you certainly cannot say that a commercial bank cannot take any proprietary positions, without making it impossible to perform necessary market-making functions in, for instance, foreign exchange and interest rate markets.

But once you have said that a commercial bank can do all of those functions, you have allowed it to do most of the activities which, pursued on a large scale and in a risky fashion, caused the crisis.[193]

## The 21st-Century Glass-Steagall Act

It is just this sort of regulation—the sort that Adair Turner finds "difficult to imagine applying"—that the latest versions of the Glass-Steagall Act propose to implement. The Warren-McCain 21st-Century Glass Steagall Act was re-introduced in April 2017 with support from both major political parties. It was described in a May 2017 *Law360* review as potentially "the most dramatic rewrite of the federal banking laws in 150 years of federal banking regulation."[194] Not only would it reinstate the prohibitions of the Glass-Steagall Act separating commercial banking from investment banking, but it would prohibit the banking industry from engaging in a wide range of longstanding banking-related securities activities.

"Notably," said the *Law360* reviewers, "the Warren-McCain bill would, for the first time since the National Bank Act created national banks in 1863, redefine by statute what constitutes — and what does not constitute — the business of banking. The 'business of banking' would be defined to include only receiving deposits, making extensions of credit, participating in payment systems, transacting in coin and bullion, and making investments in debt securities; in the latter case, only with a number of limitations."

While tightening the already-tight regulations imposed on traditional depository banks, the bill would leave the shadow banks untouched. The reviewers observed, "Companies that make loans without also taking deposits—nonbank lenders—

would not appear to be directly affected by the Warren-Mc-Cain Bill." But these are the companies that triggered the last financial crisis and are likely to trigger the next one. While no doubt well-intentioned, the bill if passed could destabilize the system while missing what should have been its target.

## The Minnesota Plan

In November 2016, Minneapolis Federal Reserve President Neel Kashkari unveiled a different sort of plan, one designed to force the largest institutions to break up of their own accord. His Minneapolis Plan would make the largest US banks hold so much capital that they would voluntarily break into smaller parts. It would also tax large shadow-bank entities (hedge funds and asset managers) to the point that they would probably break themselves up. Banks subject to the proposed rule would be those with more than $250 billion in assets, including Bank of America Corp., JPMorgan Chase & Co, Wells Fargo & Co., and Citigroup. The plan would double the amount of loss-absorbing equity capital for these large banks, to 23.5 percent. Shadow banks with more than $50 billion in assets, such as Blackrock Inc., would bear a tax of at least 1.2 percent on their debt. Banks with less than $10 billion in assets would be more loosely regulated, since they do not pose a threat to the US economy.[195]

Texas Rep. Jeb Hensarling, head of the House Financial Services Committee, has also argued for raising capital requirements to a level that would prompt big banks to split apart. Other legislation along those lines has been introduced by Senate Banking Committee members Sherrod Brown, a Democrat, and David Vitter, a Republican.[196]

Like other proposed regulations, however, increasing capital requirements to buffer against bank defaults would not have prevented the last banking crisis and is unlikely to prevent the next one. Bear Stearns and Lehman Brothers both had sufficient capital. What they lacked was sufficient liquidity: they were unable to get funds quickly when panicked investors tried to grab their money and run.[197] Rather than shrinking the too-big-to-fail banks, the increased capital requirements imposed by Dodd-Frank and Basel III have served to make them bigger by forcing the smaller banks that could not handle the higher capital requirements to sell out to the giant banks that could handle them. And if the proposed regulations did succeed in breaking up the big banks, a collection of smaller commercial banks would no doubt act much like the big banks of which they were offshoots, while lacking the big banks' ability to deal with massive international capital flows.[198]

## Defusing the Time Bomb in the Shadow Banking System

None of these proposals would prevent a banking crisis triggered by the landmines buried in the shadow banking system, where the greatest risks lie. Some curbs have been imposed on those markets, but risks and concerns remain. In a July 2017 report titled "Assessment of Shadow Banking Activities, Risks and the Adequacy of Post-Crisis Policy Tools to Address Financial Stability Concerns," the Basel Financial Stability Board observed that policy measures had reduced the shadow banking risks contributing to the last crisis but said there were potential new financial stability risks that could materialize in the future. They included "the size and considerable growth of collective investment vehicles that are susceptible to runs, such as open-ended fixed income funds, credit hedge funds, real estate funds and MMFs [money market funds]." New forms of shadow banking were also likely to develop in the future, requiring continued monitoring. The authors concluded that while "the interconnectedness between banks and other financial intermediaries has gradually declined since the crisis peak ..., the bank interconnectedness still remains higher than the pre-crisis level, due in part to continued interconnectedness with MMF's, investment funds, and broker-dealers for funding." Continued attention was therefore warranted.

Proposals for eliminating safe harbor status in bankruptcy for repos and derivatives have been made but have not yet been implemented. The Bankruptcy Fairness Act of 2016 would have required biennial reporting by the Office of Financial Research on the effects of modifying the Bankruptcy Code concerning repos and derivatives, providing a potential gateway for eliminating their safe harbors; but the legislation died in the 114th Congress.[199]

In September 2017, the Federal Reserve Board finalized a new rule to go into effect in 2019, which does modify the super-priority safety net but remains problematic. Rather than being able to grab the collateral and run, the lenders will have to wait one or two business days before canceling their contracts.[200] But critics object that if collateral flight is banned after some cutoff point (e.g. the bankruptcy filing), flight will happen before the cut-off, making the crisis worse. And waiting a day or two is not the same as losing the super-priority privilege. It still puts the favored players ahead of other creditors in bankruptcy.

Some attempt has also been made to regulate the rehypothecation of collateral used in the shadow market. Regulations have been imposed in the EU surrounding collateral and its reuse, intended to reduce systemic risk. But the result has been a reduction in the availability of collateral, leading to concerns that shortages could lead to a run on high-quality collateral. Meanwhile, according to one European source, "the use of traditional repurchase agreements ... , of which the profitability is significantly impaired by the new requirements, is slowly being replaced by synthetic repos techniques—using financial derivatives."[201] One risky practice is being replaced with another.

The EU is expected to ratify a new regulatory framework called the Securities Financing Transaction Regulation (SFTR), due to go live at the end of 2019 or in early 2020. But the regulations are aimed only at increasing transparency on the use of repos and the risks of collateral arrangements, not at eliminating them, and the reporting burden will be heavy. According to an October 2018 article in *Bloomberg*, it is not clear that US and Asian jurisdictions will ever consider that reporting route.[202]

Imposing capital requirements and other restrictions on the repo market may make it less risky, but the restrictions will also dry up the liquidity that conventional banks and capital markets require to operate.[203] Rehypothecation may be sleight of hand, but the double- or triple-counting of assets fills the gaps created by shortages in the high-quality collateral serving as money tokens for the repo system. Moreover, that gap has been widening. According to an April 2015 article in *The Wall Street Journal*:

A shortage of high-quality bonds is disrupting the $2.6 trillion U.S. market for short-term loans known as repurchase agreements, or "repos," creating bottlenecks for a key source of liquidity in the financial system and sending ripples through short-term debt markets. ... The shrinkage in bank repo balances is so acute that interest rates on repos tied to certain securities have fallen into negative territory. That means financial institutions such as banks and money funds are willing to pay up to lend their cash just so they can have access to specific securities.[204]

That explains why there is a market for some federal securities even at negative interest rates (meaning the lender pays the borrower rather than the reverse). Recall the concerns of Professor Gorton, who warned that the repo market is of critical importance to the economy. Without it, traditional banks will not lend, and the credit essential for job creation will not be created.[205] He said in an October 2012 interview on *Alphaville FT*:

> [S]hadow banking ... is real banking. The economy needs this banking system. Prior to the crisis the issuance of non-mortgage asset-backed securities was larger than the issuance of U.S. corporate bonds. So, this banking system was very large and very important. It is difficult to see how the economy can recover when this banking system is in shambles. No positive, constructive, steps have been taken to recreate confidence in this system.

What creates confidence, he said, is not "capital" but *government backing*:

Capital requirements were never the sole focus of attention for bank regulation until the 1980s. ... [T]here is a basic misunderstanding of financial crises. A bank run is a demand that all short-term debt in the banking system be turned into cash. That is simply not possible. *It would be best to create a system where such a demand does not arise because the government's oversight has created sufficient confidence. Capital per se cannot do this.*[206] [Emphasis added.]

Government is what ultimately undergirds a sound, secure monetary system. The liquidity problem can be eliminated only by replacing the repo system itself with something less risky and more functional, something as sound as the government because it is the government, a public utility operated by and for the people. How government-backed publicly owned banks could provide liquidity without sleight of hand is explored in Part II.

## When Big Is Good

An August 2016 article in *American Banker* observed that downsizing the megabanks would put the United States at a competitive disadvantage, resulting in the outsourcing of the banking business of some of America's largest companies. Large borrowers expect to have all their financial services in one place and will look elsewhere if necessary to find that arrangement.[207] Whether the biggest banks lose market share is not of concern to most people, who might be glad to see them become less powerful. But their giant size and complexity do serve some necessary functions in today's international markets.

So argued Jamie Merchant, co-founder of the Center for Progressive Strategy and Research, in a February 2016 article titled "We Don't Need to Break Up the Big Banks. We Need to Put Them under Democratic Control." For all its recklessness and complexity, he observed, the speculative global financial system is integral to the world economy:

> A giant multinational firm like Apple, for instance, relies on the whole bizarre catalogue of financial derivatives—swaps, futures, options and all of their related mutations—to coordinate its investments across a dozen or more countries. These countries all have different debt levels, currency exchange rates, interest rates and political conditions of their own that are factored into investment decisions as different forms of risk.

> Liquidity, or the ability to buy and sell financial assets at will, is the engine of this system, and the big investment banks—Morgan Stanley, Goldman Sachs, Citigroup—are its main vehicles. Their enormous size allows them to act as the oil in the gears across the global geography of production.[208]

The problem is not that the megabanks are too big to fail. It is that they are too important not to be under democratic control. Merchant argued:

> The international banks, whose outstanding derivative contracts are estimated to have a value of over $500 trillion, are the massive and powerful conduits of world capital . ... A new antitrust movement aims at breaking

the power of the largest banks by dismantling them. But while the intentions behind "breaking up the banks" are good, such a program is deeply flawed, doubling down on market competition and nationalism when we should be thinking about new forms of public control and transnational coordination.

The issue is not that big international banks have such huge amounts of capital but who has control over those resources. The giant international banks need to be put under democratic control. It sounds good in theory, but how do we get from here to there? Before the old structures can be eliminated, something more functional needs to be developed to replace them. That challenge is the subject of Part II of this book.

> *Takeaway: In some respects, regulations have made the big banks safer; but the risks have largely been transferred to the shadow banking system. The market needs liquidity to function and will turn elsewhere if credit is not accessible from commercial banks. Both the megabanks and the shadow banks serve necessary functions in today's global economy. Better than breaking them up or diluting their functions would be to make them public utilities, transferring those functions to the public domain.*

## PART II
# BANKING THAT WORKS FOR THE PEOPLE

*"You never change things by fighting the existing reality. To change something, build a new model that makes the existing model obsolete."*

—R. Buckminster Fuller, American architect and inventor, 1895-1983

## CHAPTER 7

# TO DOWNSIZE OR NATIONALIZE? ANOTHER LOOK AT THE PUBLIC OPTION

*"The bank is a utility. Why are we bailing banks out? Because when I come to Munich from New York, I would like to be able to access my checking account. It's a utility. It's like having the right to have sure water in your house."*[209]

—*Nassim Taleb (author of The Black Swan), "Time to Nationalize US Banking System?" (2009)*

**Stepping back for a look** at the big picture, banking regulations have not fixed the problem of "too big to fail" despite thousands of pages of legislation and nearly a decade of attempted reform. The regulators are pursuing faulty models. If banks were merely intermediaries, taking in the deposits of savers and lending them out again, systemic risk could be avoided by increasing capital requirements or downsizing the largest banks. But banks are not just intermediaries. They *create* deposits when they make loans. That means they create new money in the form of bank credit that did not exist before.

These bank-created deposits now compose the vast majority of the US money supply, and the loans by which they were created must be repaid; but the circulating money supply is chronically short of the money needed to repay them. The debts must be paid back with interest that was not created in the original loans; and even the money created as principal is not all spent back into the system. Some of it is "saved," held in bank accounts or investment accounts of various sorts that are outside the reach of the local productive economy where the debtor class earns most of its income. That means debtors have to continually borrow to keep up. The result is a growing pyramid of debt, which must eventually collapse of its own weight, in the familiar boom and bust pattern euphemistically called "the business cycle."

The economy needs repeated injections of new money to avoid these crises. But economists and regulators pursuing monetarist models assume that adding money to the money supply will just force prices up. When the economy hits 4.7 percent unemployment, equated with "full productivity," they hit the brakes and start raising interest rates, further squeezing an already tight local money supply.

Not just debtors and economies but banks are chronically short of money, due to a business model that relies on sleight of hand. When their deposits are insufficient to meet liquidity needs, they draw on short-term financing from a shadow banking system that is highly risky and has largely eluded the control of regulators. The shadow banks generate liquidity through a shell game called "rehypothecation," in which the same collateral purports to be under multiple shells at the same time; and it is on this money magic that we are dependent for our money supply.

Much of this interconnected web of debt is created just for speculation—money making money without increasing productivity—and the megabanks have been caught in multiple frauds.[210] But they also create the volumes of money that keep the stock market and other speculative ventures going; and speculation is now what our financialized economy is all about. It is not the economy we want, but it is the economy we have. Downsizing the biggest banks, raising their capital requirements, or eliminating safe harbor for the shadow banking system could have unintended consequences, triggering another crash by popping the fragile bank-created credit bubble that supports the economy.

Meanwhile, our financial system is fostering gross inequities. The power to create money delegated to privately owned banks allows them to extend bank-created credit to themselves and their off-balance-sheet entities very cheaply while "renting" it to individuals, businesses and local governments at much higher rates. Rentier income at interest grows exponentially while wages grow linearly, baking economic inequality into the system. Raising capital requirements or manipulating interest rates will not fix these flaws inherent in a banking system that is designed and controlled by private financiers to maximize their own profits.

We need a system that is sustainable and as safe as the federal government itself, yet not so centralized in the government that it can be usurped by big corporate interests having the power to "buy" legislators. We need a system that has the security of the government but is under local control, serving the interests of local economies. Merely breaking up the biggest banks, increasing their capital requirements or manipulating interest rates in a futile attempt to control the money supply will not achieve that result. But what are the alternatives?

## Breaking the Taboo—Nationalization

One of the options discussed by the Obama administration during the banking crisis in early 2009 was nationalization, transferring the biggest banks to public ownership.[211] But as noted in a March 2009 editorial in *The Progressive*:

> The word "nationalization" shuts off the debate. Never mind that Britain, facing the same crisis we are, just nationalized the Bank of Scotland. Never mind that Ronald Reagan himself considered such an option during a global banking crisis in the early 1980s.[212]

It sounds like a radical departure from capitalist principles, but nationalization is actually what the FDIC advocates when a major bank goes bankrupt.[213] It is one of three options open to the FDIC when a bank fails. The other two are (1) closure and liquidation, and (2) merger with a healthy bank. Most failures are resolved using the merger option, but for very large banks, nationalization is sometimes considered the best choice for taxpayers. The leading US example was Continental Illinois, the seventh-largest bank in the country when it failed in 1984. The FDIC wiped out existing shareholders, infused capital, took over bad assets, replaced senior management, and owned the bank for about a decade, running it as a commercial enterprise. In 1994, it was sold to a bank that is now part of Bank of America.[214]

In a July 2018 policy paper for the Democracy Collaborative titled "The Crisis Next Time: Planning for Public Ownership as an Alternative to Corporate Bank Bailouts," Thomas Hanna observes that nationalization has been a response to financial crises around the world for decades. The crisis that began in 2008 unleashed perhaps the most expansive wave of bank nationalizations in modern history. It included the largest bank in Belgium; Ireland's Anglo Irish Bank; Northern Rock and the Royal Bank of Scotland in the UK; Iceland's takeover of its major banks; and nationalizations in Latvia, the Netherlands, and Portugal.[215]

What did constitute a radical departure from capitalist principles in 2008-09 was an unprecedented wave of bank bailouts, sometimes called "welfare for the rich." The taxpayers bore the losses while the culpable management not only escaped civil and criminal penalties but made off with record bonuses. Banks backed by an army of lobbyists have succeeded in getting laws changed so that what was formerly criminal behavior became legal. Instead of nationalization, we got TARP, the Troubled Asset Relief Program.

Faced with the inequity of that solution, many economists recommended nationalization instead. Willem Buiter, chief economist of Citigroup and formerly a member of the Bank of England's Monetary Policy Committee, wrote in *The Financial Times* in September 2009:

> Is the reality of the modern, transactions-oriented model of financial capitalism indeed that large private firms make enormous private profits when the going is good and get bailed out and taken into temporary public ownership when the going gets bad, with the tax payer taking the risk and the losses?
>
> If so, then why not keep these activities in permanent public ownership? There is a long-standing argument that

there is no real case for private ownership of deposit-taking banking institutions, because these cannot exist safely without a deposit guarantee and/or lender of last resort facilities, that are ultimately underwritten by the taxpayer.

... Once the state underwrites the deposits or makes alternative funding available as lender of last resort, deposit-based banking is a license to print money.[216]

In a July 2012 article in *The New York Times* titled "Wall Street Is Too Big to Regulate," Gar Alperovitz, professor emeritus of political economy at the University of Maryland, concurred. He noted that the five biggest banks—JPMorgan Chase, Bank of America, Citigroup, Wells Fargo and Goldman Sachs—had amassed assets amounting to more than half the nation's GDP. He wrote:

With high-paid lobbyists contesting every proposed regulation, it is increasingly clear that big banks can never be effectively controlled as private businesses. If an enterprise (or five of them) is so large and so concentrated that competition and regulation are impossible, the most market-friendly step is to nationalize its functions. ...

Nationalization isn't as difficult as it sounds. We tend to forget that we did, in fact, nationalize General Motors in 2009; the government still owns a controlling share of its stock. We also essentially nationalized the American International Group, one of the largest insurance companies in the world, and the government still owns roughly 60 percent of its stock.[217]

Thomas Hanna adds Fannie Mae, Freddie Mac, and Citigroup to the list. The government took a 78 percent share of AIG, 74 percent ownership interest in GMAC (the former financing affiliate of General Motors), a 36 percent stake in Citigroup, and a warrant to purchase 80 percent of the common stock of Fannie and Freddie. But it did not exercise the warrant or put the companies in receivership. In each of these cases, the government effectively bought a controlling interest without taking control, providing large amounts of capital without requiring much in return. They were "bailouts" rather than nationalizations. Why? Hanna quotes Berkeley law professor Steven Davidoff Solomon, who explains that the reasons were political. The government did not want to look as if it owned these entities, and nationalizing them would have added trillions of dollars in debt to the government's balance sheet. Hanna comments:

> By going to such extreme lengths to avoid any straightforward nationalization, the U.S. government response to the Great Financial Crisis became unnecessarily complicated, totally devoid of transparency, and replete with backroom deals and perverse incentives. It is hard to believe that a pure capital for stock transaction with the government exercising full voting rights would not have been preferable to the messy, hybrid approach the government took.
>
> ... [P]ublic ownership would convert rent-seeking concentrations of private financial power into public utilities that work for the common good. It holds out the prospect of a way to fundamentally restructure and reimagine the financial sector as something that no longer fuels finan-

cialization, speculation, and consolidation, but instead works to allocate funds to real productive investment and decentralizes financial power to support prosperous and healthy local economies everywhere.

That is not, however, what economists usually meant when they called for nationalization in 2009. They meant taking over insolvent banks, cleaning up their books, and reselling them to the private sector.[218] Michael Hudson, professor of economics at the University of Missouri, Kansas City, called this "Orwellian double-think." He wrote in February 2009:

> Real nationalization occurs when governments act in the public interest to take over private property. ... Nationalizing the banks along these lines would mean that the government would supply the nation's credit needs. The Treasury would become the source of new money, replacing commercial bank credit. Presumably this credit would be lent out for economically and socially productive purposes, not merely to inflate asset prices while loading down households and business with debt as has occurred under today's commercial bank lending policies.[219]

*The government would supply the nation's credit needs, with the Treasury replacing commercial bank credit as the source of new money.* This too sounds like a radical idea; but replacing private bank credit with the government's credit would actually mean returning to our roots. In the American colonies, paper scrip was issued by the government, and retaining that right was one of the principles over which our forefathers fought the American Revolution. The notion assumes a truly representative government, which we don't have now; but freeing our elected representatives from the grip of Wall Street would go a long way toward that end.

## Practical Hurdles to Nationalization

The logic of turning banks into public utilities is compelling, but as Prof. Solomon observed, nationalizing them would have added trillions of dollars to the government balance sheet. The chief objection to nationalization in 2009 was that the banks had massive liabilities on their books, which would have been imposed on the taxpayers.[220]

That was the argument, but in a 2012 article addressing the European sovereign debt crisis, UK Professor Richard Werner proposed a way around it. The banks' bad loans would not actually need to be repaid. They could be removed from the books of insolvent banks simply by having the central bank purchase them with "free" money created on its own books, as all central banks have the power to do. He said this maneuver had been done successfully in the past, without devaluing the currency or triggering hyperinflation.[221]

Werner cited three historical precedents. The first was in Britain in 1914, when the British banking sector collapsed after the government declared war on Germany. This was not a good time for a banking crisis, so the Bank of England simply bought the banks' bad loans. There was no credit crunch, and no recession. The problem was solved at zero cost to the taxpayer.

Werner's second example was the Japanese banking crisis of 1945. The banks had totally collapsed, and they carried nonperforming loans on their books that amounted to virtually 100 percent of their assets. But like the UK before World War I, the Bank of Japan after World War II had no interest in creating a banking crisis and a credit crunch recession. It wanted to ensure that bank credit would flow again, delivering economic growth. So the Bank of Japan bought the banks' nonperforming assets, not at market value (close to zero) but significantly above market value.

Werner's third example was the US Federal Reserve's recent quantitative easing program. By 2012, when he was writing, the Fed had bought more than $1.7 trillion in mortgage-backed securities from the banks. These securities were widely understood to be "toxic" (nonperforming or unmarketable at the time).[222] The move was controversial, but the banks did not collapse, the economy got back on its feet, and QE did not trigger the inflation that critics were sure would follow. There was no inflation, says Werner, because no new money entered the nonbank economy. QE was just an accounting maneuver, an asset swap in the reserve accounts of the banks themselves. In each of these cases, he wrote:

> The operations were a complete success. No inflation resulted. The currency did not weaken. Despite massive nonperforming assets wiping out the solvency and equity of the banking sector, the banks' health was quickly restored. In the UK and Japanese case, bank credit started to recover quickly, so that there was virtually no recession at all as a result.

At that time both the UK and Japan had wartime economies, so the banks could readily be enlisted into the service of the government. But that was not true in the United States after 2008, where the rescued banks were allowed to carry on as before. As a result, the largest banks have grown larger and so have their risky bets, setting the stage for yet another crash. It is a boom and bust cycle that is likely to continue unless the megabanks can be turned into public utilities subject to public supervision and control. Their necessary functions need to be preserved while eliminating their ability to game the system. The challenge is how to harness them. They will not simply roll over and give up their power, and regulation has not worked. The banking lobbyists have just harnessed the regulators instead.

Another banking crisis may be needed before Congress is motivated to take over the biggest banks, and then it will be only those banks that have failed. But Hanna proposes some steps that should be taken in the meantime. Legislation should be pursued that requires the government to take an ownership stake with full voting rights in any financial institution that has to be bailed out or rescued due to its own fraudulent or speculative activities. To avoid the multitude of problems that arose from the government's response to the last financial crisis, the legislation should clearly establish the legal parameters for the transition to government ownership and the bank's governance. The governance framework could include establishing a single public agency to oversee the government's stake in various publicly owned enterprises. (France, Sweden and Singapore have such agencies.) Public participation in the long-term structure and mission of each new publicly owned bank should be provided for, while allowing managerial autonomy to pursue that mission once established. The legislation could also set accountability, transparency, and participation rules; set limits on executive compensation; and restrict or ban speculative activity of the sort contributing to the increased financialization of the economy.[223]

## Time to Upgrade the Model

Nationalizing the largest banks would solve a multitude of ills, but today's unprecedented debt levels could make the next financial crisis worse than the last, and waiting for it to strike before Congress acts is an ominous proposition. A less daunting alternative, if it could be pulled off, would be the proposal of Buckminster Fuller: build a better model that makes the old model obsolete. A more efficient and equitable parallel system evolved over a period of years could either phase out the megabanks simply by attrition or induce them to upgrade their own models to fit the new one. We already see that happening to some extent with developments in mobile banking, accounting software, and experiments globally in new digital currency and payment systems.

What sort of alternative system might make the old one obsolete? Various models have been proposed. At one end of the spectrum are proposals to create a parallel system of local publicly owned banks. At the other extreme are "crypto-anarchists," who trust neither banks nor government. They are designing cryptographic exchange systems that are decentralized and "trustless," obviating the need for trust because the algorithms run automatically without human intervention. Far-right crypto-anarchists favor a form of "digital gold" in fixed supply (bitcoin and its offshoots), while far-left anarchist/autonomous movements favor digital credit systems on the community currency model. Both are private currency systems independent of government.

Other proposals come from economists, academics and central bank researchers. Some argue that since all banks are underwritten by the government, they should be run as nonprofit public utilities. Others are proposing that the central bank be democratized by opening its deposit window to everyone, a privilege currently reserved to banks. Under other proposals, central banks would issue their own digital currencies, returning the power to create money to the government.

Disruptors of the conventional banking system and the big banks that dominate it are also coming out of Asia, where "global digital marketplaces" are largely bypassing the need for conventional banks. These innovative systems could be prototypes for a national mutual credit system in which money is created by users themselves by turning their own credit into something they can spend in the marketplace.

Those alternative possibilities will be reviewed here in turn, beginning with the public bank option. Chapters after that will look at new proposals and innovations in digital accounting and currency systems, both as potential disruptors of the existing financial scheme and as potential tools for the sort of banking and currency restructuring needed to bring the present outmoded system into the 21st century.

*Takeaway: Although the 2008-09 banking crisis that sacrificed generations of Main Street wealth was triggered by the speculative feeding frenzy of the mega-banks and their shadow bank counterparts, those giant institutions play necessary roles in modern financial systems and cannot simply be broken up, tied up with regulation, or abolished. The alternative is to nationalize them, something that could be done without imposing their losses on taxpayers. Nationalization may need to wait for the next financial crisis, but Congress could take action in the meantime to ensure an equitable and orderly transition when that crisis hits.*

## CHAPTER 8
# MONETIZING LOCAL CREDIT WITH PUBLICLY OWNED BANKS

*"Remember that credit is money."*

– *Benjamin Franklin, "Advice to a Young Tradesman" (1748)*

**The notion that banks** should be public utilities sounds quite foreign to the modern American capitalist mentality; but globally, over 21 percent of banks are publicly owned today.[224] In the 1970s, before the push for privatization and "liberalization" of banking laws, more than 50 percent of bank assets worldwide were controlled by the public sector.[225] Even in the ostensibly capitalist United States, the government sector is responsible for well over half of economic activity.[226]

Our "private" banks are also heavily dependent on government, as the recent banking crisis made clear.

Banks, not the government, create most of the national money supply; and they are able to do this only because of exclusive privileges and protections granted by the government. Robert Hockett, Professor of Law at Cornell University, argues that they should therefore be considered franchisees of the government and regulated under the public utility model, including a cap on profits. In a policy paper titled "Finance Without Financiers," he explains:

> That model is based on the idea that in providing a private firm with the monopoly rights to provide electricity or natural gas to homes and businesses in a certain geographical area, it is appropriate for regulators to control the amount of profit that the firm can earn from that business. ... Such an approach would have the great advantage of discouraging financial institutions from taking on higher levels of risk since they would not be able to retain profits in excess of the government set ceiling.[227]

Hockett suggests that either existing banks could be turned into government-regulated nonprofits or new publicly owned banks could be created by local or state governments that had the power to create money as credit. The result would be to restore the power to create money to the public sector, where it was originally in the American colonies.

## The Colonial Public Banking Model

The first public banking institutions in North America were established when the states were still colonies of the British. Like private banks today, they simply issued the money they lent; but they had the advantage over today's banks that they did not have to scramble to balance their books overnight by purporting to borrow the money from somewhere else. They were owned by colonial governments, which had the power to issue paper scrip directly.

The development of these colonial credit institutions was traced by Alvin Rabushka, a senior fellow at the Hoover Institution at Stanford University, in a 2003 paper called "Representation Without Taxation."[228] He wrote that there were two main ways the colonies issued paper money. Most colonies used both, in varying proportions. One was a direct issue of notes, usually called "bills of credit" or "treasury notes." These were IOUs of the government backed by specific future taxes; but the payback was deferred well into the future, and sometimes the funds never got returned to the treasury at all. Like in a bathtub without a drain, the money supply kept increasing without a means of recycling it back to its source, creating price inflation. But the funds were at least not owed back to private foreign lenders, and no interest was due on them. They were just credits issued and spent into the economy on goods and services.

The inflation problem was solved when a second method of issue was devised. Colonial assemblies discovered that provincial loan offices could generate a steady stream of revenue in the form of interest, *by taking on the lending functions of banks*. A government loan office called a "land bank" would issue paper money and lend it to residents (usually farmers) at low rates of interest. The loans were secured by mortgages on real property, silver plate, and other hard assets. Benjamin Franklin wrote, "Bills issued upon Land are in Effect Coined Land." New money issued and lent to borrowers came back to the loan office on a regular payment schedule, preventing the money supply from overinflating and keeping the values of paper loan-office bills stable in terms of English sterling. The interest paid on the loans also went into the public coffers, funding the government. Colonies relying on this method of issuing paper money thus wound up with more stable currencies than those relying heavily on new issues of bills of credit.

The most successful loan offices were in the middle colonies—Pennsylvania, Delaware, New York and New Jersey. The model that earned the admiration of all was the loan office established in Pennsylvania in 1723. The Pennsylvania plan showed that it was quite possible for the government to issue new money in place of taxes without inflating prices. From 1723 until the French and Indian War in the 1750s, except for import duties on liquor, the provincial government collected no taxes at all. The loan office was the province's chief source of revenue. During this period, Pennsylvania wholesale prices remained stable. The currency depreciated by 21 percent against English sterling, but Rabushka showed that this was due to external trade relations rather than to changes in the quantity of currency in circulation.

Before the loan office came to the rescue, Pennsylvania had been losing both business and residents due to a lack of available currency. The loan office injected new money into the economy by providing a source of low-interest credit that was not previously available. Franklin said that this money system was the reason that Pennsylvania "has so greatly increased in inhabitants," having replaced "the inconvenient method of barter" and given "new life to business [and] promoted greatly the settlement of new lands (by lending small sums to beginners on easy interest)." In 1776, Adam Smith wrote of this public banking and currency system in *The Wealth of Nations*:

> The government of Pennsylvania, without amassing any treasure [gold or silver], invented a method of lending,

not money indeed, but what is equivalent to money to its subjects. By advancing to private people at interest, and upon land security [as collateral], paper bills of credit ... made transferable from hand-to-hand like banknotes, and declared by active assembly to be legal tender in all payments from one inhabitant to another, it raised a moderate revenue which went a considerable way toward defraying ... the whole ordinary expense of that frugal and orderly government. ... [Pennsylvania's] paper currency ... is said never to have sunk below the value of gold and silver which was current in the colony before ... the issue of paper money.

The American colonies gave up their right to issue bills of credit (paper money) when they joined the Union, delegating that power to Congress. But Congress declined to take it, and private banks stepped in to fill the void. In the National Bank Act of the 1860s, Congress imposed a heavy tax to block private state-chartered banks from issuing their own banknotes. However, some banks bypassed the tax by advancing credit simply as "deposits" written into deposit accounts.

States and cities today could do the same: they could bypass the prohibition on issuing paper money by advancing credit through their own state-chartered, publicly owned banks. They would not be issuing legal tender, but they would be issuing loans; and loans create deposits, which are counted in the money supply. (See Chapter 3.) This newly created bank-money would then circulate in the community, stimulating economic activity. A growing public banking movement is advocating that approach in the United States and elsewhere today.[229]

## The Bank of North Dakota

In the 19th century, only a few states owned their own depository banks; and by the 20th century, there was only one—the Bank of North Dakota (BND). That bank, however, has survived for nearly a century and has done remarkably well. In November 2014, *The Wall Street Journal* reported that the Bank of North Dakota was more profitable than even the largest Wall Street banks, with a return on equity that was 70 percent greater than that of either JPMorgan Chase or Goldman Sachs.[230]

This stellar performance was attributed by the author to the state's oil boom; but in succeeding years the boom became an oil bust, yet the BND's profits continued to soar.[231] Oil plunged from over $100 a barrel in mid-2014 to $30 a barrel in January 2016. Yet in its annual report published in April 2016, the BND showed 2015 to be its most profitable year to date, with total assets of $7.4 billion and a return on equity of an impressive 18.1 percent. Its lending portfolio grew by 12.7 percent, with growth in all four of its areas of concentration: agriculture, business, residential, and student loans.[232] In April 2018 the BND reported record profits for its 14th straight year.[233]

In 2016, North Dakota Governor Jack Dalrymple proposed returning $200 million from the BND's profits to the state's general fund, to help make up for a budget shortfall caused by collapsing oil and soybean proceeds. He commented, "Our economic advisers have told us there is no similar state in the nation that could have weathered such a collapse in commodity prices without serious impacts on their financial condition."[234]

One of many advantages of having a cheap and ready credit line with its own bank has been to reduce the state's need for wasteful rainy-day funds invested at minimal interest in out-of-state banks. When North Dakota went over-budget in 2001 and again in 2016, the BND acted as a rainy-day fund for the state.[235] When a local city suffered a massive flood in 1997, the bank provided emergency credit lines.[236]

Ironically, the goal of the BND is not actually to make a profit. It was formed in 1919 to free farmers and small businessmen from the clutches of out-of-state bankers and railroad men. Its stated mission is to deliver sound financial services that promote agriculture, commerce and industry in North Dakota. As noted in *The Wall Street Journal* article just cited:

It traditionally extends credit, or invests directly, in areas other lenders shun, such as rural housing loans.

. . . [R]etail banking accounts for just 2%-3% of its business. The bank's focus is providing loans to students and extending credit to companies in North Dakota, often in partnership with smaller community banks.

Bank of North Dakota also acts as a clearinghouse for interbank transactions in the state by settling checks and distributing coins and currency. ...

The bank's mission is promoting economic development, not competing with private banks. "We're a state agency and profit maximization isn't what drives us," President Eric Hardmeyer said.

How then to account for the BND's remarkable profitability? Its secret seems to be its very efficient business model. Its costs are very low: no exorbitantly paid executives; no bonuses, fees, or commissions; no private shareholders; very low borrowing costs; no need for multiple branch offices; and no FDIC insurance premiums (the state rather than the FDIC guarantees its deposits). BND profits are not siphoned off to Wall Street to be invested overseas or stored in offshore tax havens. They are recycled back into the bank, the state and the community.

The BND has a massive, captive deposit base, since all of the state's revenues are deposited in the bank by law. Most state agencies must also deposit with the BND. Although the bank takes some token individual deposits, the vast majority come from the state itself. The BND also has a massive capital base. Originally capitalized with a bond issue, it has built up a sizable capital fund through years of prudent and efficient banking practices, which it can leverage many times over into loans.

## BND's Partnership Model

The BND does not compete with local North Dakota banks for deposits. Rather, it helps local community banks by providing letters of credit guaranteeing the deposits of municipal governments, which are generally reserved for local banks. In other states, community banks must post collateral equal to or greater than the deposits they take from municipal governments, tying up the deposits and limiting their use as liquidity for new loans. In North Dakota, community banks are able to avoid this requirement by substituting the BND's letters of credit for collateral.[237]

The BND also partners rather than competes with local North Dakota banks for loans. The local bank acts as the front office dealing directly with customers. The BND acts more like a "bankers' bank," participating in the loans and helping with liquidity and capital requirements. Local banks are thus able to take on projects that would otherwise either go to Wall Street banks or go unfunded, including loans for local infrastructure.

Due to this amicable relationship, the North Dakota Bankers' Association endorses the BND as a partner rather than a competitor of the state's private banks. Indeed, it may be the BND that ultimately saves local North Dakota banks from extinction, as the number of banks in the United States steadily shrinks. According to a July 2015 report by the Institute for Local Self-Reliance:

> North Dakota has more banks and credit unions per capita than any other state. In fact, it has nearly six times as many local financial institutions per person as the country overall. While locally owned small and mid-sized banks and credit unions (those under $10 billion in assets) account for only 29 percent of deposits nationally..., in North Dakota they have a remarkable 83 percent of the market.[238]

The BND also acts as a mini-Fed for the state, providing correspondent banking services to virtually every financial institution in North Dakota. It offers a federal funds program that provides secured and unsecured federal funds lines to over 100 financial institutions. It also provides check-clearing, cash management and automated clearing house services for local banks. Because it assists local banks with mortgages and guarantees their loans, local North Dakota banks have been able to keep loans on their books rather than selling them to investors to meet capital requirements, allowing them to avoid the subprime and securitization debacles.[239]

The BND also helps rural lenders with regulatory compliance. When rural banks that handled only three to five mortgages a year were losing business to out-of-state banks because they were not able to shoulder the heightened regulatory burden, the BND was directed by the state legislature to get into the rural home mortgage origination business. The Mortgage Origination Program, signed by North Dakota's governor in 2013, states that the BND may originate residential mortgages if private sector mortgage loan services are not reasonably available. Local financial institutions or credit unions can participate by assisting the BND in taking loan applications, gathering required documents, ordering required legal documents, and maintaining contact with the borrower.[240] Local banks thus get paid what is essentially a finder's fee for sending rural mortgage loans to the BND. If the BND touches the money first, the onus is on it to deal with the regulators, something it can afford to do by capitalizing on economies of scale, allowing the local bank to avoid dealing with regulatory compliance while keeping its customer.

Like public sector banks generally, the BND lends countercyclically. While Wall Street banks were being bailed out by the taxpayers and were drastically cutting back on local loans, the BND was increasing its local lending—and at the same time showing record profits. In the decade following the 2008 banking crisis, it reported an annual return on investment of between 17 percent and 23 percent.[241]

The BND passes its profits on to North Dakotans, both
as dividends to the state and by facilitating below-market
loans. Students can get favorable loans from the BND that
come without fees or the onerous conditions often imposed
by private lenders. For students who already have loans, the
BND has a student loan consolidation program that reduces
the interest rate and relieves conditions on repayment. It can
also extend credit to local businesses and smaller borrowers.
It has a loan program called Flex PACE, which allows local
communities to provide assistance to borrowers in areas of
jobs retention, technology creation, retail, small business, and
essential community services.[242] In 2015, the North Dakota
legislature established a BND Infrastructure Loan Fund
program that made $50 million in funds available to com-
munities with a population of less than 2,000, and $100 mil-
lion available to communities with a population greater than
2,000. The loans were to have a 2 percent fixed interest rate
and a term of up to 30 years.[243] At that time, the taxable rate
on infrastructure bonds in other states was 4 to 6 percent.[244]
The loans could be used for the new construction of water
and treatment plants, sewer and water lines, transportation
infrastructure and other infrastructure needs to support new
growth in a community.

## The Magic of Leverage

Policymakers have been heard to object to state bank proposals that they don't have the money to lend. "We need our
state revenues to meet our budget," they say. "We can't afford
to lend them out." But banks do not lend their deposits,
as we have seen. The deposits are available for withdrawal

on demand by the depositor—in this case the state. The state's revenues would be no less available when deposited in its own state-owned bank than when deposited in Bank of America, and no more at risk. In fact, their revenues might be more at risk in Bank of America. With the repeal of Glass-Steagall, the biggest banks can commingle their depositors' money with their speculative investments, allowing them to gamble in the sort of risky ventures in which a transparent and accountable state-owned bank would be forbidden to engage; and in a serious market collapse, the deposits could be confiscated in a bail-in. (See Chapter 5.)

It has also been argued that "politicians make bad businessmen," but a public bank would not be run by politicians. Making loans is nothing new to state and local governments, which do this routinely through loan officers who are trained in prudent lending and know the local market very well. The chief difference is that government lending programs today are typically done as revolving funds. The money has to be there before it can be lent out and must come back before it is lent again. Banks, on the other hand, can leverage their capital into roughly 10 times that sum in loans. A bank with adequate capital will lend to any creditworthy borrower without first checking its reserves. If the bank has insufficient reserves to cover the checks when the loan money leaves the bank, it can borrow from a variety of cheap sources that are normally available only to the banking club but that local governments and communities can tap into by owning their own banks.

That is one of the major benefits to the state of having its own bank: it can borrow cheaply from other banks, the money market, the Federal Reserve or the Federal Home Loan Banks. In effect, the state can borrow at bankers' rates rather than at state bond rates, getting the sort of Wall Street perks not otherwise available to governments, businesses, or individuals; and it can be backstopped by the Federal Reserve system if it runs short of funds. It can also avoid the fees related to bond issuance, maximizing the use of its resources. Rather than borrowing the whole principal of a 30-year bond and paying interest on it for 30 years before the money is actually paid out, the state or local government can stagger disbursement as the money is needed.

To see how bank leverage works, we can look at some numbers. In its annual report for 2017, the Bank of North Dakota reported that it had:

- equity (capital) of $825 million;
- total assets of $7 billion, including loans of $4.9 billion;
- deposits of $4.6 billion;
- short-and long-term borrowings, fed funds and repos of $1.6 billion;
- interest expense of $38 million;
- net interest income after provision for loan losses of $170 million;
- net income after deducting noninterest expenses (salaries, operating expenses, etc.) of $145 million.[245]

Dividing $145 million in income by $825 million in equity, the BND's net return on equity was thus about 17.6 percent. Dividing $145 million in income by $4.9 billion in loans, its net return on loans was about 3.5 percent.

Assume a local government with similar numbers. It has $1 billion in funds available to lend or invest. If it lends that

$1 billion through a revolving fund at 3.5 percent, it will earn $35 million in interest. If it uses its $1 billion to capitalize a bank, assuming the bank can duplicate the BND's low operating costs, it can earn 17.6 percent or $176 million on the same money. The bank will need deposits for liquidity, but it already has them. It just needs to transfer some of the deposits it currently holds in Wall Street banks. Note that it will earn a net return of 17.6 percent on equity *after* deducting its operating costs and cost of funds (including interest paid on its own deposits). That is five times the return it would have made on the same capital expenditure lent directly in a revolving fund.

The bank could also use its efficiency savings to make loans at lower interest than otherwise, while making 10 times as many of them. Consider the possibilities for California. It already has a bank—the California Infrastructure and Development Bank (or "IBank"). But the IBank is a "bank" in name only. It cannot take deposits or leverage capital into loans. It makes infrastructure loans at 3 percent, a good below-market rate; but the bank has a limited pot of money to lend. If it used those funds to capitalize a depository bank, it could make 10 times as many loans at 3 percent, greatly expanding its usefulness.

The easiest, most risk-free option would be for the state to refinance its own debt at below-market rates. As an example, consider California Proposition 68, a statewide ballot measure that voters approved in the June 2018 primary election authorizing $4.1 billion in bonds for parks, environmental, and flood protection programs. That was the stated cost, but the measure included $200 million per year in interest over 40 years, bringing the total expenditure to $8 billion.[246] (Financing typically accounts for half the cost of long-term projects funded through the municipal bond market.[247]) The IBank could finance the same bill at 3 percent over 30 years for $2.1 billion—a nearly 50 percent reduction in financing costs. Even more could be saved with staggered disbursements—borrowing and paying interest only as sums are actually expended—rather than borrowing a lump sum and financing it over 40 years.

Those are the possibilities if the IBank were adequately capitalized; but today it is seriously underfunded, because the California Department of Finance returned over half of its allotted funds to the General Fund to repair the state's budget after the dot-com collapse in 2001.[248] But the legislature could repay that revenue bond and expand the IBank to address California's infrastructure needs, drawing deposits and capital from its many pools of idle funds across the state, saving billions of dollars for its public clients. The IBank has 20 years' experience in making prudent infrastructure loans at below municipal bond rates, and its clients are limited to municipal governments and other public entities, making them safe bets underwritten by their local tax bases.

Many states and municipalities are now exploring the public bank option, including Washington state, Michigan, Pennsylvania, New Mexico, New Jersey, California, Arizona, Alaska, New York and others.[249] Feasibility studies done at both state and local levels show that affordable small business lending, increased employment, low-cost student loans, affordable housing and greater economic stability can all result from keeping local public dollars in the local community.

## Public Sector Banks Globally: The Sparkassen Model

The BND is an inspiring model, but it is only one bank. For others we will have to look abroad, but there they are plentiful, composing a fifth of the banking sector globally. Government-owned banks in some developing countries have had a reputation for being inefficient or corrupt, but that reputation is changing. In a 2014 research paper titled "Alternative Banking and Recovery from Crisis," Professors Kurt Mettenheim and Olivier Butzbach concluded that "alternative banks [public savings banks, cooperative banks, and public development banks] have equaled or outperformed joint-stock banks in terms of efficiency, profitability and risk management. This counters core ideas in contemporary banking theory and bank regulation about the superiority of private, market based banking."[250]

Public sector banks have been particularly successful in Germany, where they dominate the local banking scene. Like the BND, these local savings banks or Sparkassen actually outperform the private banking sector while serving the public interest. This was confirmed in a January 2015 report by the Savings Banks Foundation for International Cooperation (SBFIC, the Sparkassenstiftung für internationale Kooperation), drawing from Bundesbank data.[251] The report showed that the Sparkassen have a return on capital that is several times greater than for the German private banking sector and that they pay substantially more to local and federal governments in taxes.

The Sparkassen were instituted in the late 18th century as nonprofit organizations to aid the poor. The intent was to help people with low incomes save small sums of money and to support business start-ups. Today these savings banks operate a network of over 15,600 branches and offices, employ over 250,000 people, and have a strong record of investing wisely in local businesses. Resting on top of this pyramid of thousands of municipal savings banks are the publicly owned Landesbanken, which function as "universal" banks operating in all sectors of the financial services market. The Sparkassen network capitalizes on economies of scale to provide services to its members, including a compliance department that deals with the onerous regulations imposed on banks by the EU.

Thanks in large part to its vast network of public banks, Germany is now the largest and most robust economy in the Eurozone, an impressive feat considering that it emerged from World War II with a collapsed economy that had degenerated into barter.[252] Manufacturing composes 25 percent of Germany's GDP, more than twice that in the UK. Underlying the economy's strength is its *Mittelstand*—small-to-medium-sized enterprises—which are supported by a strong regional banking system that is willing to lend to fund research and development. According to Peter Dorman, Professor of *Economics at* Evergreen State College, writing in 2011:

If you add in the specialized publicly owned real estate lenders, about half the total assets of the German banking system are in the public sector. (Another substantial chunk is in cooperative savings banks.) They are key tools of German industrial policy.... Because of the landesbanken, small firms in Germany have as much access to capital as large firms; there are no economies of scale in finance.

This also means that workers in the small business sector earn the same wages as those in big corporations, have the same skills and training, and are just as productive.[253]

Germany has been called "the world's first major energy economy." Renewables generated 41 percent of its electricity in 2017, up from 6 percent in 2000; and public sector banks provided over 72 percent of the financing for this energy revolution.[254] They were instrumental in the transition both as lenders and as facilitators, coordinating stakeholders and setting up renewable energy cooperatives.

## Postal Banks: Saving the Post Office, Serving the Underbanked, and Funding Infrastructure

Another type of public bank that is very popular worldwide is the postal savings bank. According to the Universal Postal Union, 1 billion people now use the postal sector for savings and deposit accounts, and more than 1.5 billion people take advantage of basic transactional services through the post.[255] A Discussion Paper of the United Nations Department of Economic and Social Affairs states:

> The essential characteristic distinguishing postal financial services from the private banking sector is the obligation and capacity of the postal system to serve the entire spectrum of the national population, unlike conventional private banks which allocate their institutional resources to service the sectors of the population they deem most profitable.[256]

Maintaining post offices in some rural or low-income areas can be a losing proposition, and expanding their postal business to include financial services has been crucial in many countries to maintaining the profitability of their postal networks. Public postal banks are profitable because their market is large and their costs are low. The infrastructure is already built and available, advertising costs are minimal, and government-owned banks do not reward their management with extravagant bonuses or commissions that drain profits away. Profits return to the government and the public. Postal banking systems are ubiquitous in other countries, where their long record of safe and profitable banking has proved the viability of the model.

A century ago, postal banking was also popular in the United States. In the late 19th century, a nationwide coalition of workers and farmers united to demand postal savings banks of the sort found in most other nations. They argued that postal banks could provide depositors with basic banking services and were a safe haven against repeated financial panics and bank failures. After the private banking system crashed the economy in the Bank Panic of 1907, a postal savings alternative was established by the Postal Savings Bank Act of 1910. The US Postal Savings System was set up to get money out of hiding, attract the savings of immigrants, provide safe depositories for people who had lost confidence in private banks, and furnish depositories with longer hours that were convenient for working people. The postal system paid two percent interest on deposits annually. It issued US Postal Savings Bonds that paid annual interest, as well as Postal Savings Certificates and domestic money orders. Postal savings peaked in 1947 at almost $3.4 billion.[257]

But postal banking was under continual assault from the private banking establishment. Soon after the Postal Savings Bank Act was passed, the American Bankers Association formed a Special Committee on Postal Savings Legislation to block any extension of the new service. According to a September 2017 article in *The Journal of Social History* titled "'Banks of the People': The Life and Death of the U.S. Postal Savings System," the banking fraternity would maintain its enmity toward the government savings bank for the next 50 years.[258]

The US Postal Savings System came into its own during the banking crisis of the early 1930s, when it became the national alternative to a private banking system that people clearly could not trust. When demands increased to expand its services to include affordable loans, alarmed bankers called it the "postal savings menace" and warned that it could result in the destruction of the entire private banking system.

The response of President Franklin Roosevelt to the crisis, however, was not to expand the Postal Savings System but to buttress the private banking system with public guarantees, including FDIC deposit insurance. That put private banks in the enviable position of being able to keep their profits while their losses were covered by the government. Deposit insurance along with a statutory cap on the interest paid on postal savings caused postal banking to lose its edge. In 1957, the head of the government bureau responsible for the Postal Savings System called for its abolition, arguing that "it is desirable that the government withdraw from competitive private business at every point." The Postal Savings System was finally liquidated in 1966. One influential right-wing commentator, celebrating an ideological victory, said, "It is even conceivable that we might transfer post offices to private hands altogether."

The push for privatization of the US Postal Service has continued to the present. The nation's second largest civilian employer after Walmart,[259] the USPS has been successfully self-funded without taxpayer support throughout its long history; but it is currently struggling to stay afloat. What has driven it toward insolvency is an oppressive congressional mandate—included almost as a footnote in the Postal Accountability and Enhancement Act of 2006 (PAEA)—that requires the USPS to prefund healthcare and pensions for its workers 75 years into the future. No other entity, public or private, has the burden of funding multiple generations of employees yet unborn. The pre-funding mandate is so blatantly unreasonable as to raise suspicions that the nation's largest publicly owned industry has been intentionally targeted for takedown.

To avoid that result, legislation was introduced in Congress in 2013 that would allow the post office to recapitalize itself by diversifying its range of services to meet unmet public needs.[260] One way it could diversify would be by reviving the banking services it efficiently performed in the past. A January 2014 white paper published by the Office of the Inspector General of the USPS proposed that a system of postal banks could service the massive market of the unbanked and underbanked and provide a safe place to save money.[261] In a 2011 survey, the unbanked and underbanked included about one in four households.[262] Without access to conventional financial services, people turn to an expensive alternative banking market of bill-pay, prepaid debit cards, check cashing services, and payday loans; and they pay excessive fees and are susceptible to high-cost predatory lenders. Catering to this underserved group could not only be a revenue generator for the post office but could save that struggling sector of the population large sums in fees.

A postal bank could also appeal to other savers concerned with the safety of their deposits. Traditionally, people have deposited their money in banks for three reasons: safety from theft, the convenience of check writing and bill paying, and to earn some interest. Today, bank deposits not only earn virtually no interest but may not be safe from theft—in this case by the Wall Street megabanks that are authorized by statute to confiscate the money of their creditors in the event of insolvency. Postal banking could provide a safe, casino-free public banking alternative, as it did from 1911 until 1967. It could also provide a way to vote with our feet, moving our money out of a risky and rapacious Wall Street banking system into a network of publicly owned banks with a mandate to serve the people and the economy. In April 2018, Sen. Kirsten Gillibrand introduced legislation that would require every US post office to provide basic banking services.[263]

## Nationalizing the Federal Reserve

That brings us to the federal agency that should be at the top of the public banking pyramid, the central bank itself. Before the collapse of the gold standard in the early 1930s, central banks around the world served primarily as "banks for bankers." But in the Great Depression, central banks became responsible for setting the course of monetary policy for national economies. As a result, most central banks globally are now owned by their governments.[264] But that is not true of the US central banking system. Although the Fed's Board of Governors, Chair and Vice Chair are appointed by the president with the approval of the Senate, the twelve Federal Reserve Banks are owned by and accountable to the same commercial banks they are supposed to regulate. Instead of a national public banking system run through local post offices, as the early populists sought, what the American people got was a mostly private banking scheme backstopped by a central bank effectively controlled by the banks themselves.[265]

To gain the trust of the citizenry, the Federal Reserve needs to become a truly democratic, public institution, operated by and for the people; and discussions along those lines are happening, not just among activist groups but among economists and central bank staffers themselves.[266] The Federal Reserve citadel was breached in 2015, when Congress passed the Fixing America's Surface Transportation (FAST) Act, requiring the Fed to transfer everything in excess of $10 billion from its capital surplus to the Treasury Department. In December 2015, the Fed complied by transferring an additional $19.3 billion to the Treasury.[267] President Donald Trump has also questioned the Fed's independence, and he has the power to appoint its Board of Governors.[268]

The Federal Reserve Act was passed by Congress, and Congress can change it. A citizen advocacy group called the Center for Popular Democracy proposes that all Federal Reserve officials be made public employees, with a mandate to represent the American people. Representatives and employees of financial institutions should not serve as directors at Federal Reserve banks, and financial institutions that are regulated by the Fed should have no role in selecting the directors. Instead, the governors of the Reserve banks would be appointed by the Federal Reserve Board of Governors after consulting with elected officials, community, consumer and labor organizations, academics, and other representatives of the public within the region. The Board of Governors would choose a diverse set of directors who understood economic conditions for all sectors of the local economy. These directors, in turn, would conduct a transparent and publicly inclusive process for choosing Reserve Bank presidents.[269]

Some academics would go further. In a June 2018 policy paper titled "Central Banking for All: A Public Option for Bank Accounts," a trio of law professors and former Treasury advisors said that the underlying problem with the banking system today is that banks have privileges that individuals, businesses and local governments don't have. Only banks and other financial institutions are allowed to have deposit accounts with the Fed. They get more interest on these deposits than we get on our private bank accounts, and they pay less to borrow than we do. They get immediate transfers through their Fedwire accounts, while we must wait a couple of days for checks to clear. Banks don't have to worry about deposit insurance limits, minimum balances, deposit fees, or transfer fees. They can gamble with our deposits, and if they lose them the taxpayers must bail out the banks, or they can bail our money in. The banks' own deposits, however, are completely secure with the Fed, which cannot go bankrupt. The authors proposed democratizing these banking functions by opening the Fed's deposit window to everyone.[270] The proposal echoes that of Prof. Huber discussed in Chapter 3 and is similar to proposals now being made by some central bank researchers, discussed in Chapter 13.

Democratizing the central bank could be taken further. A truly "public" central bank could open not just its deposit window but its lending window to all, allowing it to undergird a national public banking system on the model of the colonial bank that was so successful in providing low-cost credit in colonial Pennsylvania. A democratized Fed could issue and lend national digital currency without having to borrow first from somewhere else or relying on the risky shadow banks for liquidity. The effect would be to return the power to create the national money supply to the people through their representative government.

That assumes, however, that we actually have a representative government. "Crypto-anarchists" are suspicious of proposals for a national digital currency, viewing them as simply dangerous attempts to eliminate cash and control the money taps. Their ideal is a stateless society operating independently of both government and banks.

Before getting to proposals for reforming the Fed and the national currency, the next two chapters will look at the growing movement to replace national currencies with cryptocurrencies, and at whether those innovative new currencies could indeed replace the national currency or disrupt the Wall Street-dominated banking system as claimed.

*Takeaway: Successful public banking models are available from around the world, featuring local banks that are either publicly owned or organized as nonprofits. Although the United States has a history of public banking going back to colonial times, its only model with a long-term track record today is the century-old Bank of North Dakota. That record, however, is stellar, beating some of the largest Wall Street banks for profitability while at the same time serving the needs of the local community. A growing public banking movement is seeking to expand that model to other cities and states. Proposals are also on the table for opening the banking services of a publicly owned central bank to everyone.*

## CHAPTER 9
## THE RADICAL ANARCHIST SOLUTION: BYPASSING GOVERNMENT AND BANKS WITH CRYPTOCURRENCIES

*"You don't need honor among thieves. You just need a blockchain."*

—*Robert Hackett, Fortune*[271]

**Bitcoin and the cryptocurrency movement** exploded on the scene after the 2008-09 financial crisis generated widespread distrust not just of Wall Street but of national currencies and government generally. But "crypto-anarchism" had earlier roots. The term dates back at least to 1988, when its basic principles were introduced by Timothy C. May in the "Crypto Anarchist Manifesto." In his call to arms, May wrote:

> Computer technology is on the verge of providing the ability for individuals and groups to communicate and interact with each other in a totally anonymous manner. ... These developments will alter completely the nature of government regulation, the ability to tax and control economic interactions, the ability to keep information secret, and will even alter the nature of trust and reputation.

The technology for this revolution—and it surely will be
both a social and economic revolution—has existed in
theory for the past decade. The methods are based upon
public-key encryption, zero-knowledge interactive proof
systems, and various software protocols for interaction,
authentication, and verification. ...

The State will of course try to slow or halt the spread of
this technology, citing national security concerns, use of the
technology by drug dealers and tax evaders, and fears of
societal disintegration. Many of these concerns will be valid
.... But this will not halt the spread of crypto anarchy.[272]

Twenty years later bitcoin appeared, and within a decade
the crypto movement was an international phenomenon. It
was featured in a June 2017 article in *The Guardian* titled
"Forget Far-Right Populism—Crypto-Anarchists Are the
New Masters." Jamie Bartlett wrote that crypto-anarchists
are mostly computer-hacking anti-state libertarians who
believe that digital technology is the route to a stateless par-
adise, since it undermines government's ability to monitor,
control and tax its people:

A few years ago crypto-anarchists like these were the only
people using bitcoin. ... [I]t was originally designed by
a crypto-anarchist as a neat way of undermining central
bank's control over the money supply. It is a revolutionary
idea wrapped up as efficiency gain. Bitcoin is more than
a currency, it's a new way of handling information. It
uses blockchain, which is a technique to create a massive, distributed, tamper-proof database that anyone can

add to but no one can delete, because no one controls it. Millions of pounds of investment are pouring into bitcoin and blockchain from governments, banks, IT and financial services, all excitedly eyeing up a novel way to store information or prove asset ownership securely. Specialists reckon it's as revolutionary as the internet itself.[273]

Bitcoin was a lofty idea aimed at freeing the people from the corruptions and manipulations of centralized gatekeepers. But a decade after it came online, it still has failed to achieve that democratic result.[274] Critics contend, in fact, that bitcoin is inherently undemocratic. Ownership and control are concentrated in the hands of a few very wealthy "whales" who can collude to manipulate the price, since there is no regulatory body prohibiting it.[275] Bitcoin is not a currency generated by the people who use it but is created by an elite class of miners with very expensive hardware and technical expertise beyond the reach of most people. Critics say it is a Ponzi scheme, in which cash paid to earlier investors by new investors maintains the illusion that the scheme is earning real profits; and that like all Ponzi schemes, it will collapse when sufficient sums can no longer be raised from new investors to pay off earlier ones.[276]

Disillusionment with cryptocurrencies after the soaring crypto market crashed in early 2018 underscored these hard truths. But the dream of a democratic currency created and traded by people themselves, bypassing private profit-seeking middlemen, has generated ongoing interest. Developers are still working on the technology, variations of which might yet have promising uses in a 21st-century upgrade of the monetary system.

## Crypto-mania

A cryptocurrency is defined in the Oxford Dictionary as "a digital currency in which encryption techniques are used to regulate the generation of units of currency and verify the transfer of funds, operating independently of a central bank." Blockchain, the innovative software technology that does this for bitcoin, is a digitized, decentralized, publicly shared ledger or record of all the transactions in the cryptocurrency.

Bitcoin and its blockchain software were developed by an unknown person or group called Satoshi Nakamoto, who has or have since disappeared from public view.[277] Nakamoto wrote in 2009:

> The root problem with conventional currency is all the trust that's required to make it work. The central bank must be trusted not to debase the currency, but the history of fiat currencies is full of breaches of that trust. Banks must be trusted to hold our money and transfer it electronically, but they lend it out in waves of credit bubbles with barely a fraction in reserve.[278]

The challenge for Nakamoto was to create a digital currency that would be the cyberspace equivalent of cash—something that could not be switched off by a central power, whether a bank or a government, because it was stored on millions of computers at once. The currency needed to exist on a peer-to-peer network using an open source protocol, with no central controlling authority and no single physical location. The virtual currency also needed to be hyperinflation-proof, originating in a way that avoided devaluation from the too-easy creation of monetary digits on a computer; and the currency units needed to be nonduplicable, preventing the fraud of double-spending. This feature would also prevent fractional reserve lending and the rehypothecation of collateral.

The solution Nakamoto came up with was a type of distributed ledger or decentralized database that keeps continuously updated digital records of who owns what, without relying on a central administrator in the form of a bank, government or accountant. To prevent over-issuance of the currency, Nakamoto capped the number of bitcoins that could be produced at 21 million. How bitcoin's distributed ledger works was explained by tech blogger Collin Thompson like this:

> When a digital transaction is carried out, it is grouped together in a cryptographically protected block with other transactions … . Miners (members in the network with high levels of computing power) then compete to validate the transactions by solving complex coded problems. The first miner to solve the problems and validate the block receives a reward [in the form of bitcoins] … .
>
> The validated block of transactions is then time-stamped and added to a chain in a linear, chronological order. New blocks of validated transactions are linked to older blocks, making a chain of blocks that show every transaction made in the history of that blockchain. The entire chain is continually updated so that every ledger in the network is the same, giving each member the ability to prove who owns what at any given time.[279]

Revolutionary changes were envisioned from the technology. In an April 2016 article titled "Blockchain Is the Most Disruptive Invention Since the Internet Itself," blogger Martin Hiesboeck declared that it "won't just kill banks, brokers and credit card companies. It will change every transactional process you know. Simply put, blockchain eliminates the need for clearinghouse entities of any kind. And that means a revolution is coming, a fundamental sea change in the way we do business."[280] According to an April 2017 investor website, "just about every industry is starting to use or consider the blockchain in one way or another," including 80 percent of banks; the NASDAQ stock exchange, soon to be followed by five other major stock exchanges; the Depository Trust & Clearing Corporation (DTCC), Wall Street's main clearinghouse; and CLS, the world's biggest multicurrency settlement system.[281] In an April 2017 newsletter, investment advisor Simon Black proclaimed, "The centuries-old, multi-trillion dollar banking industry is at risk of being disrupted by just 200 lines of code."[282]

Businesses may have been considering it, but the blockchain designed for bitcoin has proved to be too slow and energy-intensive for use in the billions of small-scale transactions occurring daily in large national economies. The networks that Visa and Mastercard use process more than 5,000 transactions per second, with the capacity to process many times more.[283] Facebook can process half a million "likes" per second. Bitcoin takes 10 minutes to clear and settle a single transaction, and it can handle only 7 transactions per second, a limitation inherent in the way the system was set up.[284] Contrary to earlier claims, blockchain transactions are not free, and the price has been going up.

But those concerns have not deterred the faithful. Bitcoin hit the phenomenal price of $20,000 per coin in December 2017, up from a mere $0.0007 when it was first introduced in 2009. Its success has prompted the development of over 2,000 new blockchain-based cryptocurrencies, with a market capitalization that briefly exceeded $750 billion, up from just $20 billion at the beginning of 2017.[285] By December 2018, however, the cryptomarket had dropped from that dizzying peak by 80 percent, with bitcoin at $4,000 and the crypto market cap at only $138 billion.

## Digital Cash?

Bitcoin has been called "digital cash." It is stored in "digital wallets" similar to the paper dollars in physical wallets, and it remains under the owner's sole control until it is transferred to someone else. Computers around the world record the trade, but they cannot see the parties' names or other personal identifiers, which are all coded by number. Bitcoin is often called "anonymous," but it is actually a "pseudonymous" system: the user's balance is associated not with a name but with an address and its public-private key pair. In that sense it is like a pseudonym, but if the pseudonym is ever linked to the user's identity, everything he ever wrote under it will be linked to him; and maintaining anonymity has proven to be difficult.[286]

Thus while bitcoin gets close to "digital cash," it is not really a "bearer instrument" like cash. You cannot directly transfer a bitcoin token to someone else without first having the miners validate the transactions, so there is still the need for a middleman. At best it is a hybrid between a bearer instrument and a ledger money system. For most purposes, physical cash—the legal tender issued by governments—is still the best way to conduct business independently of middlemen. But cash is difficult to carry across borders, and here bitcoin has the advantage, since it travels in cyberspace.

The downside of acting like cash is that bitcoin is also subject to its risks. The digital coins can be lost or stolen. The coded keys are generally too long to commit to memory, and there are numerous reports of computers on which the keys were stored disappearing along with the keys. Unlike with a lost checkbook or credit card, there is no bank to phone up for replacement digits. No one is keeping a central record of who owns what, and there is no FDIC insurance protecting consumers against theft or fraud.

The blockchain is said to be almost impossible to hack into, since millions of computers would need to be hacked simultaneously.[287] But while the blockchain itself cannot be hacked, the exchanges on which it operates can be and have been.[288] The computers of individuals who hold cryptocurrencies can also be hacked in order to steal their private keys. Just posting a tweet acknowledging that you have an account on an exchange can be dangerous, as one blogger complained after losing $8,000 worth of bitcoin through the theft of his cell phone number.[289]

A pseudonmymous private digital currency outside the control of government is also outside the protections of government. There is no recourse in the event of defective products or other failures to perform. There is no credit card company or Amazon that will return your money if you are not satisfied with what you got in the mail. A bitcoin deal is a deal without recourse either for the counterparties or for a government looking to unwind illegal transactions. Governments are talking about imposing reporting requirements on cryptocurrency transactions similar to those required of banks, so pseudonymity is a feature that may not be available for long.[290]

## Can Bitcoin Replace the Dollar?

Despite those concerns, bitcoin has so captured the popular imagination that many enthusiasts think it will one day replace the US dollar. They see the dollar as weak and vulnerable due to a $21 trillion national debt and the Fed's $3.7 trillion in quantitative easing, which was expected to trigger hyperinflation (although that has not actually happened). Bitcoin, the runaway leader in the cryptocurrency craze, is seen as "digital gold" that will hold its value when national currencies fail. It is said to be particularly popular in foreign countries with unstable national currencies and capital controls that prevent taking the national currency out of the country.

Critics say, however, that bitcoin could not actually replace the dollar. In a "withering" 24-page article released in June 2018 as part of its annual economic report, the Bank for International Settlements said that bitcoin and its offspring suffer from a range of shortcomings that would prevent them from fulfilling the lofty expectations prompting an explosion of interest and investment in them. "Cryptocurrencies are too unstable, consume too much energy, and are subject to too much manipulation and fraud to serve as bona fide mediums of exchange in the global economy," the researchers wrote.[291]

Analyzing what it would take for bitcoin's blockchain software to process the digital retail transactions currently handled by national payment systems, they concluded that the blockchain would eventually overwhelm everything from individual smart phones to servers. "The associated communication volumes could bring the Internet to a halt," they said. The race by bitcoin miners to be the first to process transactions consumes about the same amount of electricity as Switzerland does. The researchers said that "the quest for decentralised trust has quickly become an environmental disaster."

Environmental issues aside, bitcoin trades are too slow for ordinary store purchases. They are faster than clearing checks through a bank; but by April 2018 the average time to confirm a bitcoin transaction was 78 minutes, and sometimes it could take several days.[292] The lag time gets progressively longer as more miners join the network. According to the Bank for International Settlements, the daily volume of transactions in US dollars globally is *$4.5 trillion.*[293] Average bitcoin transactions, by contrast, were about $2 million in the first quarter of 2018.[294] Bitcoin would have to be scaled up more than 2,000 times to replace the US dollar in daily market transactions, with a lag time that would be proportionately slower. At that rate you could be waiting in line for weeks to get a cup of coffee.

The fees for bitcoin trades are also going up, particularly if you want to get to the head of the line.[295] These fees are paid to the miners for their services in working out complex cryptographic puzzles to add transactions to the blockchain. According to data from *BitInfoCharts,* in April 2018 the average fee to make a bitcoin transaction was $28. The total value of all transaction fees paid to miners hit a high that month of $11 million on a single day.[296] For large transactions, a $28 fee is reasonable, but it won't work for purchasing a cup of coffee or for the many other micropayments involved in everyday consumer purchases.

There are now bitcoin debit cards that can be used anywhere Visa and MasterCard are accepted, making transactions fast and convenient. But you are not really paying in bitcoin. You are paying in US dollars, and you're back in the conventional banking system. The Shift Visa debit card, for example, is an arrangement between Coinbase (a popular bitcoin exchange) and Visa. You buy bitcoin on the Coinbase exchange with dollars (4 percent fee), then Coinbase pays Visa, which pays the merchant in dollars. The merchant still pays the standard 2 or 3 percent Visa fee, a cost passed on to the customer in increased prices. You still pay $2.50 to withdraw cash at an ATM, and 3 percent for conversion to other currencies when using the card abroad. And when you apply for the card, you need to identify yourself to comply with Know Your Customer requirements, eliminating bitcoin's much-prized privacy.[297] You might as well just use your Visa card and save time, money and energy. A 2015 *Motherboard* article comparing bitcoin's energy cost to Visa's concluded that bitcoin was about 5,000 times more energy intensive per transaction than Visa's at then-current usage levels.[298]

Bitcoin has other features that limit its use as a national currency, and one is its extreme volatility. A currency needs to be a stable store of value if it is going to be used regularly in trade, which is probably why few merchants accept it. In a July 2017 report, Morgan Stanley analysts noted that the number of online merchants accepting bitcoin had dropped to just three, down from five a year earlier. This was after the currency had been available for nearly nine years and its value had soared to astronomical heights. But bitcoin owners evidently weren't worried, since they were not spending their digital coins anyway. The rapid appreciation of the coins has led to hoarding rather than spending them. The analysts also cited high transaction costs, long transaction times, and the lack of government oversight as factors making bitcoin unserviceable as a trade currency.[299]

In *The Guardian* in January 2016, a disillusioned senior bitcoin developer pointed to another problem with the crypto leader. Although billed as a decentralized form of money, bitcoin is actually controlled by just a handful of people—the big developers and big miners—who are resistant to the adaptations needed to increase its capacity to deal with an increasingly congested network.[300] Bitcoin replaces one currency controlled by a few rich people at the top with another currency controlled by a few rich people at the top.

Conspiracy theories have also circulated around the origins of bitcoin, whose inventor remains stubbornly elusive. The blockchain program is considered too complex and sophisticated to be the brainchild of a university student or group, and no one has stepped forward to claim the one million bitcoins the inventor is thought to have generated for his own account.[301] A case has been made that Satoshi Nakamoto is actually the National Security Agency, the largest US foreign intelligence service. The NSA has teams of cryptographers and the fastest supercomputers in the world. bitcoin's encryption algorithm, SHA-256, was developed by the NSA; and it was one of the first organizations to describe a bitcoin-like system. A 1996 white paper authored by the NSA titled "How to Make a Mint: The Cryptography of Anonymous Electronic Cash" is said to *outline a system very much like bitcoin, in which secure financial transactions are possible through the use of a decentralized network the researchers refer to informally as a Bank.*[302]

Even if bitcoin is an NSA creation, of course, it can be a very useful technological innovation. The internet itself was largely developed by the US military.[303] But the NSA connection raises questions about how secure bitcoin is. Commenting on its possible NSA roots, Mathew Sparkes wrote in *The Telegraph* in 2014 that "the protocol leaves a permanent trail of transactions that could be a very useful tool for law enforcement. Certainly, anonymity is one of the biggest myths about bitcoin. In fact, there has never been a more easily traceable method of payment. Every single transaction is recorded and retained permanently in the public 'blockchain.'"[304]

## Ethereum and "Smart Contracts"

Whatever the origins and limitations of bitcoin, its blockchain technology has triggered an explosion of interest, and thousands of cryptocurrencies involving multiple technological advances and projected uses have been devised. Bitcoin lit the match, but the innovation that set it ablaze was the development of a platform called Ethereum. Conceived by a Russian-Canadian programmer named Vitalik Buterin at the tender age of 19, Ethereum is a whole network, with its own internet browser, coding language and payment system. It takes the technology behind bitcoin and substantially expands its capabilities, enabling users to create decentralized applications ("apps") on the Ethereum blockchain.

Ethereum has its own cryptocurrency token, called Ether; but unlike bitcoin, which is solely a cryptocurrency, Ethereum supports applications beyond money systems. The supply of bitcoin has a 21 million cap, but the supply of Ether is potentially limitless. Its block mining time and the amount of computing power required are also far less than for bitcoin.[305] Ethereum's rise set off a flood of research and development by providing a place for innovative developers to build programs, businesses, and services.

Ethereum is supported by a global system of volunteers called "nodes," who download the Ethereum blockchain to their desktops and enforce its consensus rules. The rules are dictated by "smart contracts"—pre-programmable messages embedded in the chain, which contain the contract terms and are designed to automatically perform transactions when certain conditions are satisfied. According to *Cointelegraph*, a smart contract is a special computer protocol intended to contribute to, verify or implement the negotiation or performance of a contract, allowing the performance of trackable, irreversible transactions without third parties.[306]

Smart contracts are self-executing, but they are just digital arrangements with no connection to the physical world, so they still require middlemen for enforcement—a sheriff to carry out evictions and repossessions, or a county recorder to validate transfers of title. In a June 2018 article titled "The Truth about Smart Contracts," bitcoin entrepreneur Jimmy Song contends they are not really "smart" at all but are dumb and blind enforcers of the letter of the contract. If a lease says it is terminated under certain conditions, the smart contract simply locks the tenants out. There is no place for equitable excuses or extenuating circumstances of the sort considered by a judge and jury in court. Smart contracts are difficult to design securely and are only as smart as their programmers, leaving them vulnerable to attack by hackers who find loopholes in them.[307]

## The Crypto Explosion

Other second-generation cryptocurrencies were designed to overcome some of the limitations of bitcoin, substantially reducing transaction times and costs. Bitcoin Cash was the result of a split or "hard fork" in bitcoin by users who believed that the size of the blocks should be increased to speed transactions and reduce fees. Bitcoin Gold was the result of another hard fork from bitcoin. Dash and Litecoin can do transactions in seconds or minutes at a cost of between one and two cents each. Ripple is also said to do transactions in seconds, at the cost of a fraction of a penny.[308]

Nexus is a cryptocurrency on the bitcoin model developed by a company preparing to launch affordable satellites. Besides being much faster (using multiple distributed ledgers instead of one), it is claimed to be four times more secure than bitcoin and to be untouchable by regulators, since it will be broadcast from 100 miles up in space.[309]

BitShares is a cryptocurrency designed to be merchant-friendly for commercial use. Rather than limiting the number of tokens, the price of Bitshares is kept stable by pegging them to underlying fiat currencies (the US dollar, Euro, Chinese Yuan) or to commodities like gold and silver. Pegging is said to allow merchants to hold the currency rather than selling it quickly, avoiding the volatility of the first-generation

cryptocurrencies.[310] BitShares creator Dan Larrimer also created EOS, which involves both a cryptocurrency and a platform
and is claimed to be a viable competitor to Ethereum.[311]

Hashgraph, a new consensus protocol competing with
EOS, is being promoted as a technology that will make
blockchains obsolete. According to its website, it can do over
250,000 transactions per second and has bank-grade security.
It does not yet have a native cryptocurrency token but is projected to have one eventually. However, Hashgraph too has
limitations. It still has scalability problems; it is patented; and
it will be governed by a "global governing council" of up to
39 companies, which sounds a lot like a "government" rather
than a "distributed" network of independent participants. The
fact that it is patented means that its code is not open source
(freely accessible to all), it is not fully transparent, and the
patent holder can charge users as he likes.[312]

Workarounds to the scaling problems of bitcoin have
also been devised. One is to do transactions on side-chains
or in escrow-style accounts that are not part of the bitcoin
blockchain. The Lightning Network is a "second layer"
payment protocol of this sort, which operates on top of the
bitcoin or another blockchain. The arrangement has been
described as similar to opening a tab at a bar: many micropayments can be made off-chain before the tab is closed on
the blockchain itself. But the Network is still in the testing
phase, and critics say it is risky, cumbersome, centralized (operating much like a bank accounting system), and still won't
work mathematically if scaled to millions of users.[313]

Other cryptocurrencies serve particular market niches.
Among other interesting innovations are cryptocurrencies issued for free that grant users a basic income in them, includ-

ing "Grantcoin" and "EquaCoin."[314] (For more on the basic income concept, see Chapter 16.) A blockchain-based digital currency called "SolarCoin" is also given away by its creators, in this case as a reward for generating solar electricity.[315]

Other cryptocurrencies can be used for cannabis trades. As of this writing, cannabis is legal in more than half the states but is still illegal federally, so banks willing to service the business are hard to find. A cryptocurrency called "cPay" provides electronic payment processing for in-state cannabis purchases. Another digital system called "PayServices" can handle cannabis and many other sorts of trades in hundreds of different currencies without using blockchain technology, which its developers perceive to be too slow for active commercial trade.[316]

Those are just a few of the hundreds of cryptocurrencies now on the market. That any of them could replace the dollar, however, seems unlikely. As Hyman Minsky observed, anyone can create money. The trick is to get it accepted. Most of the contenders have an uphill battle just competing with bitcoin, let alone taking on the national currency. But they could serve particular markets, and the massive push to develop them is prompting banks to streamline their own software and practices.

## "Initial Coin Offerings": Democratizing the Stock Market

Some of this innovative development holds promise, but many of the new cryptocurrencies have come on the market simply to raise money for their issuers. Ethereum found its "Killer App" as a distributed platform for crowdfunding and fundraising. Capital is raised through "Initial Coin Offerings" (ICOs), an unregulated method of crowdfunding that allows cryptocurrency companies to avoid the tightly regulated process of raising capital required by venture capitalists, banks and stock exchanges. In an ICO, a portion of the newly issued cryptocurrency is given to investors in exchange for government-issued currency or other cryptocurrencies such as bitcoin or Ethereum.[317]

Advocates say ICOs have decentralized and democratized the process of raising capital, since anyone can issue "coins" or "tokens" on the Ethereum platform, and anyone can invest in the new offerings. But there are significant differences between an ICO for the sale of digital coins or tokens and the "Initial Public Offerings" (IPOs) through which stock is sold. In an IPO, investors become part owners of the company and are entitled to dividends if it makes a profit. The IPO is overseen by the Securities and Exchange Commission, which ensures that potential investors are receiving valid information about the company and are being treated fairly and honestly. This requires the company to submit audited financial statements and meet other complicated requirements. IPO investors are also required to meet certain qualifications, including having a threshold amount of money or having engaged in a certain number of financial transactions. These barriers are high, largely excluding small startup ventures and small investors from participation in IPOs; but the rules are there for a reason. They ensure that only people or groups who can afford to lose the money are investors in these very risky ventures, and that they are honestly informed of the risks.[318]

Unlike in an IPO, investors in an ICO do not legally

become part owners of the company, and they are not entitled to dividends if the company is profitable. They can make
a profit only if they can sell the coins or tokens for more
than they paid for them, or by using the coins to purchase
the goods or services the issuing company produces. If
the company does not have a viable product, the coins can
become worthless, and many have. Many are literally Ponzi
schemes. The risk is all on the investors, and unsophisticated
players who have no way of telling a fraudulent scheme from
a viable one can have their investments wiped out. For that
reason, ICOs and token offerings are expected to be regulated in the future.[319]

## Taking the Block Out of Blockchain: "Permissioned" Blockchains

Blockchain has also caught the attention of bankers and
businesses, but what they are interested in is not the bitcoin-style blockchain in which anybody can create an address and begin interacting with the network. Rather, they
are exploring the "blockchain-like" clearing networks called
"permissioned" blockchains—private ledgers requiring
permission to join. The participants already have business
relationships allowing them to trust each other. According
to a spokesperson for JPMorgan Chase's Blockchain Center
of Excellence, "you're sharing infrastructure between participants—so issuer, dealer, investors, custodians and admin-
istrators can all see one golden source of truth of a trade or
in this case a debt instrument. And being able to trust that
golden source and then correspondingly, not having to spend
as many resources reconciling deal terms, tracking and trac-

ing wires, or agreeing on interest rate calculations."[320]

In an article titled "The Trust Trade-off: Permissioned Vs. Permissionless Blockchains," Australian business designer Devon Allaby explains:

> [T]he permissioned Blockchain isn't looking to overthrow the political system, or remove the need for established financial institutions. Instead it leverages some of the other core elements of Blockchain architecture (immutability, ability to grant granular permissions, automated data synchronisation, rigorous privacy and security capabilities, process automation) to create efficiencies, reduce costs, and open up opportunities for new data-driven business models.[321]

For businesses that already have offline relationships, the use of heavy computation to create trust is not just redundant, says Allaby, but "commits the even more serious crime of being expensive." This cost gets exponentially higher for smart contracts, which execute an entire program for each transaction. As the use cases become more sophisticated, he writes, "the impact on cost, speed and throughput become untenable."

In a November 2017 article in *The Financial Times* titled "Taking the Block Out of Blockchain," Izabella Kaminska noted wryly that the blockchain was supposed to change everything. But after two years of dabbling and experimentation, "it's mostly just been changing itself (so as to become even barely usable in capital markets)." The technology has evolved into a chain without blocks, operating in a permissioned environment without "proof of work." She quotes from a blockchain update acknowledging that "it has become apparent that in capital markets, the further away you are from the original Blockchain DNA, the more likely you are to succeed."[322]

The blockchain's decentralized distributed ledger was supposed to disrupt the banking system and the dollar; but the banks have instead disrupted the blockchain model, with a version that is not "distributed" but centralized and is not "open source" but requires permission to join. As observed in a February 2018 *Investopedia* article titled "Banks Claim They're Building Blockchains: They're Not," permissionless and permissioned blockchains are technically very different beasts. For the first time, argues the author, a high-tech alternative exists to the banking system. Bitcoin's blockchain introduced a system that allows individuals to transfer funds around the world without a central, trusted authority. The established players are defusing that threat by adopting the new paradigm while taking out the parts that are disruptive for incumbents.[323]

To purists, Nakamoto's original concept has been hijacked, appropriated by corporate interests. Rather than eliminating the middlemen, it is being used by them to streamline their own procedures. The term "blockchain" is often being used just because it increases sales, though no "chain of blocks" is involved.[324] Companies are also calling their securities "cryptocurrencies" to avoid securities regulation, with the term "ICO" (Initial Coin Offering) substituted for "IPO" (Initial Public Offering).

## A Gold Rush Without Gold?

Everyone is cashing in on the crypto gold rush, but speculative bubbles aside, no one seems yet to have struck gold. As tech blogger Daniel Jeffries complained on *Hacker Noon* in

October 2017:

> Eight years into the crypto experiment, everyone is work-
> ing on the railroad tracks of the future but we don't have
> much to show for it other than speculative trading and
> some smart contracts. The apps are hideous and practi-
> cally unusable. It's nerve-wracking when you push "send"
> and blast $5000 across the web to someone. Better hope
> you copied and pasted that address right so your money
> doesn't disappear into the void![325]

In another article on *Hacker Noon* titled "Ten Years in,
Nobody Has Come Up with a Use for Blockchain", tech
blogger Kai Stinchcombe echoed that complaint, writing:

> Everyone says the blockchain, the technology underpin-
> ning cryptocurrencies such as bitcoin, is going to change
> EVERYTHING. And yet, after years of tireless effort
> and billions of dollars invested, nobody has actually come
> up with a use for the blockchain—besides currency specu-
> lation and illegal transactions.
>
> Each purported use case—from payments to legal docu-
> ments, from escrow to voting systems—amounts to a set
> of contortions to add a distributed, encrypted, anonymous
> ledger where none was needed. What if there isn't actually
> any use for a distributed ledger at all? What if, ten years
> after it was invented, the reason nobody has adopted a
> distributed ledger at scale is because nobody wants it?[326]

Bitcoin was an inspiring idea, and its developers pointed

us to the goal; but for a democratic system in which money is actually created by users themselves, it seems we will need to look elsewhere.

*Takeaway:* Bitcoin and its innovative blockchain technology may find use cases, but a national currency is unlikely to be one of them. It is too slow, expensive and energy-intensive for use on a national scale. Much of the hype around "blockchain" and its commercial uses involves "blockchain-like" digital systems that may streamline existing technology but are not actually system disruptors. There are cryptocurrencies and associated software, however, that could be potential models for a credit system operated nationally, considered next.

## CHAPTER 10
# FROM COMMODITY MONEY TO MUTUAL CREDIT: THE COMMUNITY CURRENCY MODEL

*"Cryptos fear credit, but I suspect they will soon discover that credit is a feature, not a bug, and that will require them to re-examine the implicit monetary theory that underlies their coding."*

**Prof. Perry Mehrling, Institute for New Economic Thinking, October 2017[327]**

**Technical issues aside,** there is a more fundamental reason that bitcoin and its later iterations will not work as a national currency. The very thing they seek to eliminate—an elastic, expandable money supply—is "a feature, not a bug," of modern economies. Bitcoin and its blockchain software are solely payment systems, not credit systems; and businesses, households and governments run on credit.

The need for an expandable credit system was highlighted by Barnard College professor Perry Mehrling in an October 2017 article called "Can Bitcoin Replace the Dollar?" Discussing his conversations with a group of digital technologists convinced that it could, he wrote:

[T]he technologists see themselves as creating a form of money more trustworthy than that issued by sovereign states, more trustworthy because the rules of money creation (whether proof-of-work or proof-of-stake or whatever) limit issue to a fixed and finite quantity. Scarcity of the tokens today, and confidence that scarcity will be maintained in years to come, are supposed to support the value of the tokens today. Importantly, no such confidence can be attached to state-issued money; quite the contrary, states are seen as reliable abusers of money issue for their own purposes. Cryptocurrency is digital gold while fiat currency is just paper, subject to overissue and hence depreciation.

From this point of view, current holders/users of cryptocurrency are just early adopters. Once everyone else realizes the superiority of cryptocurrency, they will all want to switch over, and the value of fiat currency will collapse.

... One of the most fascinating things about the technologist view of the world is their deep suspicion (even fear) of credit of any kind. They appreciate all too well the extent to which modern society is constructed as a web of interconnected and overlapping promises to pay, and they don't like it one bit.[328]

Prof. Mehrling, on the other hand, says he looks at "the operation of the world as it actually exists." In the real world, banking is fundamentally a swap of IOUs, and money is nothing more than the highest form of credit:

In that world, the payment system is essentially a credit system, in which offsetting promises to pay clear with only very minimal use of money. ... One can imagine automating a lot of that activity—and blockchain technology may well be useful for that task—but one cannot imagine eliminating the credit element. ... [F]rom a money view standpoint, it is the institution of credit that is the real disruptor, which is fundamentally why it is feared ....

What the concept of money-as-credit has disrupted is the prevailing monetarist dogma holding that money is a "thing" like gold that exists in perpetuity. In Mehrling's real world, money is elastic, expanding and contracting in response to the demand for credit. As he wrote in an article quoted earlier, "each of us, in our interface with the essentially financial system that is modern capitalism, operates essentially as a bank, meaning a cash inflow, cash outflow entity. ... [T]he elasticity of credit ... allows us to spend today and put off payment to the future."[329]

## Money As a Commodity Versus Money As Credit

Bitcoin has been compared to the gold-based monetary system prized by the "Austrian" school of economics. The Austrian ideal is a system in which money is an existing token in fixed supply that has to be mined or acquired from somewhere else.[330] The 21-million cap that Nakamoto put on the bitcoins that could be issued is thought to have been a direct analogy to the physical limit on the gold in the world, considered to be equivalent to a cube 21 meters on a side.[331] But this hard limit also represents a limitation on bitcoin's usefulness as a national currency, which must have some way to expand to meet the needs of trade. The reason the medieval system of gold-backed currency was able to work as long as it did was that the money supply could expand through various forms of paper money.

So argued Antal Fekete, a professor of mathematics and statistics in Newfoundland, Canada, in a 2005 article called "Detractors of Adam Smith's Real Bills Doctrine." He showed mathematically that the attempt to finance all of the stages of production in an economy by borrowing the nation's savings in gold would put a demand on gold supplies that simply could not be met. Manufacturers all along the chain of production need to pay for workers and materials before the customer pays for the finished product, which can be 30 or 60 or 90 days after being invoiced. Their work is financed with credit lines or loans, which can add up to many times the final value of the product.

Fekete used the example of a hypothetical drug that takes 91 days to produce and involves 90 firms, each one taking a day to do its work. Each adds $1 of value to the product, which ultimately sells for $100 a bottle. The first producer borrows $11 in gold for the raw materials. The second producer borrows $12 in gold to obtain the semi-finished product with the first producer's work added. The third producer borrows $13 to get the product from the second producer, and so forth. The total comes to $4,995, almost 50 times the retail value of the product. That means almost $5,000 worth of gold would be tied up for 91 days just to move one $100 bottle of drug through the production process.[332]

Fekete argued that the gold system worked historically only because the various stages of production were financed with bills of credit—paper credits representing advances against future repayment. And even with that ability to expand the money supply, restrictive gold reserve requirements triggered repeated bank runs and crises when the banks ran out of gold. The inability of the money supply to expand led to recessions, depressions, unemployment, economic stagnation, and the ultimate abandonment of the gold standard.

But gold did have the advantage that it could be traded without the validation of a middleman. It had value in itself. In order to turn our credit into a form of money that will be accepted in trade, we need the guarantee of a third party, which in the current commercial system takes the form of a bank.

The blockchain system operates outside banks, and bitcoins are not precious metals that can be worn as jewelry or have industrial uses. They are actually fiat currencies, conjured out of thin air. Satoshi Nakamoto therefore had to find another way to validate them and to avoid the "double-spending" problem—users spending the same money twice. This was achieved by incentivizing "miners" to check the transactions and continually update the ledger in return for payment in bitcoin. The miners were thus substituted for bankers as middleman guarantors.

Capping the number of coins and making the mining process slow and expensive prevented hyperinflation from the too-easy private creation of digital currency with computer keystrokes, a necessary feature of a private system; but it also made the system too slow and expensive for commercial use on a national or global scale. It is the attempt to turn abstract digits into concrete commodity money that runs up the exorbitant energy costs of bitcoin. All the "coins" that exist must be laboriously tracked in every trade to ensure there is no counterfeiting or double-spending.

In a centralized system, that complicated and expensive process is unnecessary. Japanese economists Yokei Yamaguchi and Kaoru Yamaguchi observe that if the currency is issued by a central monetary authority, inflation can be avoided simply by limiting its quantity by regulation.[333] But that sort of top-down control of the money supply also has limitations, as seen in the often-misguided policies of central banks charged with regulating the money supply today.

There is a third way the money supply can be kept in balance. It can be created at the local level through the demand for loans and extinguished when they are paid off, just as happens now. What needs to be fixed in the current banking system are not its elastic credit features but the corruptions, opacity and inefficiencies that have diverted and distorted its free flow, largely due to control by those same private middleman gatekeepers needed to validate its exchanges.

## Mutual Credit Clearing Systems: Private Digital Currencies Based on Abundance Rather Than Scarcity

There are private digital currency systems that operate on the money-as-credit model while bypassing banks and governments. These are the community currencies, also called complementary, cooperative or alternative currencies. Traditionally, community currencies have been limited by the size of the community, since they are accepted only by participating local merchants. But with the development of the internet and digital online software, their popularity and range are expanding. A new generation of currencies is emerging that combines the economic necessity served by community currencies with the technological innovation generating the cryptocurrency phenomenon.

Community currencies operate on the same sort of credit clearing system that banks use to create the "bank money" composing the majority of our money supply today, but they do it without manipulation by profiteering middlemen. Money is created as a debit in an account and is extinguished when the debt is repaid. Like bitcoin, digital community currency systems create this money without banks or governments; but unlike bitcoin, community currencies are user-generated and cannot be "scarce." As South African community currency advocate Margaret Legum puts it:

> In a community currency system, money is not used as a commodity in itself, to be lent and borrowed and kept out of use. The currency comes into existence only when a trade happens and, as a result, there is no risk of inflation or deflation since there is no such thing as too much or too little money.[334]

Community currencies have appeared historically when national systems failed to meet local needs. The local economy was short of the national currency and ways to earn it, but people still had practical skills and hours they could devote to work. Traditionally, community currencies have allowed activities like volunteering in a local garden, giving a neighbor a haircut, or reading to a homebound senior to be traded for food and other basic needs even if dollars never change hands. No interest is charged, so there is no built-in imperative for growth. Community currencies also allow communities to make decisions about where capital should flow rather than giving decision-making power solely to banks, and they foster human relationships, building community and encouraging people to interact with one another.[335]

To provide a pool of currency to get the ball rolling, participants may be given some initial amount of free credits when they join. This was done, for example, with the successful Bangla-Pesa community currency initiated in an urban slum in Mombasa, Kenya. Goods and services were available for trade, but the villagers lacked a medium of exchange. Enrollees in the currency received a certain number of vouchers and agreed to accept those of other enrollees. The vouchers thus acted as a credit mechanism for small vendors to make purchases when business was slow, to be repaid later when business picked up again. The immediate effect of distributing the Bangla-Pesa seed money was to increase local sales by 22 percent.[336]

## Digital Community Currencies Compared to Bitcoin

In a white paper titled "Mutual Credit Cryptocurrencies: Beyond Blockchain Bottlenecks," software architect Arthur Brock points to several key distinctions between digital community currencies and cryptocurrencies on the bitcoin model. Bitcoin-style currencies involve tokens or coins in limited supply and put a premium on anonymity. Digital community currencies are "mutual credit clearing systems"—basically accounting systems keeping track of credits and debits—and they put a premium on reputation. That means users have a recognized and trusted identity in the community.

In the bitcoin system, there is no mechanism for buying on credit or taking an overdraft on your account. You have to acquire the money tokens from somewhere else, and all sales are final. Because the "coins" exist independently of the trade, they can be scarce and are deliberately kept that way. In that sense, they are "commodities." But the process required to maintain that feature is cumbersome and expensive. None of that is necessary in a system that involves the simple balancing of accounts. As Brock explains:

> In a mutual credit system, units of currency are issued when a participant extends credit to another user in a standard spending transaction. Picture a new mutual credit currency with all accounts having a zero balance. The first transaction could look like this: Alice pays Bob 20 credits for a haircut. Alice's account now has -20, and Bob's has +20.

> Notice the net number of units in the system remains zero, just like the balance sheet in standard accounting must always balance to zero. That accounting practice places no limits on the amount of cash or assets a business can have; it simply means they are offset by an equal amount of liabilities or equity. Every negative balance in a mutual credit system is offset by positive balances so there is always a systemwide ZERO balance. You could think of the total number of units in circulation at any time as the sum of all the negative balances (or, if you prefer, the sum of positive balances since they are the same number).

Note that Alice in Brock's example is "spending" money she doesn't have. This sounds very like the commercial banking system, in which the bank lends money it doesn't have. The bank creates a debit in the borrower's account and issues "bank credit" or "checkbook money" against it that is accepted as money in the marketplace. The debit is extinguished when the loan is repaid, canceling the money out. The bank ensures repayment with strict underwriting standards, a written contract enforceable in court, and often with collateral (a house or a car). In a mutual credit system, the supply of currency is managed by setting credit limits, limiting how far people can spend into a negative balance. Different currency systems set different rules, says Brock, but their underlying basis is trust among community members who have a personal relationship with each other.

## Enter the Internet

The traditional problem with scaling community currencies beyond the local community is that there are only so many people you can have a personal relationship with. The use of community currencies for national or international commerce has therefore been limited. But the advent of the internet has helped mitigate this problem. Picture a sort of online Craigslist or eBay trading solely in a particular digital community currency. New currency is created by selling into the online market, and it is extinguished when purchases are made with the acquired credits. To encourage trust, rating systems can be used, similar to the reviews by multiple users on Amazon or eBay, allowing buyers and sellers to establish their credentials as reliable trading partners with a public record of their prior trading histories. Cryptographic verification systems that cannot be manipulated or altered can also minimize the need for blind trust in strangers. Another problem that has restricted the usefulness of local community currency systems is the limited range of goods and services available to community members, but the internet has expanded those possibilities.

Traditional community currencies such as LETS (local employment and trading systems) have been slow to adapt to the internet; but some are now being digitized, and software has been developed that would allow communities to create their own local currencies. Two providers offering free LETS software are *Community Exchange Systems (CES)* and *Community Forge (CF)*.[337] According to the CES website, CES and CF are working together to provide several hundred communities with a parallel financial system in which peer-to-peer credit is used as an interest-free medium of exchange. CES is international in scope, a sort of international payments system or correspondent banking system for community currencies. The user can access an internet host server that manages a particular exchange, and this access allows the user to link up with other exchanges. Database software keeps track of the currency balance of each member, and each exchange has its own currency or unit of measure to keep track of values as they are transferred.

Most community exchanges operate on principles of mutual credit or time banks. Time banks use time as the unit of value (person-hours or some other time-based unit), while mutual credit systems value their currencies based on the national currency. In order for international trade to take place, the CES applies conversion rates between the different currencies. It uses a base currency of one hour, which makes the conversion rates between time banks easy to calculate. In the case of mutual credit exchanges, an average hourly wage rate is established for the area in which the exchange operates. In this way CES allows a person in an Australian time bank, for example, to transact with a person in a South African mutual credit system. The system does not involve printed money or coins but uses computer technology to serve as an online banking system and marketplace. In 2013, the CES website reported that there were 485 exchange groups located in 53 countries hosted on its global server, with another 37 Australian exchanges on its Australian server. Registered members have access to an online community, sometimes described as an online shopping mall. They can offer goods and services on the exchange, and as their credits accumulate they can buy on it.[338]

"Interledger" is another protocol designed to facilitate trade between different ledgers.[339] The system is loosely equivalent to the SWIFT network of financial messaging. It relies on "connectors"—people who have accounts on two ledgers, who can act as intermediaries for people wanting to cross ledgers. For example, a connector might have an account on the Ithaca Hours system and an account on the Ethereum Network. If someone with Ether wanted to pay someone else in Ithaca Hours, he could transfer Ether into the connector's Ether account and the connector would transfer Ithaca Hours into the recipient's Ithaca Hours account. In this sense Interledger is loosely similar to *Hawala*, a system for transferring money traditionally used in the Muslim world. The money is paid to a trusted agent who then instructs a remote associate to pay the final recipient.

## Holochain: A Cryptocurrency Rooted in Biomimicry

Software engineer Arthur Brock has developed an alternative cryptocurrency architecture that he says is rooted in biomimicry ("how nature functions and scales"). He calls it "Holochain" to distinguish it from "blockchain." The system provides for building a tokenless cryptocurrency based on mutual credit principles operated peer to peer.[340] Holochain is not actually a blockchain; it is not a linear sequence of transactions or series of "blocks." Rather, it has been described as a mesh of transactions, providing cryptographic control of information but without requiring nearly as much storage and processing power as bitcoin or Ethereum.

In a February 2018 article titled "What Could Come After Blockchain Technology? The What and Why of Holochain," crypto-activist Tristan Roberts writes that after searching the digital universe, he settled on Holochain as the most likely new crypto technology to succeed. He describes it as "agent-centric" rather than "data-centric": rather than having to carry a slow and expensive chain of every transaction in perpetuity, as on a blockchain, each "node" (individual operator) carries only his or her own data. Roberts writes:

> Rather than spending an absurd amount of energy to craft a single record of events, Holochain allows people to write anything to their own chain. However, transactions that violate the rules of the application (such as me saying that you gave me all your tokens) won't be propagated by the network.[341]

The practical effect, says Roberts, is that "strangers can interact collaboratively in a high-trust manner, without a profit-seeking corporation sucking up all of the 'value' it can. Imagine Uber owned by the drivers and riders; AirBnb owned by the hosts and guests."

Particularly interesting for purposes of this book, Holochain users are not buying coins created by wealthy miners in faraway places. They are creating their own money simply by extending credit to other users. Roberts explains:

> [M]ost currencies, including Bitcoin, are based on fiat. They mint the tokens by a line of code, and trade the resulting tokens that are backed by nothing. This requires global consensus of the state of the ledger. This cannot be done on a Holochain ... . You can't track the coins. But you can still implement money if you re-consider what money is; a non-fiat kind of money.
>
> ... [I]nstead of coins being issued backed by nothing, they are issued by the peer, in arrangement with another peer, by creating liability/debt. Managing the currency supply in a mutual credit system is about managing credit limits—how far people can spend into a negative balance.

A comparison could be made with credit cards: you have a credit limit but can spend as you will, backed by your promise to repay at the end of the month (or pay interest thereafter). The difference is that with Holochain there is no credit card company taking a 2 or 3 percent fee from the merchant on every transaction, forcing prices up. Rather than borrowing "bank credit," you are creating your own

credit, backed by the trust of the community that you will
pay it back.

Holochain software for digitizing user-created money is
a promising development for local community currency systems that run independently of banks and governments. But
as with all private mutual credit arrangements, the system is
limited by how far the community is willing to trust strangers. Unlike with credit cards, there is no bank to ensure
payment if the borrower does not pay.

Community currencies are an innovative solution for
local communities engaging in trade peer-to-peer, but they
won't work for the large-scale credit needs of corporations
or of local governments engaging in long-term infrastructure projects. Mutual credit clearing systems, like blockchain
systems, suffer from problems of scale.

## Ripple: Reconsidering the Advantages of Centralization

The problem of scaling a private credit system was illustrated
in the evolution of Ripple, the second-ranked cryptocurrency by market capitalization as of September 2018. The
Ripple system grew out of software developed for use with
LETS community currencies in Canada by Ryan Fugger,
whose goal was to create "a system of debt money without
artificially imposed scarcity." According to a 2013 article
by blogger Morgen Peck, what that meant in practice was
*"giving individuals the power to operate as their own banks,
with the ability to issue credit."*[342] Turning the borrower's credit
into something that can be traded in the marketplace is also
the function of banks, but Fugger hoped to develop software

that would bypass banker middlemen and allow individuals to issue their own spendable credit. The bigger idea behind his original design, according to Peck, was to get rid of the need for money to settle debts, because debts can be canceled out against each other. Just as the bills of credit issued by American colonial governments circulated as money, so Fugger hoped that the digital Ripple credits would "ripple out" into a form of currency. Peck wrote:

> Embedded in the Ripple concept is the possibility that the network could become so large that its users would start to participate in a closed loop of trade, treating personally issued credit as a unique form of currency. In this scenario, rather than immediately demanding payment on IOUs, Ripple users would pass them on as payment in another transaction. And then IOUs would circulate like currency until they canceled each other out.

That was the concept, but there remained the problem of verifying the IOUs without a trusted third party. In the end, Fugger found building an economy from a network of personal acquaintances was too challenging. What the system really needed was a central clearing mechanism—a central agency such as a bank. Looking for other uses for his innovation, he eventually sold his interest to other developers; and they wound up selling their software to bankers, who were already operating clearing arrangements similar to the mutual credit clearing systems of community currencies.[343]

Banks, like community currency systems, actually issue their own private currencies.[344] This was particularly obvious in the 19th century, when banks issued promissory notes called "banknotes" with their own names on them. Transfers between the bank's own customers are balanced by double-entry bookkeeping on the bank's internal ledgers. If the bank receives checks from other banks, however, the checks need to be cleared through external ledgers maintained at the central bank as trusted third party. If checks need to be cleared internationally, they go through another set of ledgers called the SWIFT international payment system.

One problem with the SWIFT system is that transfers can take days and involve multiple gatekeepers, particularly at the international level. Ripple's "Consensus Ledger" is said to be able to settle an international payment in three seconds on average and to process a thousand transactions per second. By September 2017, Ripple was reported to be working with more than 75 banks and was already moving more money than the bitcoin network.[345]

The Ripple system uses a "reserve" token called XRP in place of the cumbersome ACH (Automated Clearing House) transactions, but it does not operate on a bitcoin-style blockchain and is not decentralized. Ripple has attracted the interest of banks because it cuts out layers of middlemen, reduces transaction times, and increases the security of transactions.[346] Ripple or similar clearing software might also be a useful tool for a digital mutual credit clearing system scaled to a national level.

Meanwhile, Fugger's original Ripple concept is being revived by Trustlines, a Berlin-based group trying to implement it on Ethereum.[347]

## Faircoin: "The First Cooperative Blockchain"

Another effort at designing a cryptocurrency on a mutual credit model is "FairCoin," called "the first cooperative blockchain." FairCoin comes out of the far-left anarchist/autonomous movements of Catalonia in Spain and has a whole philosophy behind it. It was founded by a small group of activists who sought to cooperate as peers in a direct, nonhierarchical democracy, using a currency based on social justice and equality criteria. The FairCoop ecosystem arose after bitcoin and blockchain emerged in 2008. As described in a December 2017 post called "FairCoin—Our Own Story":

> Progressively, we realized we could cut off our dependency on big corporations, the banking system and the unjust laws of the State. New technologies made possible the creation of independent networks that connected distant communities, on the one hand, and supplied tools to self-manage an autonomous and decentralized economic system on the other. Social currency was the main one (LETS), along with free knowledge repositories and means for collective creation of the commons.[348]

According to a July 2017 release by *FairCoop*:

> Unlike other cryptocurrencies, Faircoin doesn't involve mining or minting systems, which are based on competition. Transaction blocks are generated by Cooperatively Validated Nodes (CVNs). These nodes cooperate to maintain the security of the network. This is why we call the system Proof of Cooperation.

Faircoin is becoming the essential digital currency for a totally decentralized payments system that uses the minimum possible amount of processing power. ... It's the basis for FairCoop, FairMarket, FreedomCoop and also now for Bank of the Commons, an alternative banking cooperative of which FairCoop is one of the founders.

... In the Faircoin ecosystem, collective intelligence creates useful tools that people can share, including point of sale systems for merchants, prepaid cards, instant currency exchange, exchanges to euros via ATMs, payment of direct receipts and all the banking services that have until now been in the hands of an elite.[349]

Faircoin has very low transaction fees due to its high network efficiency, the relationship between trusted nodes, and minimal energy costs, making it one of the best currencies for micropayments.[350]

The concept is good, but as with other private cryptocurrencies, Faircoin has limitations. For one thing, according to reviewer Joe Blankenship, it is complicated. "It is extremely difficult for a layman to first understand how all of this works and then to become involved as either a developer, investor, and/or user." As with most blockchain systems, users are limited by "everything from digital divide to merchant acceptance in their locale of FairCoin." What Blankenship sees as the biggest conceptual problem, however, involves governance. By administering the FairCoop ecosystem democratically by boards and committees, the core blockchain technology of "trustlessness" is lost. "[I]n the process of implementing democratic-based actions for shifts in the blockchain protocol," says Blankenship, "you have reinvented the bureaucracy of centralized governance atop a blockchain protocol ... ."[351]

A system governed by elections and boards is no longer a decentralized system, but it can be a more localized system than a Wall Street bank or national government. It can respond to local needs. The software developed for FairCoin, like that for Holochain and similar digital ledger systems, also holds promise for a larger mutual credit system, perhaps even one on a national level governed democratically with elections and boards.

## Bancor: Eliminating Market Makers and Trade Barriers Between Currencies

Bitcoin has held its position as undisputed market leader although newer cryptocurrencies have more efficient, functional designs, and one reason is that it is the "reserve" cryptocurrency for the others. Only a few merchants take cryptocurrency, and they take bitcoin. There are also some bitcoin ATMs. The more obscure cryptocurrencies generally must be traded for bitcoin in order to get into or out of the dollar market.[352] But that could change. In the blockchain bestseller *The Internet of Money* (2016), Andreas Antonopoulos envisions interfaces that would allow users to fluidly move from one cryptocurrency to another. Participants could use bitcoin, Ethereum or another digital currency as appropriate for the trade. He writes:

> I can see a world in which we can smoothly move between currencies in a multimodal way. ... There's a very

real possibility we're going to have an index currency: a currency that is not in itself tradable, that has no intrinsic use as a transactional commodity, but instead is only used to express the purchasing power vis-à-vis the various coins in our wallets.[353]

This sounds very like the "Bancor" proposed by British economist John Maynard Keynes for use as a supranational reserve currency for international currency conversion after World War II. The Keynesian Bancor was not actually a currency but was a unit of account, to be used in tracking international flows of assets and liabilities through an International Clearing Union.

In June 2017, a software protocol that was called "Bancor" in honor of Keynes's proposal took investors by storm. It raised about $147 million in its initial coin offering, then the second-largest fundraising campaign in blockchain history. The digital Bancor uses a blockchain system operating on Ethereum and is said to automatically provide a price for any digital currency, without the need for a buyer or seller to complete the trade.[354]

Setting the price of a commodity or currency has traditionally been done by "market makers," who thrive in volatile markets and seek to maximize their profits from advance knowledge. Bancor automates market making, eliminating this speculative manipulation. The Bancor team includes Bernard Lietaer, the former Belgian central banker quoted in Chapter 3, who has written extensively on mutual credit systems. He says the Bancor system eliminates the spread between "bid" and "ask," where speculative arbitrage occurs between exchange rates.[355] According to Bancor architect

Eyal Hertzog, prices are determined from actual economic activity rather than by market makers whose job is to speculate on trends in order to increase personal gains. "Bancor's code simply constantly readjusts the price toward an equilibrium between buys and sells," he says. "The strategy of the Bancor protocol is to constantly seek a 'balance of trade' equilibrium between different assets with no labor or strategic thinking required."[356]

If it works, Bancor could remove a major barrier to trading either in private cryptocurrencies or in digital community currencies, allowing those with any sort of value to trade with each other and with the national currency. But investors remain skeptical. One critic says Bancor is unnecessary because the Ether token can be used for the same purpose. By November 2017, Bancor's market value had dropped by more than half, in one of the most dramatic collapses in the short history of the cryptocurrency phenomenon, until bitcoin itself collapsed by two-thirds from its high in February 2018.[357]

Unlike some ICOs that have soared spectacularly and then crashed because they had no demonstrated function, however, the Bancor protocol has since proved its usefulness with a live product and live users. Filling the role of automated market maker, it provides a token that is always available to trade, encouraging investment by allowing traders to exit their positions quickly. That makes it appealing for little-known tokens with too little demand to be accepted by other exchanges. As of June 2018, Bancor was actively trading 90 tokens and was doing nearly $2.8 million in coin trades daily.[358]

In June 2018, the Bancor exchange announced that it was adding to its network the "Bangla-Pesa" complementary currency traded in a Bangladesh slum in Mombasa, Kenya.

Bancor is seeding the project by adding capital generated from its $153 million ICO. Its new Director of Community Currencies, Will Ruddick, says his team will use the Bancor protocol to expand its existing paper currency system, now serving over 1,000 businesses and 20 schools in Kenya, into a blockchain-based network. The pilot is said to mark the first time a local currency will function with market-based price discovery and convertibility into other cryptocurrencies, allowing users globally to support the communities from afar.[359]

The next chapter will look at some recent innovations coming out of Asia, which are disrupting the commercial banking system in another way.

*Takeaway: A currency used for commerce needs to be able to expand and contract naturally to meet the needs of trade, and digital community currencies can do this. Community currencies are user-generated and abundant, arising with the trade. But like bitcoin, they are unlikely to replace the dollar. They rely on the trust of community members, since there is no bank to ensure repayment, and the size of the community that people will trust is necessarily limited. Community currencies cannot satisfy large-scale or long-term credit needs such as those of large corporations and local governments, but they can offer prototypes for how a national credit clearing system might work.*

## CHAPTER 11

# ASIAN PAYMENT AND CREDIT ECOSYSTEMS: HOW CHINA AND INDIA ARE DISRUPTING THE TRADITIONAL BANKING MODEL

*"India may have leapfrogged the U.S. technology industry with simple and practical innovations and massive grunt work. It has built a digital infrastructure that will soon process billions more transactions than bitcoin ever has. With this, India will skip two generations of financial technologies and build something as monumental as China's Great Wall and America's interstate highways."*

*-- Prof. Vivek Wadhwa, The Washington Post, January 2017[360]*

**While Western bankers are speculating** about what can be done with the new digital software, some developing countries are busy doing it. They are not opposed to centralization, and they have masses of hungry mouths to feed. Their out-of-date banking systems are primed for an upgrade.

In August 2016, *EconoTimes* reported that Tunisia was replacing its eDinar digital currency with a "blockchain-based" version. The eDinar is centralized and only the government can issue it, so it is not actually a blockchain on the bitcoin model; but it is a significant innovation for the national payments system. It can be used for mobile money transfers, managing identification documents, paying bills, and more. The app for the digital currency was created by La Poste Tunisienne, the national post office, which has control of its circulation and issuance. Monetas, the company creating the digital platform, is reported to be working with other African partners as well, with the aim of bringing more than 300 million people into "financial inclusion," ensuring access to financial products and services to all sectors of the population.[361] Senegal became the second country to issue this type of national digital currency early in 2017.

In late 2017, Venezuelan President Nicolas Maduro announced that his government would issue *El Petro,* a digital coin backed by Venezuela's oil reserves. Other countries are also considering the launch of state-sanctioned digital currencies, including Sweden, Estonia, China, Russia, Japan, the UK, Uruguay, and Israel.[362] (See Chapter 12.)

In Kenya, financial inclusion is happening by mobile phone. Although not the first mobile money transfer system in the world, Kenya's M-Pesa was the first to operate on a large scale and is considered the most successful. The "M" stands for "mobile" and *Pesa* is Swahili for "money." As reported by *BBC News*:

> Since 2007, Kenya has been leading the way with an innovative mobile phone technology that has transformed the lives of millions of people and businesses.
>
> Mobile money transfer allows those without a bank account to transfer funds as quickly and easily as sending a text message. ...

Over 50% of the adult population use the service to send money to far-flung relatives, to pay for shopping, utility bills, or even a night on the tiles and taxi ride home. ...

To use the service, customers first register with Safaricom at an M-Pesa outlet, usually a shop, chemist or petrol station. They can then load money onto their phone. The money is sent onto a third party by text message. The recipient takes the phone to their nearest vendor, where they can pick up the cash.[363]

The BBC article quotes an enthusiastic user who says, "I don't need to go to the bank when I have the bank in my phone."

The most dramatic developments, however, are in India and China, which have leapt headlong into national digital credit systems. With large segments of the population having little access to credit or banking services, they had no real retail payments network to disrupt; so when smart phones came on the market, the opportunity was created for mobile payments to take off. Consumers could bypass checks and credit cards and go straight to mobile payments.

## India and Its 50-Year Push for Financial Inclusion

Financial inclusion has been a goal of the Indian government ever since 1969, when the banks were nationalized under Prime Minister Indira Gandhi. The recent revolution in banking technology has provided the machinery to realize that vision.[364] India's new digital credit system is not perfect. It has suffered from coding glitches and hackers, and the recent "demonetization" of its largest paper bills has been widely criticized. But the country has made impressive progress in giving people access to credit who never had it before.

India's historical challenges have been huge. It is home to over 1.2 billion people, including an estimated one-third of the world's poor.[365] In its last major famine in 1943, between seven and ten million people died.[366] When the country gained independence from British rule in 1947, the government could not afford the luxury of a banking system that put priority on inflated returns for a nonproducing investor class. Its priorities had to be on feeding and housing its burgeoning masses. The trend after independence was therefore to move banking into the public sector.

In 1955, the government nationalized the Imperial Bank of India, renaming it the State Bank of India; and in 1969, Prime Minister Indira Gandhi nationalized fourteen major banks. This bold step was taken not because the banks were bankrupt—the usual justification for nationalization today—but to ensure that credit would be allocated according to planned priorities, including getting banks into rural areas and making cheap financing available to Indian farmers.[367] Today it would be the equivalent of the US president nationalizing the largest Wall Street banks, not because they had failed but because the poor needed affordable credit facilities. The dramatic move drew enthusiastic support from the Indian people and had a major economic impact. According to a 2004 MIT research paper:

> After nationalization, the breadth and scope of the Indian banking sector expanded at a rate perhaps unmatched by any other country. Indian banking has been remarkably

successful at achieving mass participation. Between the time of the 1969 nationalizations and the present, over 58,000 bank branches were opened in India; these new branches, as of March 2003, had mobilized over 9 trillion Rupees in deposits, which represent the overwhelming majority of deposits in Indian banks.[368]

A major shift also occurred in the types of lending pursued:

At the time of nationalisation the priority sector concept was introduced by bringing agriculture, small-scale industry, retail trade, small business and small transport operators under its fold. The list widened with the passage of time. It was made mandatory for banks to provide 40 per cent of their net credit to these "priority" sectors.[369]

Jobs were created, putting millions of people to work; and the increase in bank deposits increased investment in the economy. As the nationalized bank branches proliferated, people who had never before had a bank account started putting their money in banks. Money once hidden at home became the deposit base for extending credit far and wide, increasing the money supply and the credit available for industry, trade, agriculture and infrastructure.

After a new round of bank nationalizations in 1980, the Indian government controlled over 91 percent of the country's banking industry.[370] The 1980s were also when India's economic growth took off. With the push for privatization in the 1990s, government ownership shrank, but today it still accounts for about 70 percent of all banking assets in India.[371]

Providing adequate credit at reasonable cost for farmers and small businesses, however, continued to be a major problem. Before 2009, nearly half the Indian population did not have any form of identification, since they were born without hospitals or government services and did not have birth certificates. That meant they could not open a bank account or get a loan. For financial services, they had to patronize India's version of "payday lenders," who charged exploitative interest and fees. Having no identification or traceable bank accounts also meant that most Indians were outside the tax system, a matter of obvious interest to the government. As late as 2016, only 2 to 3 percent of the population actually paid taxes. This was partly due to the lack of bank records, but it was also because the Indian government had made a policy decision not to tax the poor, and the majority of the population fell in that class.[372] The whole sector needed to be lifted out of poverty, and access to affordable credit was a major step in that direction.

## The Digital Technology Making Financial Inclusion Possible

"One seldom associates the terms 'innovation' and 'disruption' with the government of a country," declared a March 2017 article on the groundbreaking project known as India Stack; but "the government has taken on the role of a startup in India." Begun as a collaborative project between iSPIRT (Indian Software Product Industry Roundtable) and the government, India Stack is a set of open APIs (application program interfaces) made of different layers, called the Presence-less, Paperless and Cashless Layers.[373]

The first, Presence-less layer solved India's personal identification problem with a massive government undertaking
called Aadhaar. Twelve-digit identification numbers were
issued to nearly the entire population, based on demographic
data, fingerprints and iris scans. (Contrary to what you see in
sci-fi movies, iris scans do not involve lasers and are non-in-
vasive. They are just photos of the outside of the eye.[374] Iris
and fingerprint scans can be captured by any modern device
with a camera, such as a smartphone or laptop.)

The Aadhaar data was collected by the Unique Identification Authority of India (UIDAI), a statutory authority
established in January 2009 by the Indian government. By
2016, the program had issued identification numbers to 1.1
billion people. According to Prof. Vivek Wadhwa in a January 2017 article in *The Washington Post*, it was the largest and
most successful I.T. project in the world, creating the foundation for a digital economy.[375] The technology has glitches,
including complaints of stolen identities and surveillance
concerns, but the new system has rapidly brought India into
the 21st century digital economy.

The second, Paperless layer of India Stack consists of
the "digital locker" and "digital signature" components. The
digital locker is a set of digitized documents issued to a particular Aadhaar number, commonly referred to as the e-KYC
(Know Your Customer) bundle. These documents can be
issued by the government or third parties and are stored in
either a shared or an independent repository. The Paperless
layer has allowed everyone to have access to a bank account.
Eleven "payment banks" were opened that could hold money
but did not make loans, although they did provide overdraft
coverage (a form of loan).[376]

The third, Cashless layer of India's new digital infrastructure is its Unified Payment Interface (UPI). Called "the most disruptive technology in Fintech so far," it allows direct money transfer based on a single identifier such as the Aadhaar number. The UPI system eliminates middlemen and brings transaction costs close to zero. The customer just needs to download a free app and enter his identification number and bank PIN. He can then instantly transfer money to anyone, regardless of where the recipient banks. Transfers can happen in seconds without transaction costs, making them faster and cheaper even than credit card payments. Recall that US merchants are charged fees for credit card purchases averaging 2.75 percent per transaction, a charge that is indirectly passed on to customers, making it the equivalent of a private sales tax on every purchase. UPI eliminates this private tax.

"India Stack" combines these three layers into a series of secured and connected systems that allows the storage and sharing of personal data such as addresses, bank statements, medical records, employment records and tax filings. It enables the digital signing of documents, with electronic signatures authorized biometrically; and it circumvents the cumbersome process of opening a mobile phone account, which can now be done in minutes with a thumbprint or iris scan. An important feature is that the user controls what information is shared and with whom, allaying privacy concerns.

Of particular interest for purposes of this book, India Stack allows the instant approval of credit. The borrower is able to turn his own credit into money, simply through an app on his mobile phone. Prof. Wadhwa declared:

India Stack will ... transform how lending is done. The typical villager currently has no chance of getting a small-business loan, because he or she lacks a credit history and verifiable credentials. Now people can share information from their digital lockers, such as bank statements, utility bill payments and life insurance policies, and loans can be approved almost instantaneously on the basis of verified data. This is a more open system than the credit-scoring services that U.S. businesses use.[377]

These loans might be coming from nonbank peer-to-peer lenders or from banks; but assume they are coming from banks (which in India are mostly publicly owned). We have seen that banks do not actually lend their deposits but rather create deposits when they make loans. Thus when a borrower takes out a bank loan, he is actually "monetizing" his own IOU or promise to pay, validated by the bank as "trusted third party." Using the Indian digital financial system, the borrower can turn his promise to pay into a form of digital currency that is authenticated automatically by cryptographic software.

An example from the India Stack website shows a woman street vendor obtaining a one-day loan in the morning, perhaps to purchase her wares wholesale, then paying off the loan in the evening with her profits. This is a clear case of simply monetizing her own credit, since the bank does not have to balance its books until the end of the day. Its books will show only a debit balanced by a credit, netting to zero—no need for the bank to borrow from anywhere to balance its books. The vendor has just turned her own credit into money, mediated automatically through digital software. As a *Wharton Fintech* article describes this system-changing innovation: Suddenly, we go from the world where a small street vendor does not even have a bank account to the world where the same vendor now conducts all his transactions digitally, uses the information to obtain credit, grows his business and even invests his savings profitably.[378]

## User-created Money: A Comparison with Credit Cards

To better understand the mechanism behind this user-created money, a useful comparison is with how credit cards work. The credit card company grants the cardholder credit instantly, based on a credit line authorized up to a certain limit when the user opened an account with the credit card company. The company then turns the user's promise to pay into a "negotiable instrument" acceptable in the payment of debt. A negotiable instrument is anything that is signed and convertible into money or that can be used as money. Under Article 9 of the Uniform Commercial Code, when you as cardholder sign the merchant's credit card charge receipt, you are creating a "negotiable instrument or other writing which evidences a right to the payment of money."[379] In effect, your promise has become money.

This negotiable instrument is deposited electronically into the merchant's checking account, a special account required of all businesses that accept credit. The account goes up by the amount on the receipt, indicating that the merchant has been paid. The charge receipt is forwarded to an "acquiring settlement bank," which bundles your charges and sends them to your own bank. Your bank then sends you a statement and you pay the balance with a check or bank account transfer, causing your transaction account to be debited at your bank.

The net effect is that your charge receipt (a negotiable instrument) has become an "asset" against which credit has been advanced. The bank has simply monetized your IOU, turning it into money. The credit cycle is so short that this process can occur without the money of the bank or its depositors even being involved. Debits and credits are just shuffled back and forth between accounts.

Timothy Madden is a Canadian financial analyst who built software models of credit card accounts in the early 1990s. He estimates that payouts from the bank's own reserves are necessary only about 2 percent of the time, and the merchant's fee is sufficient to cover those occasions. The "reserves" necessary to back short-term advances are thus built into the payments themselves, without drawing from anywhere else.

As for the interest, Madden maintains:

> The interest is all *gravy* because the transactions are funded in fact by the signed payment voucher issued by the card-user at the point of purchase. Assume that the monthly gross sales that are run through credit/charge-cards globally double, from the normal $300 billion to $600 billion for the year-end holiday period. The card companies do not have to worry about where the extra $300 billion will come from because it is provided by the additional $300 billion of signed vouchers themselves.[380]

The 2.75 percent fees imposed on merchants and the average 16 percent interest imposed on borrowers are made possible because the market is monopolized by a tiny number of credit card companies, and entry is difficult. To participate, it is necessary to be part of a network; and the network requires that all participating banks charge a pre-set fee. Private startups cannot compete with Visa and MasterCard, but a national digital payment system similar to India Stack could. Transaction fees could be eliminated and interest charges could be significantly reduced, since they would need to be only high enough to cover defaults. A national mutual credit system run largely on digital software could thus be a major step toward building the sort of banking model that would render the commercial banking behemoths obsolete.

## Demonetization: An Unnecessary Misstep?

India has the technology and the political will to achieve financial inclusion, but in 2016 most Indians still remained outside the digital payments system. That plus a concern for rampant corruption prompted a radical move by Prime Minister Narendra Modi in November of that year, when he shocked the country and the world by eliminating from circulation all 500- and 1,000-rupee notes, comprising 86 percent of the country's circulating money supply. The stated intent was to speed digitization, flush out "black money," and "bring the parallel sector into the mainstream economy."[381] The withdrawn currency was supposed to be replaceable with new 500- and 2,000-rupee notes, but the transition was poorly executed. The printing presses could not keep up, and chaos ensued. It was particularly hard on the poor, the very sector financial inclusion was supposed to serve, since they operated in a virtually all-cash economy. Reportedly, 97 percent of the recalled cash managed to find its way into banks by the deadline on December 30, 2016; and Modi's government was victorious in the midterm state-level elections, which was seen as a referendum on its unprecedented action.[382] But critics said the step was a major miscalculation and was not necessary to achieve financial inclusion, which was already happening in India.

Some suspicious Western observers have seen this and other efforts at demonetization as calculated moves toward a global New World Order, in which money will be entirely digital. Governments will then have the power to turn off access to it by political dissidents or to confiscate deposits by imposing negative interest or bail-ins.[383] Those concerns will be addressed in a later chapter; but if that was the intent in this case, it failed. Cash is still king in India, which remains far behind the United States and the United Kingdom with their roughly 95 percent digital currencies. Other commentators have seen the massive push to go digital as just an effort to catch up. "Putting aside the policy missteps," wrote one analyst, it was "a shot in the arm to the ecosystem around digital payments and consumer-and-context-friendly technology."[384]

India's new digitized system has not yet eliminated banks, but it has made major upgrades to a banking system in serious need of improvement. India's banks are undercapitalized and have a reputation for being inefficient and corrupt, dating back to a 19th century colonial system inherited from the British.[385] The country needs to catch up, and financial technology is speeding it forward in that race. The new digitized system has greatly expanded the availability of credit for small and medium-size businesses and for individuals. Mountains of paperwork have been eliminated and the regulatory burden that often prevents banks from lending locally has been relieved, with "Know Your Customer" requirements met automatically with digital identification. Agreements can be signed digitally, and payments can be made without traveling to the bank. The new technologies allow bankers to focus on the more personal aspects of banking, the parts that cannot be performed by computer software.

In an August 2017 press release titled "The Revolution in Banking Sector Technology," V. Srinivas, Chairman of the Tax Board of the northern state of Rajasthan, declared that "the new paradigm in banking is, *banking is necessary, not banks.*" He wrote:

> The Reserve Bank of India has accepted that there has been a paradigm shift in the banking sector and has urged banks to take full advantage of the technological developments, enmesh them to meet customer expectations. The success of Fintech companies has been a game changer for small businesses and reshaping the financial services industry radically. The Reserve Bank of India's medium term plan for financial inclusion is that by 2021, over 90 percent of the hitherto under-served sections of society would become active stakeholders in economic progress.[386]

## China's Mobile Ecosystems

An even greater threat to the traditional banking model than India's digital payment system may be China's new mobile payment ecosystems. According to a May 2018 article in *Bloomberg* titled "Why China's Payment Apps Give U.S. Bankers Nightmares":

> The future of consumer payments may not be designed in New York or London but in China. There, money flows mainly through a pair of digital ecosystems that blend social media, commerce and banking—all run by two of the world's most valuable companies. That contrasts with the U.S., where numerous firms feast on fees from handling and processing payments. Western bankers and credit-card executives who travel to China keep returning with the same anxiety: Payments can happen cheaply and easily without them.[387]

The nightmare for the US financial industry is that a major technology company—whether one from China or a US giant such as Amazon or Facebook—replicates the success of the Chinese mobile payment systems, cutting banks and processors out of the lucrative fees they normally charge for card and payment services.[388]

According to John Engen, writing in *American Banker* in May 2018, China processed a whopping *$12.8 trillion* in mobile payments in the first ten months of 2017. Today even merchants on the street don't want cash. Payment for everything is with a phone and a QR code (a type of barcode). More than 90 percent of Chinese mobile payments are run through Alipay and WeChat Pay, rival platforms backed by the country's two largest internet conglomerates, Alibaba and Tencent Holdings. Alibaba is the Amazon of China, while Tencent Holdings is the owner of WeChat, a messaging and social-media app with more than a billion users. The American equivalent would be Amazon and Facebook serving as the major conduits for US payments.

WeChat and Alibaba have grown into full-blown digital ecosystems—around-the-clock hubs for managing the details of daily life. WeChat users can schedule doctor appointments, order food, hail rides and much more, through "mini-apps" on the core app. Alipay calls itself a "global lifestyle super-app" and has similar functions. In the United States, PayServices is a digital ecosystem that works on the same principle; but unlike in China, it must compete with well-established card payment systems and is little known.

Alipay and WeChat Pay have flourished by making mobile payments cheap and easy to use. Consumers can pay for everything with their mobile apps and can make person-to-person payments. Everyone has a unique QR code, transfers are free, and users don't need to sign into a bank or payments app when transacting. They simply press the "pay" button on the ecosystem's main app and their unique QR code appears for the merchant to scan. Engen writes:

> A growing number of retailers, including McDonald's and Starbucks, have self-scanning devices near the cash register to read QR codes. The process takes seconds, moving customers along so quickly that anyone using cash gets eye-rolls for slowing things down.

> Merchants that lack a point-of-sale device can simply post a piece of paper with their QR code near the register for customers to point their phones' cameras at and execute payments in reverse.

A system built on QR codes might not be as secure as the near-field communication technology used by ApplePay and other apps in the U.S. market. But it's cheaper for merchants, who don't have to buy a piece of technology to accept a payment.

The mobile payment systems are a boon to merchants and their customers, but local bankers complain that they are slowly being driven out of business. Alipay and WeChat have become a duopoly that is impossible to fight. Engen writes that banks are often reduced to "dumb pipes"—silent funders whose accounts are used to top up customers' digital wallets. The bank bears the compliance and other account-related expenses, and it does not get the fees and branding opportunities typical of cards and other bank-run options. The bank is seen as a place to deposit money and link it to WeChat or Alipay. Bankers are being "disintermediated"—cut out of the loop as middlemen.

If Amazon, Facebook or one of their Chinese counterparts duplicated the success of China's mobile ecosystems in the United States, they could take $43 billion in merchant fees from credit card companies, processors and banks, along with about $3 billion in bank fees for checking accounts. In addition, there is the potential loss of money market deposits, which are also migrating to the mobile ecosystem duopoly in China. In 2017, Alipay's affiliate Yu'e Bao surpassed JPMorgan Chase's government market fund as the world's largest money market fund, with more than $200 billion in assets. As Engen quotes one financial services leader, "The speed of migration to their wealth-management and money-market funds has been tremendous. That's bad news for traditional banks, where deposits are the foundation of the business."[389]

An Amazon-style mobile ecosystem could challenge not only the payments system but the lending business of banks. Amazon is already making small-business loans, finding ways to cut into banks' swipe-fee revenue and competing against prepaid card issuers; and it evidently has broader ambitions. Checking accounts, small business credit cards and even mortgages appear to be in the company's sights.[390]

In an October 2017 article titled "The Future of Banks Is Probably Not Banks," tech innovator Andy O'Sullivan observed that Amazon has a relatively new service called "Amazon Cash," where consumers can use a barcode to load cash into their Amazon accounts through physical retailers. The service is intended for consumers who don't have bankcards, but O'Sullivan notes that it raises some interesting possibilities. Amazon could do a deal with retailers to allow consumers to use their Amazon accounts in stores, or it could offer credit to buy particular items. No bank would be involved, just a tech giant that already has a relationship with the consumer offering him additional services. Phone payment systems are already training customers not to need bankcards, which means not to need banks.[391]

Taking those concepts further, Amazon (or eBay or Craigslist) could set up a digital credit system that bypassed bank-created money altogether. Users could sell goods and services online for credits, which they could then spend online for other goods and services. The credits of this online ecosystem would constitute its own user-generated currency, of the sort envisioned by Ryan Fugger in his effort to set up a digital community currency that was independent of banks and governments.

An Amazon-style credit clearing system would be independent of both banks and government, but Amazon itself is a privately owned for-profit megalithic system. Like its Wall Street counterparts, it has a shady reputation, being variously charged with exploitation, unfair trade practices, environmental degradation, and extracting outsized profits from trades.[392]

A nonprofit public utility could be designed in a way that eliminated these flaws. Rather than bypassing government and banks, a national credit clearing system might succeed in recapturing them as public utilities that served the economy and the people, using modern technology to replicate the system of publicly issued credit in colonial Pennsylvania. Nothing like that has evolved yet, but central bankers are taking a keen interest in digital currencies, discussed next.

*Takeaway: India and China have developed comprehensive digital payment ecosystems that could disrupt banking as we know it. Users conduct transactions by mobile phones in which their personal data is stored, cutting out bankers and their steady stream of fee income. Although the new digital ecosystems still have technological glitches and shortcomings, they have vastly increased financial inclusion and could be prototypes for a credit clearing system projected to a national scale.*

## CHAPTER 12

# CENTRAL BANK DIGITAL CURRENCIES: PROMISE OR THREAT?

*"[O]n the one hand, governments can be bad actors and, on the other hand, some citizens can be bad actors. The former justifies an anonymous currency to protect citizens from bad governments, while the latter calls for transparency of all payments. The reality is in between, and for that reason we welcome anonymous cryptocurrencies but also disagree with the view that the government should provide one."*
—*"The Case for Central Bank Electronic Money and the Non-case for Central Bank Cryptocurrencies," St. Louis Federal Reserve, February 2018*[393]

**Central bank researchers** have also been studying digital currencies.[394] The extent of this interest was suggested in June 2017, when Olga Skorobogatov, Deputy Chairman of the Russian Central Bank, declared, "Regulators of all countries agree that it's time to develop national cryptocurrencies; this is the future."[395] But the digital currencies they are considering are not the sort of cryptocurrencies that are decentralized, anonymous and "permissionless." In a February 2018 review of central bank electronic money, researchers at the St. Louis Federal Reserve observed:

Some central banks supposedly are evaluating the issuance of a central bank cryptocurrency. However, a closer look at these projects reveals that these are not cryptocurrencies according to our definition .... The projects usually are highly centralized. ... Once we remove the decentralized nature of a cryptocurrency, not much is left of it.

No reputable central bank, said the researchers, would have an incentive to issue an anonymous virtual currency:

The reputational risk would simply be too high. Think of a hypothetical "Fedcoin" used by a drug cartel to launder money or a terrorist organization to acquire weapons. Moreover, commercial banks would rightfully start asking why they have to follow KYC ("know your customer") and AML ("anti-money laundering") regulations, while the central bank is undermining any effects of this regulation by issuing an anonymous cryptocurrency with permissionless access.[396]

The government currencies being proposed are simply central bank digital currencies (CBDCs)—digital currencies issued by a government through its central bank. Most currency today is digital, but it is issued privately by the commercial banks that have usurped the field. The distinction is evident from a look at Russia's proposed new "CryptoRuble." According to an October 2017 article in *Business Insider*:

Russian President Vladimir Putin has reportedly decided that the time has come for a national cryptocurrency called the CryptoRuble. ...

Details regarding the CryptoRuble are scarce, but it looks like it will keep some aspects normally associated with cryptocurrencies, while getting rid of others. The CryptoRuble will reportedly use blockchain technology. But instead of being mined, it will be issued and tracked just like regular currencies.

Rubles and CryptoRubles will be able to be freely exchanged. But, to deter money laundering and black market activities sometimes associated with cryptocurrencies, there will be a 13 percent tax if proof of legal origin cannot be produced.[397]

Currency that is not "mined" but is "issued and tracked just like regular currencies" is not on a blockchain. It is simply a digital ruble. The article goes on:

Russia's Minister of Communications and Mass Media, Nikolay Nikiforov said that Russia's creation of the CryptoRuble was for one simple reason: "If we do not, then in 2 months, our neighbors in the Eurasian Economic Community will do it."

That is one possible motive, but another was suggested in a November 2017 article in *Forbes*:

Russia has been at the forefront of encouraging a national cryptocurrency as a way to avoid Western sanctions and economic influence. To this goal, Putin has met with Vitalik Buterin, founder of the second largest cryptocurrency Ethereum, and discussed its possible implementation in Russia. ...

A key vulnerability in the Russian economy is the access to SWIFT, the standardised network for interbank transactions. ... It has sometimes been called the "nuclear option" of economic warfare to block a state from its access to SWIFT ... .[398]

Economic warfare aside, the SWIFT system is slow and in need of upgrading. As British financial writer Frances Coppola observed in a 2018 article on central bank digital currencies:

Digital currencies are already created by both central banks and commercial banks. But some think global payments could be faster, more efficient and more secure if they were entirely handled by central banks, rather than by a combination of central banks, commercial banks and payments service providers. Central banks are therefore looking seriously at adopting the new technologies that are revolutionizing the global payments arena.[399]

In a June 2016 article in *American Banker,* Caitlin Long discussed the possibility of a "blockchain-dollar" that would bypass the need for the SWIFT system by allowing direct settlement in a global currency. She noted that the blockchain was originally developed so that bitcoin could be traded digitally across borders. She wrote:

A blockchain-dollar could ... become truly global money. ... Were a blockchain-dollar to exist, regional and community banks in the U.S. could settle directly with the Fed. Or companies could use the blockchain-dollar themselves, just as some companies use Swift directly today. Or individuals could use blockchain-dollars. Bank of England official Ben Broadbent has broached that idea, imagining a possibility in which "everyone—including individuals—would be able to hold such balances" at a central bank.[400]

Again, this could be done with digital dollars without putting them on a blockchain, since there is no need for a distributed ledger when there is a central authority keeping track of the funds. More interesting in the proposal of Dr. Broadbent was the novel idea that *everyone could have an account at the central bank.* Universal access to the central bank's deep pocket would eliminate the fear of bank runs and "bail-ins," since central banks can create the national currency without purporting to borrow it from somewhere else. Accounts could be held at the central bank not just by small depositors but by large institutions, eliminating the need for the private repo market to provide a safe place to park their funds. And no government deposit insurance would be necessary, since the central bank cannot run out of money, even in a major bank run.

The proposal raises another interesting possibility. The only central bank currency that is available to individuals today is the physical cash that composes a very small percentage of the money supply. A central-bank-issued digital currency could increase that percentage significantly, to the point where it might even squeeze out the riskier commercial-bank-created "checkbook money" altogether. Assuming the central bank were a true public utility harnessed to serving the public, this systemic upgrade could transfer the power to create money from private commercial banks back to the governments that most people think issue it now.

## Should Privately Owned Banks Create Money? The Debate Over "Narrow" Banking

Ben Broadbent is Deputy Governor of Monetary Policy at the Bank of England. In a March 2016 lecture at the London School of Economics, he said that while digital currencies and distributed ledgers are new, they raise issues that have long been debated:

> Some admirers of Bitcoin see it as a means of bypassing central banks altogether. They are in some ways the descendants of the supporters of "free banking" in the 19th century. Conversely, others see the distributed ledger as an opportunity for the central bank to expand its role, via a "central bank digital currency" available to a much wider group of counterparties. If it were a close substitute for bank deposits, a CBDC would represent a shift towards a "narrower" banking system. This too is an old debate in economics: should banks be prevented from creating liquidity, or is maturity transformation an inevitable and necessary feature of market economies?[401]

"Maturity transformation" is a euphemistic term for how banks create money by turning short-term deposits into long-term loans, something they do by issuing deposits in excess of their reserves. "Narrow" banking proposals and their modern-day variations would remove depository banks from the money-creation process and limit them to the narrow business of storing and transferring deposits. Broadbent went on:

"[M]aturity transformation"—the combination of on-demand liabilities [deposits] and illiquid assets [loans]—imparts an inherent fragility to commercial banks' balance sheets. If everyone tried simultaneously to withdraw a bank's deposits, it wouldn't have enough liquid resources with which to meet the demand. That's why banks are vulnerable to "runs". ...

By contrast, the central bank essentially holds nothing but liquid assets—largely government securities .... Shifting deposits away from commercial banks, and towards the central bank, would therefore make for a "narrower" banking system—a "narrow" bank being one whose assets are as liquid as its liabilities. In principle, it would also make for a safer one. Backed by liquid assets, rather than risky lending, deposits would become inherently more secure. They wouldn't be vulnerable to "runs" and we would no longer need to insure them.

He noted that narrow banking proposals go back as far as the classical economists Adam Smith and David Ricardo. The "Chicago Plan," proposed by a group of economists at the University of Chicago during the Great Depression, recommended that banks be required to hold 100 percent reserves against their deposits, eliminating fractional reserve banking altogether.

Modern "Sovereign Money" proposals are a modification of this theme. Rather than requiring full reserve banking, they would move deposits onto the balance sheet of the central bank. The effect would be to eliminate the "split-circuit" system of reserves trading separately from deposits. As Joseph Huber explains, the proposal "abandons the split-circuit structure based on a mixed money supply of deposits and reserves in favor of a single circuit on the basis of sovereign money only, issued by the central bank." As in full-reserve proposals, banks could not create money as loans. All new money would be created by a central monetary authority. Bank loans would be limited to recirculating the existing money of investors through investment accounts that operated in a way similar to mutual funds.[402]

Narrow banking and Sovereign Money proposals have seen a revival since the financial meltdown in 2008.[403] They include the National Emergency Employment Defense Act (the NEED Act), submitted by then-US Congressman Dennis Kucinich in 2011; the "limited purpose banking" advocated by Lawrence Kotlikoff in his 2010 book *Jimmy Stewart Is Dead*; Prof. Huber's *Sovereign Money: Beyond Reserve Banking;* and the dynamic Sovereign Money movement of the *Positive Money* group in the UK.[404] The government of Iceland has explored an alternative system in which all money would be created by the central bank, and Swiss advocates brought a referendum along those lines in June 2018.[405] But none of these proposals has yet been implemented by policymakers.

## Opening the Fed's Deposit Window

Dr. Broadbent noted that full-reserve and Sovereign Money proposals can only be implemented "by regulatory fiat," a legislative hurdle that is hard to overcome. But that hurdle could be avoided, he said, by "nationalization of deposit-taking by the central bank": the central bank could simply open its deposit window to everyone. Commercial banks could carry on as they do now. They would just attract fewer deposits, since most depositors would be likely to opt for the ultra-safe central bank.

That was also the proposal of the St. Louis Fed researchers writing on CBDCs in February 2018, cited earlier. They said:

> We believe that there is a strong case for central bank money in electronic form, and it would be easy to implement. Central banks would only need to allow households and firms to open accounts with them, which would allow them to make payments with central bank electronic money instead of commercial bank deposits.[406]

The researchers noted that this idea differed from the Chicago Plan, which would have eliminated the fractional reserve system by imposing 100 percent reserves on commercial bank deposits. Under the CBDC plan, commercial banks could continue to offer bank deposits and to lend as they do now. Central bank deposit accounts would just be an option not previously available to the public. The effect would be to increase the stability of the financial system by having a disciplining effect on commercial banks:

> To attract deposits, they would need to alter their business model or to increase interest rate payments on deposits to compensate users for the additional risk they assume. The disciplining effect on commercial banks will be reinforced by the fact that, in the event of a loss of confidence, customers' money can be quickly transferred to central bank electronic money accounts. In order to avoid this, the banks must make their business models more secure by, for

example, taking fewer risks or by holding more reserves and capital, or they must offer higher interest rates.[407]

The researchers said that central bank electronic money accounts would be used only for making payments. The central bank would not make commercial loans. "No credit can be obtained," they said, "and so almost no monitoring is needed."

## Curbing Bad Governments

Skeptical commentators worry that the real push behind central bank digital currencies is for a "cashless society," in which a controlling Deep State can turn off the money of dissidents at will. But the St. Louis Fed researchers said that Fed accounts would not be mandatory, and that cryptocurrencies could still be used as a safety valve to protect citizens against bad governments. You would not be required to move your physical cash into a digital account. You could just transfer the digital money in your current bank account into an account at the central bank. The result would be to trade digital currency representing only a bank's promise to pay in legal tender for the "real" legal tender of the central bank.

Even without darker motives, however, there is the problem that in some countries merchants are refusing cash because digital money is easier to deal with, putting goods and services out of reach of the unbanked. To circumvent this problem, the Positive Money group recommends that governments update the legal definition of "legal tender" to require retailers to accept physical cash as a means of payment.[408]

That assumes, of course, that the government actually wants to preserve cash as an option. Our money can always be turned off by a government determined to do it. The vast majority of the US money supply is already digital, existing on the servers of commercial banks that can and have refused to allow depositors to withdraw their own money under a variety of conditions, including simply being over a certain arbitrary withdrawal limit. Physical cash, too, can be confiscated. It can be and has been forcibly taken by governments, as happened in India in November 2016.[409] Gold can also be confiscated, as happened in the 1930s when President Roosevelt took the dollar off the gold standard. People were ordered to turn over their gold coins and gold certificates (paper money that the government was required to trade for gold on demand). They got dollars in exchange. The price of gold was then increased by 69 percent.[410]

Wht about cryptocurrencies? These too are not safe from action by governments, which can regulate them, tax them, and shut down the exchanges and bitcoin ATMs. As Izabella Kaminska notes in *The Financial Times,* most people keep their bitcoin on exchanges, since they don't trust themselves to store their own private keys; and exchanges operate a lot like banks without their legal protections. The coins could be re-lent and gambled with just as commercial banks do with their deposits. She writes:

> [M]ost exchanges manage daily transfers and withdrawal requests out of a much smaller pot of liquid bitcoins they control directly on users' behalf, depositing and receiving sums as and when client liquidity requires, whilst supposedly parking the excess safely in storage. ... But of course

since many of these exchanges aren't subject to public audits or disclosures, it's hard to know if the balances are really being segregated or reserved as claimed. They could, for example, be being re-lent for other purposes. There is, as with banking, a huge temptation to put those idle reserves to better use.[411]

Joseph Stiglitz, former chief economist of the World Bank, warned in July 2018 that central banks have not yet clamped down on bitcoin and other leading crypto-coins only because the market is still relatively small. Once they become significant, he said, regulators will "use the hammer."[412]

No form of money is safe from a government bent on destroying it or confiscating it. For true security, we need to reclaim our government and our financial system by making them true public utilities. An essential step in that transformation is to reclaim the power to create money from the powerful private cartel that has it now; and a CBDC system could facilitate that process. As observed in an August 2018 article on the European website *Banking Hub*:

Unlike traditional fiat currency systems, the CBDC system will be based on an asset class held outside of the traditional banking system. Thus, any conversion of existing noncash assets into the Central Bank digital currency will cause outflow of financial assets from [the] existing banking system. Another distinctive feature of this system will be to conduct payments directly between participants, without engagement of third parties (such as clearing houses, settlement institutions, payment systems operators, etc.). This would lead to the elimination of all intermediaries that are currently present in traditional payment systems and revenues generated from them, also by banks.[413]

Rather than being limited to coins and paper bills, "legal tender" could be expanded through a CBDC system to include digital cash exchanged without banks or other intermediaries. As in India and China, it could be traded peer-to-peer on cell phones; and unlike with private digital currencies, it would be backed by the full faith and credit of the government. Cumbersome and energy-intensive blockchains would not be necessary, and the currency would be accepted without reliance on a limited circle of community members willing to take it. Some broader implications of opening the central bank's facilities to the public are explored in the next chapter.

*Takeaway: Central bank researchers in a number of countries are studying the possibility of issuing their own central bank digital currencies, for a variety of reasons. By issuing the national currency in digital form, a government acting through its central bank could reclaim the power to issue money that has now been ceded to private commercial banks. To protect against bad governments, people can hold cash, gold and cryptocurrencies; but no currency is really safe from a rogue government. To ensure the safety of our money and our livelihoods, we need to reclaim our government as an institution that is responsive to the will of the people, and reclaiming the money power is a major step in that direction.*

## CHAPTER 13
# A CENTRAL BANK FOR MAIN STREET: DEMOCRATIZING THE FED

*"The difficulty lies not in the new ideas, but in escaping from the old ones."*

— *John Maynard Keynes, preface to The General Theory of Employment, Interest and Money (1935)*

**A central bank** operated as a public utility could do much more to fire up the engines of productivity than merely tampering with interest rates or propping up Wall Street with quantitative easing. Opening the Fed's facilities to all would allow it to stimulate the economy directly. It would also allow individuals, businesses and local governments to share in the perks that today are the exclusive domain of the banking club. This could all be done without issuing a FedCoin or other special digital currency that competed with the private cryptocurrency market. We could keep our cash and our gold and our cryptocurrencies as stores of value and buffers against currency collapse. But if the banking system were reclaimed as a public utility, those stores would not need to be tapped. Bank runs would be prevented and bailouts and bail-ins would not be necessary, because the central bank cannot go if bankrupt and there would be no need to prop up a private banking system that was no longer "systemically important." A central bank operated as a public utility would have other tools for protecting the value of the currency, maintaining full employment, and stimulating the economy.

## Eliminating Bank Favoritism: A Public Option for Bank Accounts

Opening the Fed's deposit window to everyone would "democratize" deposit accounts, giving individuals and businesses the same privileges that banks have now; and one of those perks is the right to receive substantial interest on their deposits. Ever since the 2008 credit crisis, the Fed has been paying banks IOER (interest on excess reserves). As of November 2018, it was paying 2.2 percent on over $2 trillion in bank reserves. If rates go to 3.5 percent, as the Fed says it is targeting by 2020, the windfall will be $77 billion annually, most of it going to Wall Street megabanks.[414]

In their February 2018 policy review, researchers at the St. Louis Fed noted that this bank favoritism could be eliminated if individuals, businesses and local governments were allowed access to the Fed's deposit window. They wrote:

> There is a political economy issue with [IOER] payments since, as of today, they are paid only to the few financial intermediaries that have access to central-bank electronic money. The general public might not consider such large payments equitable or beneficial, and there is a high risk that it will trigger political controversies that have the

potential to affect central-bank independence. ... Central bank electronic money is an elegant way of avoiding possible political upheavals with regard to these interest payments, by allowing the whole population to have access to these interest payments and not just a small group of commercial banks.[415]

Commercial banks in the United States currently handle over $12 trillion in deposits, paying an average rate on checking accounts of a mere 0.05 percent and on savings accounts of 0.08 percent. If the central bank were to pay 2.2 percent on $12 trillion in deposits, the interest cost would be over $264 billion annually. But the Fed's unlimited deep pocket can handle any sized expenditure. The question is not where to get the money but whether direct money injections of that sort would result in price inflation.

As shown in Chapter 1, there is currently a $2 trillion gap between potential and real US productivity. That gap would need to be filled *every year* before the economy would be running at full capacity. Up to that saturation point, adding money (demand) will not drive up consumer prices. It will drive the creation of new supply, keeping prices stable. For evidence, we can look at China. In the last 20 years, its M2 money supply has grown from just over 10 trillion yuan to 80 trillion yuan ($11.6T), a nearly 800% increase.[416] Yet as of December 2018, the inflation rate of its Consumer Price Index (CPI) remained a very modest 1.9 percent.[417] Why has all that excess money not driven prices up? The answer is that China's Gross Domestic Product has grown twelve-fold in the same period.[418] Supply (GDP) has risen to meet demand (money), keeping prices stable.

The potential benefits of opening the Fed's deposit window to everyone were the subject of another policy paper published in June 2018. Titled "Central Banking for All: A Public Option for Bank Accounts," it was written by a team of law professors and former Treasury advisors headed by Morgan Ricks. They pointed to other benefits enjoyed by banks with central bank accounts besides higher interest on their balances, including:

> Payments between these accounts clear instantly; banks needn't wait days or even minutes for incoming payments to post. On top of that, central bank accounts are pure money—economically equivalent to dollar bills—meaning they are fully sovereign and nondefaultable no matter how large the balance. By contrast, federal deposit insurance for ordinary bank accounts maxes out at $250,000—a big problem for institutions with large balances.[419]

Additional benefits in which consumers and retailers could share if allowed access to central bank accounts included that there would be no fees or minimum balances and no interchange fees on debit card transactions.

The Ricks team said the central bank would not need to issue a special digital currency. Just allowing everyone to open an account at the Fed would do it. Most of the money supply is already digital, created by banks when they make loans; and this digital money is designated in dollars. Opening the Fed's deposit window would simply allow the public to transfer their existing digital dollars from commercial banks into accounts at the central bank. The researchers proposed calling these accounts "FedAccounts." They observed that the

Fed already processes payments by its account holders through Fedwire, its real-time payments network, to the tune of *$3 trillion per day.*

The Ricks team acknowledge that the FedAccount program would incur some expenses, including those for complying with the Bank Secrecy Act, money laundering, and anti-terrorism regulations. But the program was expected to reduce compliance expenditures for the financial sector as a whole, due to economies of scale and reductions in duplicative reviews and the need for complicated banking regulations.

Responding to concerns over whether the Fed would be competent to manage a system like FedAccount, they argued that it would:

> At bottom FedAccount is a system for payments and accounts: a ledger combined with processes and protocols for debiting and crediting balances. The Fed already does this very efficiently on a huge scale. Today it maintains account liabilities totaling about $2.5 trillion, and it has vast and longstanding expertise in transaction processing. While the Fed does not have experience in *retail* operations, all sorts of governmental entities already interface directly with the public. Notably, the U.S. Treasury Department processes over one billion payments per year and disburses benefits to millions of Social Security and pension recipients each month. Treasury also settles claims resulting from forged, lost, and stolen benefit checks and collects monies from parties liable for fraud. ... [T]he U.S. Digital Service ("USDS") ... has dramatically improved direct services in areas ranging from the Educa-

tion Department's $1 trillion student loan program to the Department of Homeland Security's immigration program. The USDS could be enlisted to help set up FedAccount's consumer interface.[420]

The "distributed ledger" technology being proposed for central bank digital currencies they said would not be necessary. "FedAccounts would plug seamlessly into our existing, ubiquitous, time-tested money-and-payment system, rather than requiring widespread adoption of new, unfamiliar, and possibly unsound technologies."

To interface with the public, they proposed enlisting the physical plant and personnel of the US Postal Service. Like the St. Louis Fed researchers, they did not recommend giving FedAccounts a consumer lending component. The arrangement would therefore not be responsive to the credit needs of low-income households; but they said it would be compatible with consumer lending programs, including the sort of small-dollar lending that could be done through the Post Office.

The legislative changes needed would be minor. The central bank is already authorized to maintain accounts for depository institutions, as well as for the US government and certain of its instrumentalities, government-sponsored enterprises, and financial market utilities. The list would just need to be expanded to include all US persons, and to require the Fed to provide accounts to all qualifying applicants. Existing law also empowers the Fed to pay interest on balances maintained "by or on behalf of a depository institution." This provision could be adjusted to empower the Fed to pay interest on balances maintained by all US persons, and to require it to pay a uniform rate to all its account holders.

The researchers concluded:

> Money is often described as a public good, and FedAccount would bring this conception to full realization by transforming the U.S. account-money system into public infrastructure akin to roads, sidewalks, public libraries, the judicial system, and law enforcement.

> ... It is no exaggeration to say that FedAccount could rival the 1933 advent of federal deposit insurance as a stabilizing force. By making pure sovereign money widely available in "account" form, FedAccount would crowd out runnable cash equivalents, all but eliminating a primary cause of macroeconomic disasters.[421]

## Would Opening the Central Bank's Deposit Window Choke Off Credit?

The problem foreseen by Dr. Broadbent with allowing everyone to bank at the central bank was that if depositors moved their money en masse into central bank accounts, commercial banks would not have the liquidity needed to fund loans, and credit markets would dry up. Banks don't actually need deposits to make loans, but they do need liquidity to cover their outgoing checks, and deposits are the cheapest and most stable source of that liquidity. If banks lose their deposit base and the central bank is not allowed to make loans, where will credit come from?

Sovereign Money advocates have addressed the credit

problem by proposing that the government issue central bank digital currency through a federal monetary authority of some sort. This new currency would be delivered to the government for injection into the economy, where it would presumably find its way into banks for loans. The monetary authority would turn the money tap on as necessary to meet loan demand.

In a 92-page July 2016 Bank of England Staff Working Paper 2016 titled "The Macroeconomics of Central Bank Issued Digital Currencies," John Barrdear and Michael Kumhof proposed that new CBDC could be issued in a sum equal to 30 percent of Gross Domestic Product, an amount loosely equivalent to the QE conducted by various central banks over the last decade.[422]

On that model, based on a GDP of $18.56 trillion in 2016, US central bank digital currency could be issued of $5.57 trillion, which would be delivered to the government to spend on various programs. The recipients would then either spend the money, invest it, or deposit it in a transaction account, but these deposits could not be expanded into loans. However, individuals could choose to put their money in "savings banks" that could make loans. Savings banks could lend at interest but could not draw on demand deposits for the loans and would not have FDIC insurance coverage. If the loans went bad, the investors would simply lose their money.

Critics contend, however, that relying on this "trickle-down" approach could choke off the free flow of credit. People might not be willing to put their money into savings accounts that were being used for potentially risky bets. Would credit card users need to call the bank every time they wanted to make a charge, to see if the bank had savings sufficient to cover it? Richard Murphy, professor of economics at the University of London, argues that "there is no way that a central committee can anticipate the needs of the finance system for money in the following month. There will, inevitably, be credit rationing as a result for productive activities."[423]

Commenting on narrow banking proposals, the Ricks team maintained that if FedAccounts were broadly adopted, full-reserve savings banks would not be necessary. The deposits of people and businesses would be held directly at the central bank, where banks could borrow as needed to fund their loans. The Fed would be required to extend its discount window loans to all banks. That accommodation might just be temporary, but they said it could be advantageous to leave a substantial quantity of discount window credit outstanding indefinitely. They called this "portfolio management outsourcing." Commercial banks would be making loans with central bank liquidity, while the central bank avoided the appearance of political meddling and favoritism.

That could work, but it would leave us where we are now: banks would still be in the privileged position of being able to borrow cheaply from the central bank and make loans to the public at substantially higher rates; they could fund the loans that were most lucrative for their shareholders, bypassing the needs of local businesses, local governments and local communities; and they could speculate with the central bank's cheap credit, create asset bubbles, and continue to financialize the economy at the expense of productive enterprise.

## Another Option: The Central Bank As Commercial Lender

A more equitable approach would be for the central bank to open not just its deposit window but its lending window to everyone. The central bank would not be able to handle an entire nationwide lending business itself, but the "portfolio management outsourcing" suggested by the Ricks group could be done by a network of local banks operated as nonprofit franchises of the public system, as recommended by Prof. Hockett.[424] (See Chapter 8.) These nonprofits could be federal postal banks, local publicly owned banks, or local privately owned public benefit banks.

That idea has historical precedent. The central banks of the United States, Australia, New Zealand, Canada, and many other countries have successfully assumed commercial as well as central bank functions in the past.[425] In the United States, this change in policy might not even require an act of Congress.

In 1934, Section 13(b) was added to the Federal Reserve Act, authorizing the Fed to "make credit available for the purpose of supplying working capital to established industrial and commercial businesses." This long-forgotten section remained in effect for 24 years. According to David Fettig in a 2002 article on the Minneapolis Fed's website called "Lender of More Than Last Resort," 13(b) allowed Federal Reserve banks to make loans directly to any established businesses in their districts, and to share in loans with commercial lending institutions if the latter assumed 20 percent of the risk. No limitation was placed on the amount of a single loan.[426]

Fettig wrote that "the Fed was still less than twenty years old and many likely remembered the arguments put forth during the System's founding, when some advocated that the discount window should be open to all comers, not just member banks."

Section 13(b) was eventually repealed, but the Federal Reserve Act retained enough vestiges of it to allow the Fed to intervene to save a variety of nonbank entities from bankruptcy. Fettig wrote:

> Section 13(b) may be a memory, ... but Section 13 paragraph 3 ... is alive and well in the Federal Reserve Act. ... [T]his amendment allows, "in unusual and exigent circumstances," a Reserve bank to advance credit to individuals, partnerships and corporations that are not depository institutions.[427]

In 2008, the Fed bailed out investment company Bear Stearns and insurer AIG, neither of which was a bank. Bear Stearns received almost $1 trillion in short-term loans, with interest rates as low as 0.5 percent. The Fed also made loans to other corporations, including GE, McDonald's, and Verizon.

The chief problem with Section 13(3) was that the tool was applied selectively. The recipients were major corporate players, not local businesses or local governments. The section was therefore amended in the 2010 Dodd-Frank Act to read:

> Only Broad-Based Facilities Permitted. Section 13(3) is modified to remove the authority to extend credit to specific individuals, partnerships and corporations. Instead,

the Board may authorize credit under section 13(3) only under a program or facility with "broad-based eligibility."

What exactly does that mean? Law professor Tim Canova is an expert in Federal Reserve legislation and history. He interprets the amended section to mean that lending solely to a specific auto company (GM) or to a specific utility company (GE) is prohibited. But lending to all auto companies or to all utility companies might be allowed.[428] Arguably, then, loans could be extended to anyone who demonstrated creditworthiness and the ability to pay the loan back, so long as everyone in that category had access to the lending facility on equal terms.

In her discussion of CBDCs, Frances Coppola noted that a major obstacle to ending commercial bank responsibility for money creation is the problem of credit risk. Taxpayers ultimately back central banks and could end up with the losses from loan defaults."[429] But as Prof. Werner observes, the central bank does not actually need to balance its books. Bad loans could just be written off. (See Chapter 7.) Borrowers who defaulted on their loans would lose their credit rating and access to central bank credit for a time, as happens in bankruptcy proceedings today; and as with any default, some extra money would remain circulating in the system in the form of newly created loan money that was not repaid. But as observed in Chapter 3, we actually need some extra money in the economy to cover growth and to compensate for the interest that was not created in the original loans, as well as for the money that is unavailable for loan repayment because it is sitting idle in bank accounts, stashed under mattresses, captured in the speculative financial casino, or sent abroad. How to deal with the chronic shortage of money available to repay our mounting debt burden is discussed further in Chapter 15.

For borrowers who did not qualify for central bank loans or who simply chose not to bank there, the public credit facility would not be their only alternative. They could still borrow from commercial lenders, venture capitalists, loan funds, and the like. Speculators borrowing outside the guidelines of the public banking system could still gamble. They just could not do it with central bank credit created on the books of financial institutions backed by the full faith and credit of the federal government.

## Evolving a National Community Currency System

A digital currency backed by the central bank would be the equivalent of a national mutual credit clearing system—a community currency in which the community was the whole nation. The currency would be universally accepted and it could not be "scarce." As in our current banking system, it would come into existence when lent and would disappear when the loan was repaid. But there would be no need for nonprofit franchisee lenders to scramble to borrow overnight to balance their books, returning the money the next morning. Money would be acknowledged to be just the "monetization" of the borrower's own promise to pay, turning it into credit that can be spent in the marketplace.

"Remember," said Benjamin Franklin, "that credit is money." Credit and debt are just accounting entries—functions of the double-entry bookkeeping on which banking has been based since the Middle Ages. Blockchains and distributed ledgers are said to allow "triple-entry" bookkeeping, with the trustless, automatic, immutable distributed ledger replacing fallible, corruptible human middlemen. But blockchains and distributed ledgers are not scalable to the national level. This is also true of digital community currencies. Ryan Fugger's vision for his Ripple cryptocurrency was to create a digital currency that could not be scarce, that came into existence as it was traded, generated by the participants themselves; but there was no way to ensure that the obligations of strangers at a distance would be repaid. Participants had to rely on the trust of community members who knew each other or knew others who knew them, limiting the currency's use.

The scaling problem could be avoided by expanding the community to the size of a country, creating a mutual credit clearing system operating on a national digital ledger that was open, transparent, and "trustless" because the program largely ran automatically without human manipulation. Human professionals would still be needed to carry out those functions that computer programs cannot do, but they would be public servants on a salary rather than private corporate monopolists extracting rent on money conjured on their own books.

To make all this work would require a central bank mandated to serve the public interest, and transforming that institution into a true public utility would need to be the first order of business. But with sufficient political will this could be done, as was demonstrated by the early 20th-century populists who set up the Bank of North Dakota as the state's own widely trusted "mini-Fed." Opening the central bank's services to the public, as the Ricks team observed, "could play some role, however modest, in restoring doubting Americans' faith that the government can make a positive difference in their daily lives. This would be no small accomplishment."[430]

*Takeaway: The central bank's tools for achieving its statutory objectives could be expanded considerably if it were to open both its deposit and its lending windows to the public. Bank runs could be eliminated, bail-ins would not be necessary, and depositors could get perks that are now available only to banks, including substantial interest on their deposits. Central bank lending to the public has historical precedent, is operationally feasible, and need not expose taxpayers to credit risk.*

# CHAPTER 14

## WHAT THE FED COULD DO WITH ITS NEW TOOLS: ENGINEERING A DEBT JUBILEE

*I have never yet had anyone who could, through the use of logic
and reason, justify the Federal Government borrowing the use
of its own money. ... I believe the time will come when people
will demand that this be changed. I believe the time will come
in this country when they will actually blame you and me and
everyone else connected with the Congress for sitting idly by and
permitting such an idiotic system to continue.*

— *US Rep. Wright Patman, 1941*[431]

**Allowing the central bank** to lend directly to businesses, individuals and governments could solve a host of other problems, and one of them is disposing of a federal debt that has become impossible to repay through taxes or budget cuts. The US federal debt has topped $22 trillion, and under the current scheme it will continue to grow, along with its mounting interest burden. Some pundits warn darkly that the only option will be a government default. But there is more than one way to skin a debt created with accounting entries. An enlightened central bank could eliminate the debt in the same way it was created, by simply "monetizing" it—turning it back into what it arguably should have been all along, interest-free Greenback dollars. The bonds could be bought back with new money issued by the Federal Reserve or the Treasury.

The argument invariably raised against this solution is that it would trigger runaway inflation, but the evidence of the Fed's own quantitative easing programs indicates otherwise. The central bank has already monetized $2.7 trillion of the federal debt, while struggling to hit even its modest 2 percent inflation target.[432] Asset bubbles have occurred in the stock and housing markets, but they have been attributed chiefly to ZIRP—the Fed's zero interest rate policy—which drove bondholders into the stock market, encouraged large investors to borrow with reckless abandon, and allowed corporate executives to engage in share buybacks, driving up stock prices.[433] The money for these purchases was not created by the central bank but was created by commercial banks in the form of cheap bank credit; and it was advanced not for productive purposes but to purchase existing assets from prior owners, driving up prices without increasing GDP.

## QE Opens the Door

Although quantitative easing fell short of its inflation target, it did succeed in showcasing what the Fed has the power to do. QE revealed to the world that the central bank has a limitless ability to issue new money, and that it can exercise that tool without collapsing the currency or the economy. It also demonstrated that there was no need for the federal government to borrow from the bond market. The government could borrow from its own central bank interest-free, and it could do this to the tune of trillions of dollars without triggering runaway inflation.

QE1 was aimed chiefly at cleaning up bank balance sheets by transferring "toxic" mortgage-backed securities onto the balance sheet of the Fed, saving the big banks from insolvency without imposing their debts on the taxpayers. (See Chapter 7.) But QE2 turned out to be something quite different. Then-Chairman Ben Bernanke announced that the Fed would be using its asset-purchasing power to buy federal securities on the open market. The bond dealers selling the securities would presumably buy more Treasuries, increasing overall Treasury sales. The result was to relieve the government of a potentially crippling interest burden, since the Fed returns its profits to the Treasury after deducting its costs.[434]

At first, the Fed resisted buying the government's debt with QE. In January 2010, Chairman Bernanke told Congress:

> *We're not going to monetize the debt.* It is very, very important for Congress and administration to come to some kind of program, some kind of plan that will credibly show how the United States government is going to bring itself back to a sustainable position.

But the federal debt had increased by more than 50 percent from 2006 to 2010, due to a collapsed economy and the highly controversial decision to bail out the banks. By the end of 2009, the debt was up to $12.3 trillion. The interest paid on it ($383 billion) was actually less than in 2006 ($406 billion), because interest rates had been pushed to extremely low levels; but even at those rock-bottom levels, interest was still eating up nearly half of federal personal income tax receipts. If interest rates were to rise, it was thought that the impact on taxes would be crushing. With an increase of just a few percentage points, debt service could consume over 100 percent of income tax receipts; and taxes might have to be doubled.[435]

Bernanke's concern was that the impasse in Congress over tough spending cuts and tax increases would force the Fed to accommodate the budget deficit by printing money and buying Treasury bonds.[436] And that is exactly what happened. In November 2010, Republicans swept the House. There would be no raising of taxes on the rich, and the gridlock in Congress meant there would be no budget cuts either.

The Fed was also dealing with global monetary issues. Over the previous six months, China had stopped buying US debt, reducing inflows by about $50 billion per month. The Fed wound up buying $600 billion in long-term government bonds at the rate of $75 billion per month, effectively filling the hole left by China. An estimated $275 billion were also rolled over into Treasuries from the mortgage-backed securities the Fed bought during QE1, which were then reaching maturity. Bernanke said more QE was possible if unemployment stayed high and inflation stayed low.

Alarmed critics warned that the central bank was planning to monetize the whole deficit for the next eight months. Bill Bonner wrote in *The Daily Reckoning*:

> If this were Greece or Ireland the government would be forced to cut back. The politicians would have no choice. The markets would speak. They would have to listen. For where else would they get more money to squander? But now ... with quantitative easing ready ... there is no need to face the music.[437]

True, but why pay interest to investors and foreign central banks when you can get the money virtually interest-free from your own central bank? The Fed alone among the government's creditors returns its profits to the government after deducting its costs, and the Fed's cost of funds is zero.[438]

So monetize the debt the Fed did. When the QE program was officially halted in October 2014, the US central bank had accumulated $4.5 trillion in assets, $2.7 trillion of which were federal securities.[439] It wound up owning more Treasuries than China and Japan combined, making it the largest holder of government securities outside the government itself and its agencies.[440] The result of this exercise was that the government was able to double its debt after 2008 without increasing the interest owed by the taxpayers. QE had opened the door to funding the government's budget with dollars created on a computer screen.

In November 2010, Dean Baker, co-director of the Center for Economic and Policy Research in Washington, wrote in response to the debt ceiling crisis:

> There is no reason that the Fed can't just buy [federal] debt (as it is largely doing) and hold it indefinitely. If the Fed holds the debt, there is no interest burden for future taxpayers. The Fed refunds its interest earnings to the Treasury every year. Last year the Fed refunded almost $80 billion in interest to the Treasury, nearly 40 percent of the country's net interest burden. And the Fed has other tools to ensure that the expansion of the monetary base required to purchase the debt does not lead to inflation.[441]

In 2011, Republican presidential candidate Ron Paul proposed dealing with the debt ceiling by simply voiding out the $1.7 trillion in federal securities then held by the Fed. In an article on Paul's proposal in *Time Magazine*, Stephen Gandel explained that the Treasury pays interest on these securities to the Fed, which then returns 90 percent of the payments to the Treasury. Despite this shell game of payments, the $1.7 trillion in US bonds then owned by the Fed were still counted toward the debt ceiling. Paul's plan:

> Get the Fed and the Treasury to rip up that debt. It's fake debt anyway. And the Fed is legally allowed to return the debt to the Treasury to be destroyed.[442]

Congressman Alan Grayson (D-FL) also endorsed this proposal.[443] Needless to say, however, Congress did not act on it. The argument was that the central bank needed to be able to sell the debt back into the economy to counteract the "overheating" that was sure to follow. But the anticipated overheating never came. Why? As explained on *CNBC.com* by John Carney and Warren Mosler, co-founder of Modern Monetary Theory, QE was just an asset swap in bank reserve accounts:

> Quantitative easing is about the Fed buying Treasury securities. When you (voluntarily) sell them to the Fed, at current market prices, the Fed just shifts your dollars from your securities account to your bank's reserve account, all at the Fed. So why should that do anything to the economy? You have the same amount of dollars, and you could have shifted them in the same market place any time you wanted in any case.[444]

Government securities are considered "near money," something readily convertible to bank money. When they are turned into bank money, the seller is no richer than before, and he has no more incentive to spend on goods and services than before. Savers who sold their bonds to the Fed would probably just park the money in some other form of liquid investment, perhaps municipal bonds, corporate bonds, or the stock market. And getting more money into those capital markets should be good for the economy, increasing productivity, employment and the tax base.

If the federal government does not need to borrow in the bond market, why do it? Recall the contention of former Fed Chairman Marriner Eccles that it was mandated in 1930s legislation to appease the big bond-dealing banks by giving them a cut. (Chapter 1.) The result of that concession, however, has been to drive up the interest tab on the debt to the point that by 2027, the taxpayers could be paying $1 trillion annually just in interest, on a debt that can never be repaid but simply gets rolled over from year to year.

That massive interest bill is unnecessary. The government does not need to sell bonds at all. It could just run up an overdraft on its account at the central bank. So argued UK economist Richard Murphy in a June 2018 post, drawing on Modern Monetary Theory. He wrote:

> [I]f a government with its own currency in which it requires settlement of tax liabilities wants taxation to be paid then it must first of all spend to put the currency in question into circulation. ... The difference between new money created by government spending and taxation revenue received is at present made good by the issue of

government bonds, although this is not strictly necessary: except for EU legislation that prevents direct lending from the central bank to the government that owns it this shortfall could, instead, be managed by an overdraft arrangement between the government and the central bank on which no interest would need to be paid.[445]

EU governments, like the US government, cannot spend by writing an overdraft on their central bank accounts just because self-imposed legislation forbids it. If the US government could avoid paying interest on its bonds, the taxpayers could have saved $460 billion in 2017 and could save an estimated $1 trillion annually by 2027. To avoid that interest tab, the Fed could buy the government's debt from the bondholders as it did in its quantitative easing programs, returning the interest to the Treasury as it does now. Arguably the Fed could buy up the *entire* $21 trillion federal debt, gradually as the bonds came due, and the chief effect on the economy would just be to relieve the taxpayers of the interest on it. For future congressional budgets, the Treasury could run up a tab on its Fed account interest-free. How it could avoid "overheating" the economy is discussed in Chapters 16 and 17.

Although the government would not need to borrow on the open market to fund its budget, government securities do serve useful purposes in the current economy. As Murphy observed in a November 2018 article, they give people a safe place to save, they give pensioners a guaranteed income stream, and they provide the banking sector with a mechanism for collateralizing overnight deposits.[446] Those purposes could all be met, however, by a national public banking system in which the central bank's services were open to the public. Savers and pensioners would have a safe place to save their money and earn a fair return on it, and banks in the public system would not need to rely on private collateral to back deposits, since they would have access to the central bank's vast liquidity pool.

## Avoiding Housing Bubbles

The Fed's massive bond-buying program has not inflated the Consumer Price Index, but asset bubbles did occur in real estate and the stock market after that program was implemented. These have chiefly been attributed to ZIRP, but QE could have played a role. New money created by the Fed as bank reserves cannot be lent or spent into the broader economy, but that does not mean QE cannot increase the money supply. As John Carney explained on *CNBC.com* in December 2013:

> When the Fed buys a Treasury or an agency security from a primary dealer, the dealer has to acquire that security from somewhere. Some of the securities sold to the Fed come from inventory the primary dealers already had but a good portion is acquired by the dealers from other security holders, such as nondealer banks, investors and large funds. The primary dealer pays for the security by crediting a deposit account of whoever—a bank, a household, a pension fund—is selling the security. So the Fed gets the Treasury, the dealer gets a reserve injection and the Treasury seller gets a deposit. So we see, QE creates deposits. ...

These deposits created through QE are real bank deposits. They are M-1. The funds in them can be withdrawn
as cash currency, spent, invested, or held in the deposit
accounts. ... And, if investors were so inclined, they can
be used to purchase financial assets from high yield bonds
to stocks. They could, theoretically, produce assets bubbles and even inflation, if the deposits were just spent on
consumer goods.

This doesn't mean that this is happening now. I suspect a
lot of QE-created deposits simply remain as deposit assets
of the Treasury sellers. Some of it, however, probably goes
into assets that are close substitutes for Treasurys.[447]

To the extent that new deposits have been created by
the Fed's asset purchases, they are unlikely to have inflated
consumer prices, because the money is unlikely to have gone
into consumer purchases. Bond investments are typically
the savings of people and institutions that do not need the
money for everyday consumption. If the bonds get sold, the
money is just reinvested in other income-earning assets that
are close substitutes for Treasuries. That could include stocks,
which are liquid like bonds; but it would be unlikely to include real estate, which is a less liquid asset.

The real estate bubble is thus likely to have been created
by ZIRP. The issue was highlighted in written testimony
to the UK Treasury in March 2017 by researchers from the
Positive Money group in the UK, where housing bubbles
are also a major problem. In a detailed review of post-2008
monetary policy, the researchers showed that while the very
low interest rates after the 2008 crisis were intended to

boost bank lending, most new lending actually went toward nonproductive sectors—mortgages, consumer credit and financial businesses. Banks would rather make loans that are secured against existing property or to other financial institutions than make riskier loans to businesses engaged directly in productive activity. As a result, the low interest rates since 2008 have boosted asset prices and inflated the housing market without stimulating productivity.[448]

While very low rates probably caused the problem, the researchers said that raising rates now won't fix it, because even a small rate rise would be unaffordable for many borrowers. Keeping rates low, on the other hand, risks fueling a further buildup of private debt by encouraging new lending into financial and property markets. To boost demand and directly stimulate the productive, nonspeculative economy, the central bank needs new tools. The researchers attached a letter from 42 leading economists suggesting that rather than curtailing its money creation policies, the central bank would better serve the economy by getting newly created money directly into it. They wrote:

> A fiscal stimulus financed by central bank money creation could be used to fund essential investment in infrastructure projects—boosting the incomes of businesses and households, potentially assisting the UK's green economic transition, and increasing the public sector's productive assets in the process. Alternatively, the money could be used to fund either a tax cut or direct cash transfers to households, resulting in an immediate increase of household disposable incomes.[449]

## Federal Debt Jubilee: Japan Takes the Lead

The Japanese government has demonstrated that the productive economy can be stimulated with a direct injection of money without triggering price inflation. "Abenomics," the economic agenda of Japan's Prime Minister Shinzo Abe, combines central bank quantitative easing with fiscal stimulus (government spending). It has been declared a success even by the once-critical International Monetary Fund.[450]

When Shinzo Abe crushed his opponents in a snap election in October 2017, the win was attributed largely to the success of his economic agenda.[451] Noah Smith wrote in *Bloomberg*, "Japan's long-ruling Liberal Democratic Party has figured out a novel and interesting way to stay in power—govern pragmatically, focus on the economy and give people what they want." He said everyone who wanted a job had one; small and midsized businesses were doing well; and the BOJ's unprecedented program of monetary easing had provided easy credit for corporate restructuring without generating inflation. Abe had also vowed to make both preschool and college free.[452]

Abenomics has achieved more, however, than just stimulating economic growth. By selling its debt to its own central bank, which returns the interest to the government, the Japanese government has in effect been *canceling* its debt. Until recently, it was doing this at the rate of a whopping $720 billion (¥80tn) per year. According to fund manager Eric Lonergan in a February 2017 article:

> The Bank of Japan is in the process of owning most of the outstanding government debt of Japan (it currently owns

around 40%). BOJ holdings are part of the consolidated government balance sheet. So its holdings are in fact the accounting equivalent of a debt cancellation. If I buy back my own mortgage, I don't have a mortgage.[453]

If the Federal Reserve followed suit and bought 40 percent of the US national debt, it would be holding *$8 trillion* in federal securities, three times its current holdings from its quantitative easing programs. Yet liquidating a full 40 percent of Japan's government debt has not triggered inflation. To the contrary, as of April 2017, the country had a *record low inflation rate* of .02 percent.[454] That's not 2 percent, the Fed's target inflation rate, but *1/100th of 2 percent*—almost zero. Japan also had an unemployment rate that was at a 22-year low of 2.8 percent, and the yen was up nearly 6 percent for the year against the dollar.[455]

Selling the government's debt to its own central bank did not drive up Japanese prices although that was the BOJ's expressed intent. Prices did not go up but productivity did. In a February 2017 article in *Mother Jones* titled "The Enduring Mystery of Japan's Economy," Kevin Drum noted that over the past two decades, Japan's gross domestic product per capita has grown steadily and is up by 20 percent. He wrote:

> It's true that Japan has suffered through two decades of low growth … . [But] despite its persistently low inflation, Japan's economy is doing fine. Their GDP per working-age adult is actually higher than ours. So why are they growing so much more slowly than we are? It's just simple demographics … Japan is aging fast. Its working-age population peaked in 1997 and has been declining ever since.

Fewer workers means a lower GDP even if those workers are as productive as anyone in the world.[456]

Former World Bank economist Joseph Stiglitz concurs. In a June 2013 article titled "Japan Is a Model, Not a Cautionary Tale," he wrote:

> Along many dimensions—greater income equality, longer life expectancy, lower unemployment, greater investments in children's education and health, and even greater productivity relative to the size of the labor force—Japan has done better than the United States.[457]

Not that all is idyllic in Japan. Forty percent of Japanese workers lack secure full-time employment, adequate pensions and health insurance.[458] But the point underscored here is that large-scale digital money-printing by the central bank to buy back the government's debt combined with fiscal stimulus by the government (spending on "what the people want") has not inflated Japanese prices, the alleged concern preventing other countries from doing it.

In an October 2017 article in *The Week* titled "The Magic of Abenomics," Pascal-Emmanuel Gobry said Abenomics was a "smashing success," noting that Japan had enjoyed strong growth and that unemployment was down to a remarkable 2.8 percent. Gobry asked, "So why don't we implement Abenomics in the West? Because we'd have to slaughter too many ideological sacred cows. The left hates supply-side reform, and the right hates fiscal stimulus."

Abe came under political attack in 2018, and allegations of corruption unrelated to his economic policy have sub-

stantially diminished his popularity.[459] But while the Bank of
Japan has been under heavy pressure to join the other central
banks in tightening the money supply and reversing the "ac-
commodations" made after the 2008 banking crisis, it is still
holding firm. According to a September 2018 *Reuters* article,
the BOJ has recently slowed its rate of bond purchases; but
BOJ Governor Haruhiko Kuroda insists that buying less is
not the same thing as selling bonds back into the market.
The Reuters article concluded that "Japan is nowhere near an
exit from ultraloose monetary policy."[460]

Other central banks might do well to take a lesson from
Japan and try canceling their own governments' debts. We
have entered a new century and a new millennium. Ancient
civilizations celebrated a changing of the guard with widespread debt cancellation. It is time to declare a debt jubilee
and reset the playing field for the 21st century.

> *__Takeaway__: The US central bank could reduce or
> eliminate the government's impossible-to-repay $21 tril-
> lion federal debt by gradually buying it from bondhold-
> ers with QE, as it has already done to the tune of $2.7
> trillion without triggering unwanted inflation. Japan's
> central bank has gone even further, buying 40 percent of
> its federal debt without triggering inflation. It has done
> this through a successful economic policy that combines
> QE with fiscal stimulus (government spending), some-
> thing our government could do as well. That possibility is
> explored next.*

## CHAPTER 15

# "QUALITATIVE EASING": INJECTING MONEY DIRECTLY INTO THE VEINS OF THE ECONOMY

*"[W]e may have to resort to QE yet again. If so, let us stop buying bonds, and stop creating windfall profits for the holders of assets in the hope that some largesse will trickle down. If we have to do it again, let us inject the money directly into the veins of the economy ... ."*
—*Ambrose Evans-Pritchard, UK Telegraph, November 2014*[461]

**Quantitative easing has not inflated** consumer prices because the new money it created has been trapped in bank reserve accounts or has otherwise not trickled down to the consumer marketplace. But what about injecting money directly into the veins of the economy, as urged by Ambrose Evans-Prichard? The central bank could inject money to build infrastructure, make interest-free loans for state and local governments, or make low-interest loans to targeted economic sectors and local businesses. All of these options would increase employment, fulfilling one of the Fed's dual mandates. But under classical monetarist theory, consumer prices would also shoot up.

That is the theory, but empirical data refutes it. As John Maynard Keynes observed, when money is injected for productive purposes and workers and materials are available, supply and demand will increase together and prices will remain stable. Rather than supply creating demand ("Say's law"), demand creates supply. New money injected into the economy triggers the production of new goods and services to satisfy the demand.[462]

Historical data confirms this premise.[463] Among other noteworthy examples is the Bank of Canada's monetary policy from 1935 to 1973, when the central bank was not "independent" but actually served the government and the public. As Joyce Nelson explains in *Bypassing Dystopia* (2018), the Bank of Canada Act gave Canada's publicly owned central bank the power to make near-zero interest loans to federal and provincial governments for infrastructure and health care spending. It did that successfully for nearly 40 years, funding the St. Lawrence Seaway, the Trans-Canada Highway, the construction of coastal ports and airports, and many other public building ventures, without incurring debt to commercial lenders and without creating inflation problems. But in 1974, the Bank for International Settlements, the World Bank, the International Monetary Fund, and a variety of corporate think-tanks persuaded countries including Canada to stop their central banks from making interest-free loans. Instead, governments were to do most of their borrowing from commercial banks. Since then, Canada's federal debt has skyrocketed, and its taxpayers have paid about $1.5 trillion in interest on it, most of which could have been saved if the federal government had continued to borrow from its own central bank.[464]

## China's "Qualitative Easing"

More recent empirical evidence for the viability of central bank money injections comes from China, where the People's Bank of China is engaging in a form of QE that Citigroup chief economist Willem Buiter calls "qualitative easing." According to an August 2014 article in the *Wall Street Journal*:

> In China's context, such so-called qualitative easing happens when the People's Bank of China adds riskier assets to its balance sheet—such as by relending to the agriculture sector and small businesses and offering cheap loans for low-return infrastructure projects—while maintaining a normal pace of balance-sheet expansion [loan creation].[465]

The Citigroup economists said that Chinese-style "qualitative easing" was actually less inflationary than the "quantitative easing" engaged in by Western central banks. The low Chinese inflation rate, at 1.9 percent as of December 2018, is particularly remarkable considering that the Chinese money supply has increased eight-fold in the last 20 years. The key, as noted in Chapter 13, is that its GDP has increased at an even faster rate. Supply (GDP) has risen along with demand, keeping prices stable.

Under the Chinese program, policymakers have sought not only to bolster lending to small and medium-sized enterprises but to support national goals such as the One Belt, One Road initiative through which China is developing infrastructure along its old Silk Road trade routes.[466] This massive $1 trillion undertaking includes highways, pipelines, transmission lines, ports, power stations, fiber optics, and railroads connecting China to Central Asia, Europe and Africa. Dan Slane, a former advisor on President Trump's transition team, was quoted in a January 2018 article as calling it "the largest infrastructure project initiated by one nation in the history of the world … designed to enable China to become the dominant economic power in the world." He added, "If we don't get our act together very soon, we should all be brushing up on our Mandarin."[467]

## Solving the US Infrastructure Crisis: PPPs or QE?

In February 2018, President Trump's own infrastructure initiative was finally unveiled. Perhaps to trump China's $1 trillion mega-project, the president upped the ante from the $1 trillion promised in his campaign speeches to $1.5 trillion. That is how the initiative was billed, but only $200 billion was to come from federal funding, and less than that after factoring in the billions in tax cuts for infrastructure-related projects. The rest of the $1.5 trillion was to come from cities, states, and private investors; and since city and state coffers are depleted, that chiefly means private investors.[468]

The United States needs a full $5 trillion to rebuild its airports, bridges, tunnels, roads and other infrastructure over the next decade.[469] But instead of funding these infrastructure needs with direct loans from federal financial institutions, as the Chinese are doing, the push has been for privatization or for public-private partnerships (PPPs), letting private investors reap the profits. Moving assets off the government's balance sheet by privatizing them looks at-

tractive to politicians concerned with this year's bottom line,
but it's a bad deal for the public. Privatization means selling
public utilities to investors who then rent them back to the
public, squeezing profits from high user fees and tolls.

Private equity investment generates an average return of
about 11.8 percent annually on a 10-year basis.[470] That puts
the cost to the public of financing $1 trillion in infrastruc-
ture projects over 10 years at around $1.18 trillion, more
than doubling the cost. Decades from now, people will still
be paying higher tolls for the sake of Wall Street profits on
an asset that could and should have belonged to the public
all along.

Studies have found that on average, private contractors
charge more than twice as much as the government would
have paid federal workers for the same job.[471] Countering
the dogma that "private companies can always do it better
and cheaper," a 2011 report by the Brookings Institution
found that "in practice [PPPs] have been dogged by contract
design problems, waste, and unrealistic expectations."[472] In
their 2015 report "Why Public-Private Partnerships Don't
Work," Public Services International said that experience
over the last 15 years shows that PPPs are an expensive and
inefficient way of financing infrastructure and divert government spending away from other public services. They conceal
public borrowing while providing long-term state guarantees
for profits to private companies.[473]

One example is the Dulles Greenway, a toll road outside
Washington D.C. nicknamed the "Champagne Highway"
due to its extraordinarily high rates and severe underutiliza-
tion in a region crippled by chronic traffic problems. Local
officials have tried in vain for years to either force the private

owners to lower the toll rates or have the state take the road into public ownership.[474] In 2014, the private operators of the Indiana Toll Road, one of the best-known public-private partnerships (PPPs), filed for bankruptcy after demand dropped, due at least in part to rising toll rates. Other high-profile PPP bankruptcies have occurred in San Diego, California; Richmond, Virginia; and Texas.[475]

PPPs also divert public money away from the neediest infrastructure projects, which may not deliver sizable returns, in favor of those big-ticket items that will deliver hefty profits to investors. To the extent that private equity firms are interested in public assets, they are more interested in privatizing existing infrastructure than in funding the new development that is at the heart of President Trump's plan. Local officials and local businessmen have grown leery of privatization deals, having learned the hard way that the price of quick cash is to be bled dry with user charges and profit guarantees.

The White House said its initiative was not a take-it-or-leave-it proposal but was the start of a negotiation, and that the president was open to new sources of funding. Perhaps it is time to look more closely at how China is doing it. While American politicians are busy arguing about where to find the money, the Chinese are busy building.

A case in point is the 12,000 miles of high-speed rail they constructed in a mere decade, while American politicians were still trying to finance much more modest rail projects. According to *The Wall Street Journal*, the money largely came from loans from China's state-owned banks.[476] The country's five largest banks are majority-owned by the central government, and they lend principally to large, state-owned enterprises.[477] We have seen that banks do not merely recycle existing deposits but actually create the money they lend, and in China's case the government can aim the money created by its state-owned banks at its most pressing national needs.

## What About China's Bad-Debt Problem?

Critics say China has a dangerously high debt-to-GDP ratio and a "bad-debt" problem, meaning its banks have too many "nonperforming" loans. But according to financial research strategist Chen Zhao in a Harvard review called "China: A Bullish Case," these factors are being misinterpreted and need not be cause for alarm. China has a high debt-to-GDP ratio because most Chinese businesses are funded through loans rather than through the stock market, as in the United States. China's banks are able to engage in massive lending because the Chinese chiefly save their money in banks rather than investing it in the stock market, providing a huge source of liquidity for loans.

Most of China's "public debt," says Zhao, is money created on bank balance sheets for economic stimulus. He writes:

During the 2008-09 financial crisis, the U.S. government deficit shot up to about 10 percent of GDP due to bail-out programs like the TARP. In contrast, the Chinese government deficit during that period didn't change much. However, Chinese bank loan growth shot up to 40 percent while loan growth in the U.S. collapsed. These contrasting pictures suggest that most of China's four trillion RMB stimulus package was carried out by its

state-owned banks. ... The so-called "bad debt problem"
is effectively a consequence of Beijing's fiscal projects and
thus should be treated as such.[478]

China calls this government bank financing "lending"
rather than "money printing," but the effect is very similar
to what European central bankers are calling "helicopter
money"—central bank-generated money that does not need
to be repaid.[479] If the Chinese loans do get repaid, great; but
if they don't, it is not a major problem. The nonperforming
loans merely leave extra money circulating in the economy,
helping to create the extra demand needed to fill the gap
between wages (demand) and GDP (supply). And China's
economy particularly needs that boost today, when shrinking
global markets have caused demand to shrink following the
2008-09 crisis.

In a December 2017 article in *The Financial Times* called
"Stop Worrying about Chinese Debt, a Crisis Is Not Brew-
ing," Zhao wrote:

> [S]o-called credit risk in China is, in fact, sovereign risk.
> The Chinese government often relies on bank credit to
> finance government stimulus programmes. ... China's
> sovereign risk is extremely low. Importantly, the balance
> sheets of the Chinese state-owned banks, the government
> and the People's Bank of China are all interconnected.
> Under these circumstances, a debt crisis in China is al-
> most impossible.[480]

Chinese state-owned banks are not going to need a Wall
Street-style bailout from the government. They *are* the gov-

ernment, and the Chinese government has a massive global account surplus. It is not going bankrupt any time soon. Consumer prices have not shot up despite some extra money circulating in the market from the bank-generated loans that were not repaid, because the money has gone into productive enterprises. Demand and supply have risen together, keeping prices stable as Keynes predicted.

## "QE-Muni": Qualitative Easing for Municipal Governments

In an October 2012 editorial in *The New York Times* titled "Getting More Bang for the Fed's Buck," Joseph Grundfest and co-authors proposed a form of QE for the United States that was similar to China's. They noted that Republicans and Democrats alike had been decrying the failure to stimulate the economy through needed infrastructure improvements, but shrinking tax revenues and limited debt service capacity had tied the hands of state and local governments. The authors proposed that rather than buying mortgage-backed or federal securities from banks, as the Fed was then doing through its QE program, it should do some "QE-Muni"—interest-free or low-interest loans made directly to municipal governments. An injection of cheap loans from the Fed could restock state and local treasuries. Lowering borrowing costs for states, cities and counties would forestall tax increases, which dampen individual spending, and would make it easier for local governments to pay for infrastructure improvements, teachers, police officers and firefighters.[481]

The authors acknowledged that their QE-Muni proposal faced legal hurdles. The Federal Reserve Act prohibits the central bank from purchasing municipal government debt with a maturity of more than six months, which is too short for the long-term projects expected to generate beneficial effects from QE-Muni. But Congress wrote the Federal Reserve Act and could amend it. Congress was then trying to avoid the "fiscal cliff," so all options were on the table. The fiscal cliff continues to come around, with threats of the debt ceiling dropping on an embattled Congress. It could be time to look again at "QE for Munis."

## A Better Way to Design an Infrastructure Bank

Another option for funding infrastructure is a federal infrastructure bank, something the Trump team has suggested in the past. Details remain vague, but former conceptions have envisioned a "quasi-bank" rather than a physical, deposit-taking institution, which would be seeded by the federal government, possibly from taxes on repatriated offshore corporate profits.[482] The bank would issue bonds, tax credits, and loan guarantees to state and local governments to leverage private sector investment, relying on public-private partnerships and private investors for funding.

There are other ways, however, that a national infrastructure bank could be set up. In a policy paper published by the New America Foundation titled "The Public Option: The Case for Parallel Public Banking Institutions," Prof. Tim Canova proposed a national infrastructure bank capitalized with money simply generated on the central bank's books.[483] The Federal Reserve could purchase shares, whether as common stock, preferred stock or debt, either in a national infrastructure bank or in a system of state-owned banks that funded infrastructure in their states. This could be done without increasing taxes, adding to the federal debt or hyperinflating prices.

Another alternative for financing infrastructure construction without dipping into taxes would be a federal system of depository banks that took private deposits through the US Postal Service. The Japanese have done this through Japan Post Bank (JPB), the largest depository bank in the world. Although a federal budget crisis after the Fukushima nuclear disaster led to its partial privatization, JPB is still majority owned by the government.[484] By investing its deposits in government securities, JPB has allowed the government to draw on its massive deposit base.[485] The deposits of the nation's savers are invested in government securities that are in turn invested in the nation.

In a July 2013 article titled "Delivering a National Infrastructure Bank ... through the Post Office," Frederic V. Rolando, president of the National Association of Letter Carriers, suggested something similar for the US Postal Service, which has branches in nearly every community. He noted that the idea of forming a national infrastructure bank (NIB) had bipartisan congressional support, with senators from both parties introducing bills. Rolando wrote:

> An NIB would provide a means to channel public funds into regional and national projects identified by political and community leaders across the country to keep the economy healthy. It could issue bonds, back public-private partnerships and guarantee long-term, low-interest loans to states and investment groups willing to rebuild our schools, hospitals, airports and energy grids. An NIB with

$10 billion in capital could leverage hundreds of billions in investments.[486]

Bills for a national infrastructure bank have been blocked in the past by opposition to using tax money for the purpose. But Rolando asked:

[W]hat if we set up the NIB without using taxpayer funds? What if we allowed Americans to open savings accounts in the nation's post offices and directed those funds into national infrastructure bonds that would earn interest for depositors and fund job-creating projects to replace and modernize our crumbling infrastructure?

A post office bank ... would not offer commercial loans or mortgages. But it could serve the unbanked and fund infrastructure projects selected by a non-partisan NIB.

## How Roosevelt Did It: The Reconstruction Finance Corporation

Rolando's proposal is similar to a massive government project that channeled savings and public funds into infrastructure and development all across the United States in the 1930s and 1940s, at a time when the commercial banks were insolvent. The publicly owned Reconstruction Finance Corporation (RFC) was not called an infrastructure bank and was not even a bank, but it served the same basic functions. It was a remarkable publicly owned credit machine that allowed the government to finance the New Deal and World War II without turning to Congress or the taxpayers for appropriations. First instituted in 1932 by President Herbert Hoover, the RFC was continually enlarged and modified by President Roosevelt to meet the crisis of the times, until it became America's largest corporation and the world's largest financial organization. Its semi-independent status let it work quickly, allowing New Deal agencies to be financed as the need arose.[487]

The RFC Act of 1932 provided the RFC with capital stock of $500 million and the authority to extend credit up to $1.5 billion (subsequently increased several times). The initial capital came from a stock sale to the US Treasury. With those resources, from 1932 to 1957 the RFC loaned or invested more than $40 billion. A small part of this came from its initial capitalization. The rest was borrowed, chiefly from the government itself. Bonds were sold to the Treasury, some of which were then sold to the public; but most were held by the Treasury. The RFC ended up borrowing a total of $51.3 billion from the Treasury and $3.1 billion from the public.[488]

Thus the Treasury was the lender, not the borrower, in this arrangement. Where did it get the money to lend without going to Congress or the taxpayers? Evidently it borrowed from the bond markets. As the self-funding loans were repaid, so were the bonds, leaving the government with a net profit. The RFC was the lender for thousands of infrastructure and small business projects that revitalized the economy, and these loans produced a total net income of $690,017,232 on the RFC's "normal" lending functions (omitting such things as extraordinary grants for wartime). The RFC financed roads, bridges, dams, post offices, universities, electrical power, mortgages, farms, and much more; and it funded all this while generating income for the government.[489]

## Direct Money Injections for Infrastructure: Historical Precedents

There are other historical precedents in which governments have successfully funded infrastructure and other budget needs not just with loans but with direct injections of new money issued by their treasuries or central banks. Examples include money printed to pay for critical infrastructure in the island state of Guernsey in the 19th century, the Bradbury Pound issued in the UK during the First World War, the "MEFO" bills stimulating German economic recovery in the 1930s, and infrastructure funded with central-bank-issued money in Australia, New Zealand, Canada, China, and elsewhere in the 20th century.[490]

A remarkable example drawn from US history was the funding of the transcontinental railroad with interest-free US Notes issued under the Legal Tender Act of 1862. Abraham Lincoln's government printed $450 million of these Greenbacks, effectively doubling the money in circulation. The money supply went from $484.4 million in 1861 to $931.3 million in 1863.[491] This huge injection of new money not only allowed the North to win the Civil War without incurring crippling war debts but helped to fund a period of extraordinarily rapid economic growth, including the construction of the transcontinental railroad. As that transformative project was reported by Clyde Prestowitz in *The Betrayal of American Prosperity* (2010):

> [I]n the summer of 1862, Abraham Lincoln pushed through Congress the Pacific Railroad Act, which called for the chartering of two separate companies—the Cen-

tral Pacific and the Union Pacific—to lay tracks from the
Missouri River to Sacramento. After much delay and stu-
pendous feats of engineering, the Central Pacific's engine
Jupiter and the Union Pacific's engine 119 stood nose to
nose on May 10, 1869, at Promontory Summit, Utah. The
nation was tied together, coast to coast, by a ribbon of
steel. Amazingly, although the government had loaned the
companies more than $64 million, it earned more than
$103 million in return and did so by the end of 1869.
More significantly, the railroad led to the creation of huge
new markets and cities and transformed the country into
a true continental powerhouse of a nation.[492]

As with the Reconstruction Finance Corporation in the
1930s and 1940s, the government was the lender, not the
borrower, on this giant infrastructure project; and it earned a
60 percent return on the railroad in just 17 years. The project
has been criticized for its large land grants to private railroad
companies, but the grants played only a minor role in its
financing.[493] The transcontinental railroad remains a stellar
testament to the ability of a sovereign nation to rebuild its
infrastructure, not only without going into debt but while
making a substantial profit on the venture.

What about the inflationary impact of doubling the
money supply during the Civil War? If that were done today,
it would mean adding *$13 trillion* to the money in circu-
lation. Under classical monetarist theory, the result would
be massive hyperinflation; but in the 1860s, the predicted
hyperinflation did not result. There was some price inflation
due to shortages and a flight to gold; but according to Irwin
Unger in *The Greenback Era* (1964), "It is now clear that

inflation would have occurred even without the Greenback issue."[494] War is always an inflationary venture. Historian J. G. Randall observed in 1937:

> The threat of inflation was more effectively curbed during the Civil War than during the First World War. Indeed as John K. Galbraith has observed, "it is remarkable that without rationing, price controls, or central banking, [Treasury Secretary] Chase could have managed the federal economy so well during the Civil War."[495]

The Greenbacks suffered a significant drop in value as against gold, but this was true of all US paper currency during the Civil War. In *A Monetary History of the United States, 1867-1960*, Milton Friedman and Anna Jacobson Schwartz showed that this relative drop in value was not a domestic issue due to "printing money" but was due to trade imbalances with foreign trading partners on the gold standard, especially England.[496]

## Green New Deal Proposals

Lincoln and Roosevelt succeeded in getting their sweeping monetary reforms implemented because the country was facing a national emergency. Proponents of a "Green New Deal" argue that the climate crisis we are facing today ranks as a national emergency as well, warranting similar radical funding mechanisms for resolution.

Various plans have been proposed. In the UK, a Green New Deal group was convened in 2007 and published a report through the New Economics Foundation in 2008. In

2010, Richard Murphy and Colin Hines, two of the group's founders, proposed funding a Green New Deal with what they called "Green Quantitative Easing."[497] In 2012 and 2016, Green Party presidential candidate Jill Stein made a Green New Deal a central part of her campaign.[498] Stephanie Kelton, professor of economics and public policy at Stony Brook University and an economic advisor to Bernie Sanders in his 2016 presidential race, advocated a Green New Deal funded on the principles of Modern Monetary Theory. In a November 2018 article in *The Huffington Post*, she and co-authors wrote that a Green New Deal could be financed in the same way Roosevelt's original New Deal was:

> The government didn't go out and collect money—by taxing and borrowing—because the economy had collapsed and no one had any money (except the oligarchs). The government hired millions of people across various New Deal programs and paid them with a massive infusion of new spending that Congress authorized in the budget. FDR didn't need to "find the money," he needed to find the votes. We can do the same for a Green New Deal.[499]

In November 2018, newly elected congresswoman Alexandria Ocasio-Cortez launched a resolution to create a House Select Committee on a Green New Deal, which soon attracted 45 House supporters. The proposal addresses not just the climate crisis but social justice issues, giving the committee "a mandate that connects the dots between energy, transportation, housing, as well as healthcare, living wages, a jobs guarantee" and more. Critics said the program was so sweeping that it would crush the taxpayers who had to finance it, but the drafters had other funding sources in mind. The resolution said the money would primarily come from the federal government, "using a combination of the Federal Reserve, a new public bank or system of regional and specialized public banks," and other federal sources.[500] The central bank's well of liquidity is deep enough to fund all these programs, implemented through a network of regional public banks.

## The Trillion-Dollar Coin Alternative

Quantitative easing is the province of the central bank, which is technically independent of political interference and control. But if the Fed cannot not be persuaded to engage in QE for funding infrastructure development and other critical congressional projects, the US Treasury could take on that project itself. It could resort to the same device Lincoln used—just issue the money. Congress has delegated the constitutional power to "coin money [and] regulate the value thereof" to the Treasury Secretary, and the Constitution sets no limit on the face amount of the coins. The power just needs to be exercised, something the president could instruct the Treasury Secretary to do by executive order. The Treasury could then issue a few one-trillion-dollar coins, deposit them in an account, and start writing checks.[501]

It sounds like sleight of hand today; but when the Founding Fathers gave Congress the power to coin money and regulate its value, precious metal coins were the official money of the realm. In the 19th century, coins and paper banknotes issued privately on the "fractional reserve" model made up roughly equal portions of the money supply. Coins are now all that is left of the Treasury's money-creating power, and they compose only about $50 billion of a money supply exceeding $14 trillion in 2018.[502] The government not only has the ability to reclaim the money power but needs to reclaim it, in order to ensure the universal rights to "life, liberty and the pursuit of happiness" set forth the Declaration of Independence.

The idea of minting large denomination coins to solve economic problems was suggested by a chairman of the Coinage Subcommittee of the U.S. House of Representatives in the early 1980s. He pointed out that under Article 1 of the Constitution, the government could pay off its entire debt with some billion-dollar coins. That option was largely curtailed by legislation initiated in 1982, in which Congress chose to impose limits on the amounts and denominations of most coins. The one exception was the platinum coin, which a special provision allowed to be minted in any amount for commemorative purposes (31 U.S. Code § 5112).

Philip Diehl, former head of the US Mint and co-author of the platinum coin law, confirmed in 2013:

> In minting the $1 trillion platinum coin, the Treasury Secretary would be exercising authority which Congress has granted routinely for more than 220 years. The Secretary authority is derived from an Act of Congress (in fact, a GOP Congress) under power expressly granted to Congress in the Constitution (Article 1, Section 8).[503]

## Filling the Gap Between Wages, Debt and GDP

The transcontinental railroad, Roosevelt's New Deal, Canada's early twentieth century development boom, and China's qualitative easing offer empirical support for Keynes's theory that adding money to the economy for productive, nonspeculative purposes will not drive up prices so long as materials and workers (human or mechanical) are available to create the supply necessary to meet demand. At one time, major lags in supply were created while it caught up with demand; but today we have such efficiencies of scale that "just-in-time" delivery is commonplace, allowing companies to receive goods as and when needed in the production process. There will always be price increases in particular markets when there are shortages, bottlenecks, monopolies or patents limiting competition, but these increases are not due to an economy awash with money. In fact, the consumer economy is chronically short of money, as shown in Chapter 3. The money may be somewhere in the system—held in savings accounts, brokerage accounts, the bond market, or offshore tax havens—but it is not in the local economy available to pay back personal, business and local government debt; and that is why debt levels are so high.

In an economic system in which most money is created as debt that must be paid back with interest to commercial lenders, there is never enough money in the hands of the indebted sector to extinguish the debt, which just continues to grow. Underemployed and underpaid workers must borrow just to meet survival needs. How that chronic gap could be filled without creating price inflation is the subject of the next chapter.

*Takeaway:* Contemporary data from China and Japan, along with historical examples from the United States and many other countries, confirm that new money can be injected directly into the economy for infrastructure and other productive uses without triggering unwanted inflation. The income generated by the products of these "self-funding" loans can be used to repay the loans, extinguishing the new money they created. In this way infrastructure can be built that is ultimately cost-free to the taxpayers; in fact, the resulting economic stimulus would create a net revenue gain for the government.

## CHAPTER 16

# HOW TO FUND A UNIVERSAL BASIC INCOME WITHOUT INCREASING TAXES OR INFLATION

*"There is nothing wrong with the real economy. Its factories, transport and communications infrastructure, skilled labour, restaurants etc. are all fully operational and highly efficient. There is also plenty of real demand for goods and services, especially globally from developing country consumers. It is purely the financial system which is disabling the real economy, and it is the financial sector which therefore urgently needs re-engineering."*

—*UK economist Geoff Crocker, "The Economic Necessity of Basic Income"*[504]

The central bank could fund infrastructure with a form of quantitative easing without triggering inflation, because the loans would be "self-funding," repaid through the fee proceeds of the infrastructure they built. But what about dropping money directly into the wallets of the people, perhaps as a universal basic income, a national dividend, student debt relief, or free state college tuition? It will be argued here that this too could be done without triggering price inflation, raising taxes or driving up the federal debt. Injected in proper proportions, the new money would just fill the gap between wages and GDP, keeping prices stable.

## When Machines Make Jobs Obsolete

A universal basic income (UBI) is a sum of money given equally to all adults, with perhaps half that sum allotted for children. In effect it is social security, not just for the elderly but for all—no strings attached on how it can be spent, no requirement to demonstrate need. The pros and cons of a federally funded UBI or national dividend are a hot topic today, as workers are increasingly being replaced by machines. The issue is not just social but economic. Machines do not buy food, clothing, or electronic gadgets. Demand must come from the consuming class, and for that they need money to spend. As the problem was framed in a November 2016 article titled "Will a Robot Replace You?":

> The paradox of automation ... has been very eloquently articulated by an apocryphal conversation that purportedly took place in the 1950s between Henry Ford II and the leader of the automobile workers union Walter Reuther. The two rival men, it is said, were touring a newly built and highly automated factory, with shiny robots lining the assembly hall; when Henry Ford mused: *"Walter, how are you going to get those robots to pay your union dues?"* Whereupon Walter Reuther replied: *"Henry, how are you going to get them to buy your cars?"*[505]

In May 2017, a team of researchers at the University of Oxford published the results of a survey of the world's best artificial intelligence experts to find out when machines would be better than humans at various occupations. The researchers predicted that there was a 50 percent chance of

AI outperforming humans in all tasks within 45 years. All
human jobs were expected to be automated in 120 years,
with Asian respondents expecting these dates much sooner
than North Americans.[506] In theory, that means people can
soon retire and enjoy the promised age of universal leisure.
But the immediate concern for most workers is that they
will be losing their jobs to machines.

Outsourcing is another problem. The opening of global
markets and access to the internet have created a glut not
only of manual workers but of college graduates, whose skills
can be accessed from anywhere in the world. Foreign workers willing to work for less, both skilled and unskilled, are
squeezing out local labor.

In response to these concerns, various forms of UBI
have been proposed and are being tested. A successful pilot
study is ongoing in Brazil, and a UBI has been proposed in
Switzerland. Trials are planned in Oakland, California; three
cities in Ontario, Canada; and Utrecht in the Netherlands.
Two local authorities in Scotland have announced such
plans, and politicians across Europe have spoken in favor of
the concept.[507]

Debate has largely focused on whether a UBI would
stimulate or kill incentive, whether it would free people or
make them dependents of the "nanny state," and whether
it would bankrupt the government trying to pay for it. A
known problem with government welfare programs is that
they can discourage people from seeking work, since welfare
payouts go down as incomes go up. But studies have shown
that a UBI distributed equally regardless of income does not
have that result. These studies go back as far as 1968, when
President Richard Nixon initiated a successful trial in which

8,500 people were given a basic income of around $1,600 a year for a family of four (equivalent to $10,000 today). The trial showed that the money had little impact on the working hours of the recipients. People who did reduce the time they worked engaged in other socially valuable pursuits, and young people who were not working spent more time getting an education.

Canada ran a similar trial in the 1970s, in which 30 percent of the people in the small town of Dauphin, Manitoba, were given $15,000 each. A 2011 analysis of the experiment found that employment rates among young adults did not change, high-school completion rates increased, and hospitalization rates dropped by 8.5 percent.[508] Larger experiments run more recently in India have reached similar results.[509]

## UBI as Monetary Policy

The chief roadblock to implementing a UBI today is where to find the money. Heavily indebted governments cannot raise taxes or incur additional debt in sums sufficient to provide for the survival needs of the whole population. The once-derided "helicopter money" is therefore getting a second look.[510] Milton Friedman said the direct way to reverse deflation (a shortage of money in the economy) is to "drop money from helicopters," and dropping it right into people's pockets could be the most democratic way to distribute it. Dropping digital dollars into digital wallets could be done with a few computer keystrokes, eliminating the need to send out millions of dividend checks.[511] European economists are considering that approach, not as welfare but as a key policy tool for stimulating the economy.[512]

In a now-famous speech in Washington titled "Deflation: Making Sure 'It' Doesn't Happen Here," then–Fed
Governor Bernanke stated that the central bank would not
be "out of ammunition" to counteract deflation just because
the federal funds rate had fallen to 0 percent. Lowering
interest rates was not the only way to get new money into
the economy. Using Friedman's helicopter-drop analogy, he
said, "the U.S. government has a technology, called a printing press (or, today, its electronic equivalent), that allows it
to produce as many U.S. dollars as it wishes at essentially no
cost." The government can just print the money.

The speech was actually directed at the Japanese, who
were then struggling with massive deflation. Consumers
were not spending and the Japanese economy was stagnant.
QE had been tried, but the money was not getting into people's pockets. Bernanke therefore suggested a more uncon-
ventional approach: give Japanese households cash directly.
Consumers could use the new windfalls to spend their way
out of the recession, driving up demand and raising prices.

Bernanke's speech was the subject of a 2014 article in
*Foreign Affairs* titled "Print Less but Transfer More: Why
Central Banks Should Give Money Directly to the People."
Political economist Mark Blyth and hedge fund manager
Eric Lonergan admonished:

> It's well past time ... for U.S. policymakers -- as well as
> their counterparts in other developed countries -- to con-
> sider a version of Friedman's helicopter drops. In the short
> term, such cash transfers could jump-start the economy.
> Over the long term, they could reduce dependence on the
> banking system for growth and reverse the trend of rising

inequality. The transfers wouldn't cause damaging inflation, and few doubt that they would work. The only real
question is why no government has tried them.[513]

It is a good question. Cynical commentators suggest that
the intent of current policies is to keep people poor, since the
poor are willing to work for minimal wages. Well-fed people
can demand their fair share of the pie.

Proposals for a basic income guarantee or national
dividend are far from new. A similar approach was advocated nearly a century ago by Major C. H. Douglas in his
books *Economic Democracy* (1920) and *Social Credit* (1924).
His proposals grew from the observation that the price of
goods and services necessarily exceeds the wages available to
purchase them. Partly this is because some wages are saved
rather than spent, and partly it is because producers must
set their prices to cover costs other than labor and materials,
including the cost of financing.[514] The gap between prices
and wages is filled by additional borrowing, until debt spirals
out of control. To avoid that unsustainable result, Douglas
argued, the gap needs to be regularly filled by a distribution
of new money made directly to the people.

Other 20th-century thought leaders who advocated
a universal basic income included Nobel Prize-winning
American economists Paul Samuelson, Milton Friedman,
and Friedrich Hayek.[515] These men were not "socialists." In
fact, Hayek was one of the founders of Austrian economics.
He wrote in his 1973 book *Law, Legislation and Liberty*:

The assurance of a certain minimum income for everyone,
or a sort of floor below which nobody need fall even when

he is unable to provide for himself, appears not only to
be wholly legitimate protection against a risk common to
all, but a necessary part of the Great Society in which the
individual no longer has specific claims on the members
of the particular small group into which he was born.

## A Remarkable Historical Precedent—The G.I. Bill

That investment in "human capital" can pay major dividends
was demonstrated by the dramatic effects of the G.I. Bill.
The Servicemen's Readjustment Act of 1944 is estimated to
have cost $50 billion in today's dollars and to have returned
$350 billion to the economy, a nearly sevenfold return.[516]
    The intent of the Bill was to mitigate the potentially
damaging economic impact of 15.7 million returning veterans looking for scarce jobs and housing as World War II
ended. The G.I. Bill offered them regular readjustment payments until they could find a job. Conservative congressmen
worried that this might create a "freeloader mentality," but
only about half of returning veterans received even a single
unemployment payment. By far the most popular benefits
of the program were financial assistance for education and
housing. Over half of G.I.s took advantage of this educational provision, with 2.2 million attending college and 5.6
million opting for vocational training. At the time, there were
serious shortages in student housing and faculty; but colleges
and universities expanded to meet the increased demand.[517]
    The G.I. Bill's educational benefits helped spur postwar
economic growth by training legions of professionals. Historian Milton Greenberg estimates that the G.I. Bill enriched
the economy and the culture by producing 450,000 engi-

neers, 240,000 accountants, 238,000 teachers, 91,000 scientists, 67,000 doctors and 22,000 dentists, earning them the title of the "Greatest Generation."[518]

Tuition was free in a number of state colleges and universities for decades after World War II. Compare that to the situation today, when US higher education is so expensive that the collective student debt burden is over $1.5 trillion. Student debt is now the second highest US consumer debt category, behind only mortgage debt. It has risen nearly 164 percent in 25 years, while median wages have increased only 1.6 percent.[519] More than 2 million student loan borrowers have student loan debt greater than $100,000, with 415,000 of that total holding student loan debt greater than $200,000.[520] Worse, these debts may be carried for life, since *students cannot file for bankruptcy.* That discriminatory regulation is part of the Bankruptcy Reform Act of 2005, the same Act that put derivative and repo investors at the head of the line in grabbing the collateral of bankrupt corporations.[521] Student incomes today are largely invested in paying off debts rather than in buying homes, cars, and consumer goods.

Student debt is bundled as asset-backed securities and sold to investors, similar to the mortgage-backed securities that the Fed bought from the banks in its first round of QE. The Fed could buy up student debt in the same way. If it held the securities on its books without collecting on them, it could bring about a student debt jubilee.

One problem without sort of targeted debt forgiveness, however, is that people with other types of debt might complain of favoritism. A UBI for all would be a more equitable way to dispense debt relief, allowing people to pay down their debts or not as they chose.

## Why "QE for the People" Need Not Be Inflationary

The G.I. Bill confirmed that investment in human capital can return to the economy many times over, repaying the outlay without driving up prices. The objection of economists to any sort of "qualitative easing," whether in the form of a UBI or debt cancellation or infrastructure spending, is that it cannot be "sterilized" in the way that conventional QE can. When the money supply grows too large and consumer prices shoot up, the process cannot be reversed. If the money is spent on a national dividend, infrastructure, or the government's budget, it will be left circulating in the economy and will not be retrievable. As explained in a 2015 editorial in the *UK Register*:

> QE is designed to be temporary, ... because once people's spending rates recover we need a way of taking all that extra money out of the economy. So we do it by using printed money to buy bonds, which injects the money into the economy, and then sell those bonds back once we need to withdraw the money from the economy, and simply destroy the money we've raised. ... If we don't have any bonds to sell, it's not clear how we can reduce [the money supply] if large-scale inflation hits.[522]

And that is why QE has not worked to stimulate the economy—because the money the productive economy desperately needs has been "sterilized," kept out of circulation. Large-scale inflation was widely predicted from QE, but this has not happened despite 10 years and $3.7 trillion in "money printing." Yet the Federal Reserve is still bent on "quantitative tightening"—raising interest rates and reducing the money supply by selling bonds– in anticipation of that event.

As noted in Chapter 1, GDP remains well below both the long-run trend and the level predicted by forecasters a decade ago. In 2016, real per capita GDP was 10 percent below the 2006 forecast of the Congressional Budget Office, and it shows no signs of returning to the predicted level.[523] In 2017, US gross domestic product was $19.4 trillion. If that sum was 10 percent below full capacity, the money circulating in the economy would need to be increased by another $2 trillion to create the demand to bring it to full capacity. This money could well come in the form of a UBI.

In *The Road to Debt Bondage*, Derryl Hermanutz proposes a central-bank-issued UBI of $1,000 per month.[524] Assuming it went to all US residents over 18, or about 250 million people, the outlay would be about $2.5 trillion annually. The money would be transferred digitally into their bank accounts; and for people with overdue debt, Hermanutz proposes that it automatically go to pay down those debts. *Recall that money is created as loans and extinguished when they are repaid. The portion of a UBI used to pay down debts would therefore be extinguished along with the debt.*

People who were current on their debts could choose whether or not to pay them down, but many would also no doubt go for that option. In 2018, credit card debt alone exceeded $1 trillion, and auto loan debt exceeded $1.1 trillion. Hermanutz estimates that roughly half of a UBI payout could be extinguished in this way through mandatory and voluntary loan repayments.

Another third would go to "savers" who did not need the money for expenditures. This money, too, would not be likely to drive up consumer prices, since it would go into investment and savings vehicles rather than circulating in the consumer economy. That leaves only about one-sixth of payouts, or $400 billion, that would actually be added to the circulating money supply, and that sum could easily be absorbed by the *real* "output gap"—the $2 trillion gap between actual and forecasted productivity.

Not only *could* this money be added but it actually needs to be, in order to bring the economy to full capacity. If demand (money) is not increased, supply and GDP will not go up. New demand needs to *precede* new supply. The money has to be out there searching for goods and services before employers will add the workers needed to create more supply. If the money is not there, the Federal Reserve (which has a mandate to pursue full employment) needs to fill the breach by issuing it and circulating it in some way.

As for the official unemployment figures, they are clearly misleading. As of May 2018, the rate of unemployed or underemployed US workers was actually 7.6 percent when short-term discouraged workers were included, double the widely reported rate.[525] When long-term discouraged workers were included, the real unemployment figure was 21.5 percent.[526] In addition to that large untapped pool of workers, there is the expanding labor potential of robots, computers and innovations such as 3D printers, which can work 24 hours a day without overtime pay or medical insurance. A vast workforce is thus available to create the supply needed to respond to any new demand generated by a UBI or other "qualitative easing," keeping prices stable.

Only when demand is saturated and productivity is at full capacity will consumer prices be driven up; and that sort of large-scale inflation need not happen for a long time, if ever. Just as loans increase the money supply and repaying them shrinks it again, so taxes repaid to the government will shrink a money supply inflated by the government; and increased productivity will cause the tax base to increase naturally. In fact a UBI, like the G.I. Bill, might actually pay for itself. As explained by Joseph Stiglitz in *The Guardian*, money invested in the economy by the government circulates and recirculates:

> The result of that is that the economy grows by a multiple of the initial spending, and public finances turn out to be stronger: as the economy grows, fiscal revenues increase, and demands for the government to pay unemployment benefits, or fund social programmes to help the poor and needy, go down. As tax revenues go up as a result of growth, and as these expenditures decrease, the government's fiscal position strengthens.[527]

Economic growth drives tax revenues up without the need to raise taxes. An August 2017 report from the Roosevelt Institute found that a UBI of $1,000 per month to all adults would grow the US economy by $2.5 trillion in eight years.[528]

According to the Heritage Foundation, total tax revenue as a percentage of GDP is now 26 percent.[529] Thus one new dollar of GDP results in about 26 cents of increased tax revenue. A working paper published by the San Francisco Federal Reserve in 2012 found that one dollar invested in infrastructure generates at least two dollars in GSP (state

GDP), and "roughly four times more than average" during economic downturns.[530] Whether that means $4 or $8 is unclear, but assume it's only $4. Multiplying $4 by $0.26 in taxes would return the entire original dollar to the government in an economic downturn and would return half of it to the government in good economic times. Any shortfall could be made up in other ways, including closing tax loopholes or taxing the $21 trillion or more that is hidden in offshore tax havens. Shortfalls could also be made up through a system of public banks that would collect interest that was returned to the government.

Even if taxes were insufficient to bring demand in balance with supply, the government would not need to rely on the Fed for "quantitative tightening" in order to pull the money back. Taxes could simply be adjusted to balance the money supply; and as shown in the next chapter, this could be done by an automatic digital program that actually reduced the tax burden for most people.

What of the concern that supplementing people's incomes will lead to increased consumption, exhausting already-limited natural resources? That too need not happen if the funds are properly directed. Money going to pay off debt will be voided out with the debt. Beyond that there is a whole range of services that do not use natural resources— education, research, childcare, eldercare, sanitation, music, art, and the like—on which people could be put to work if the money were available to fund them. Putting new money into infrastructure, research and development can actually save natural resources, by making their use more efficient.

The specter invariably raised to deter legislators from issuing new money for public purposes is the fear of repeating the notorious hyperinflations of history—those in Weimer Germany, Zimbabwe and elsewhere. But according to Professor Michael Hudson, who has studied the question extensively, those disasters were not due to government money-printing to stimulate the economy. He writes:

> Every hyperinflation in history has been caused by foreign debt service collapsing the exchange rate. The problem almost always has resulted from wartime foreign currency strains, not domestic spending. The dynamics of hyperinflation traced in such classics as Salomon Flink's *The Reichsbank and Economic Germany* (1931) have been confirmed by studies of the Chilean and other Third World inflations. First the exchange rate plunges as economies pay for foreign military spending during the war, and then—in Germany's case—reparations after the war ends. These payments led the exchange rate to fall, increasing the price in domestic currency of buying imports priced in hard currencies. This price rise for imported goods creates a price umbrella for domestic prices to follow suit. More domestic money is needed to finance economic activity at the higher price level. This German experience provides the classic example.[531]

Six men now own as much wealth as half the global population.[532] There is no way the people at the top of the income pyramid can spend enough on consumer goods and services to generate the demand necessary to keep half the population employed. As robots increasingly take over human jobs, the choices will be a UBI or to let half the population starve. A UBI could be paid simply as a dividend for living in the 21st century, when mechanization has minimized the need for human labor, finally freeing us to enjoy some leisure and pursue more creative endeavors.

*Takeaway: To satisfy its mandate to maintain full employment, the central bank needs to generate the demand (money) necessary to prompt producers to produce; and the most direct way to do that is to simply drop new money into consumers' bank accounts. A central-bank-funded UBI would not create price inflation if maintained in proper proportions. Money used to pay down debt would be extinguished along with the debt, and money spent on goods and services would create the demand to drive new GDP, balancing supply with demand and keeping prices stable. New GDP would also increase the tax base, shrinking the money supply as those taxes returned to the government.*

## CHAPTER 17

# ELIMINATING THE INCOME TAX AND POPPING THE FINANCIALIZATION BUBBLE

*"The hardest thing in the world to understand is the income tax."*
—*Attributed to Albert Einstein*

**Summing up from the previous chapters**, harnessing the Federal Reserve into the service of the public would allow the central bank to maintain full employment and the stability of the currency while at the same time providing a public option for banking services, preventing bank runs, eliminating "too big to fail," providing the liquidity necessary to fund a government budget that met the needs of the people and the economy, and retiring the federal debt. But that still leaves the risky derivatives and repo markets, which are so intertwined with the sovereign debt of nations that they could take down the global economy the next time a big derivatives bank went bankrupt or skittish repo investors pulled their money out *en masse.* How can those time bombs be defused?

To a large extent, the demand for repos and derivatives could be expected to shrink simply by attrition, as a public banking system backed by the unlimited reserves of the central bank made them no longer necessary. The central bank would provide boundless liquidity, and there would be no need for FDIC insurance, since the central bank could not go bankrupt. Large institutional investors would be comfortable parking their money there without resorting to the riskier repo market, and the need for derivatives as insurance against risk would be significantly reduced by reducing the risks they were designed to alleviate. The risk of bank defaults and bank runs would be eliminated, since the central bank has unlimited liquidity. The market for interest rate swaps, which now accounts for over 75 percent of the derivatives market,[533] would also shrink, since the central bank would have other tools for stabilizing the money supply besides manipulating interest rates. That point was actually made on a July 2016 blog for Bank of England staff, in an article aptly titled, "Central Bank Digital Currency: The End of Monetary Policy as We Know It?"[534]

The real concern, however, is not with this sort of "honest" derivatives intended to ensure against real market risks. It is with the speculative casino that makes up the vast majority of the derivatives market, in which money makes money by skimming it from other players. There will always be gamblers looking for those opportunities, which drain profits from the productive economy without producing new goods and services. Financial speculation of this sort has created gross disparities between rich and poor, allowing the financial economy to grow at the expense of the productive economy and the wage-earners who depend on it.

## From Income Tax to Financial Transactions Tax

One alternative for curbing the financialization bubble is to restructure the tax system. High-frequency program trading and other forms of short-term gambling could be taxed out of existence with a financial transactions tax (a tax on all financial settlements), while speculative trading of other types could be tamed with an appropriately targeted punitive capital gains tax.

Financial settlements occur any time money changes hands, including sales of stocks, bonds, repo, derivatives, and currency trades, which currently escape taxation altogether. Projections are that a financial transactions tax (FTT) of a mere 0.1 percent could replace all other taxes. It would be easy to implement in a digital system, and it would go a long way toward killing the financialization that is killing the economy. A major objection to an FTT is that it would also kill the repo market on which banking today depends; but if there were something better to replace it, eliminating that risky part of the shadow banking system could be a desirable outcome.

In a 2017 book called *The Economist's Tale: How Technology Enables a National Income, the End of Income Taxes, and a Balanced Budget* (2017), financial entrepreneur Scott Smith presents some compelling data. Smith helped pioneer structured finance on Wall Street in the 1990s and was an independent candidate for US president in 2016. He observes that US personal income in 2016 totaled only $16 trillion, a very small pie to fund a $4 trillion US national budget. A much bigger pie would be available if the government were to tax all payments of every sort. He calculated that annual payments in the United States, including all those financial transactions that currently bear no sales tax, are now more than *five quadrillion* dollars—that's 5,000 trillion dollars. It's hard to believe, but he gives the following figures for 2015, with sources:

Table 11 in the Bank for International Settlements Red Book shows CHIPS, Fedwire, checks, ACH, and on-us payments in 2015 totaled $1,567 trillion among banks (http://www.bias.org). Table 8 shows the use of payment instruments, ACH, cards and checks in 2015 totaled $171 trillion among non-banks. Table 21 shows transactions at the NSCC and FICC in 2015 totaled $1,231 trillion. Table 26 shows transactions at the DTC and the Fed in 2015 totaled $408 trillion. Table 18 shows trades on the NYSE and NASDAQ in 2015 totaled $36 trillion. Table 6 in the BIS' FX Turnover Publication shows US FX trades at $311 trillion in 2015. Table D12.2 in the BIS' OTC IR Derivative publication shows US trades at $310 trillion in 2015. The CME Group has publicly reported trades exceeding $1,000 trillion annually since 2014 (http://openmarkets.CMEgroup.com/9685/todays-number-more-than-1-quadrillion-traded-in-2014). The grand total is $5,034 trillion—and this is not an exhaustive list of the flow of money in the monetary economy.[535]

The bulk of these payments are not for goods and services. They are for financial speculation—money transferred from one pocket to another without adding real value to the economy. While sales of the consumer goods that people use and need are taxed at around 10 percent, speculative financial trades are not taxed at point of sale at all. Smith contends that a tax of a mere 1/10th of 1 percent imposed on all trades would generate enough money to cover not only the existing federal budget but free health care for all, free higher education for all, and an unconditional basic income for all.

True, the pool of trades available to tax would shrink substantially if an FTT were imposed, since many of these speculative trades generate less than 1/10th of 1 percent in profit. Their profits come from volume, e.g. from high-frequency program trading. But the collective value of taxable trades could be reduced by a full 60 percent and the payments tax would still generate $8 trillion in revenues—double the current federal budget—without taxing incomes at all. And killing high-frequency program trading would be an economic good in itself. Making money by expropriating it from other players acts as a parasite on productivity, draining resources away.

Financial transactions taxes have been successfully imposed in various countries historically, including the United States. In 1914, the US government instituted a transfer tax on all sales or transfers of stock in the amount of 0.2 percent of the transaction value. In 1932, in response to the Great Depression, this tax was doubled to 0.4 percent. The tax remained in force until 1966. In 1936, John Maynard Keynes advocated the wider use of financial transaction taxes. In 1972, influenced by the work of Keynes, James Tobin suggested a more specific currency transaction tax for stabilizing currencies on a larger global scale.[536] In 2013, the European Commission entertained a proposal for a financial transactions tax for eleven of the Member States of the European Union, in which all financial transactions would be taxed at 0.1 percent.[537] After repeated delays, in May 2018 the finance ministers of ten EU countries announced that they were resuming their negotiations for an FTT.[538]

## Squeezing the Repo Market

One objection that has been raised to a European FTT is that it could hurt the repo market. In a May 2013 article on *Alphaville FT* titled "How to Kill the European Repo Market in 10 Easy Steps," Izabella Kaminska warned:

> ICMA's European Repo Council ... says if the tax is implemented, it would likely contract the short-term repo market by at least 66 per cent. ...
>
> ... There is ... little incentive for dealers to continue to make repo markets once a tax is introduced, especially if you consider their other key revenue sources, rehypothecation and relending, have already been severely hit by the trend towards segregated accounts in the market. ...
>
> In a market that is already experiencing collateral scarcity — meaning some are having to pay to lend — this sort of additional cost could be a death knell for the private collateral markets.
>
> ... [W]ith private repo markets frozen, *the only alternative to monetise collateral rather than to liquidate would be to repo it with the central bank*. Since not all institutions have access to central bank repo facilities, this leaves the system vulnerable to collateral liquidation.[539] [Emphasis added.]

If all institutions *did* have access to central bank repo facilities, however, a death knell for the highly risky private repo market could be a good thing. It could die a natural death, replaced by a stable, secure, transparent financial system available to all. Recall the dire warnings of the *Zero Hedge* article titled "Desperately Seeking $11.2 Trillion in Collateral, Or How 'Modern Money' Really Works":

> [T]he money held in the shadow banking system ... is literally created in a limbo where "confidence" is really the only collateral. ...
>
> "[H]igh quality collateral" [backstops] trillions of rehy-pothecated shadow liabilities all of which have negligible margin requirements (and thus provide virtually unlimited leverage) until times turn rough and there is a scramble for collateral .... .
>
> [S]hould the system finally wise up and remove the black box gimmick of rehypothecation which is literally "ac-counting magic" (and also financial fraud), the Fed and its peer central banks would need to fill a hole as large as $10 trillion![540]

Although that sounds daunting, the Fed succeeded in coming up with *$29 trillion* in liquidity for the banks after the 2008 banking crisis, seemingly without breaking a sweat.[541] Generating $10 trillion in central bank liquidity could be just as doable, providing a more stable and less risky option than relying on the rehypothecated shadow liabilities propping up the financial markets today.

In fact, the Federal Reserve is already a major player in the repo market, and that market is already feeling the competitive squeeze. The Fed has been engaging in "reverse repo" to drain money from the economy and give big players a safe alternative for parking their funds, using some of the nearly $4 trillion in securities it acquired through quantitative easing. In an August 2014 blog, Yves Smith observed that the Fed appears to be intentionally competing with the shadow banks, since it is offering better terms than in the private market. She quoted from the *Wall Street Journal:*

> Large market participants like money-market funds are increasingly trading from the Fed, rather than with banks—a move Fitch Ratings attributes to comfort with the central bank, better terms and regulatory changes that are altering how financial firms participate in the market.[542]

Yves Smith commented:

> The wee problem is that even in good times, there is counterparty risk in the repo market. The Fed is the best counterparty imaginable. So given the choice between doing a repo with a bank versus doing a repo with the Fed on the same terms, anyone with an operating brain cell will go to the central bank. And the Fed was willing to experiment in size, so it's now become a big part of the repo market.[543]

*The Fed is the best counterparty imaginable.* It also has plenty of high-quality collateral. Arguably not just the repo market but the exploding derivatives market could be downsized if the Fed actively competed for scarce collateral. Yves Smith observed:

... [T]he big use of collateral is to secure derivatives positions. Derivative experts like Satyajit Das attest that the main uses of derivatives aren't for socially productive hedging (and related trading to make enough in the way of markets) but speculation, and accounting, tax, and regulatory arbitrage. ... [M]aking collateral less available (or more costly) is another way to crimp derivatives activity.[544]

## No More IRS Filings!

There are other advantages to a financial transactions tax, and one is that it would be much easier and cheaper to collect and to pay than income taxes. The Tax Foundation reports that in 2016, Americans spent more than 8.9 billion hours toiling over IRS tax filing requirements at a cost of $409 billion to the US economy, in addition to the annual cost of maintaining the Internal Revenue Service itself. A financial transactions tax could be shaved automatically from every digital trade, without the need for paperwork of any sort (unless payment were made in cash). Scott Smith contends that this shaved portion would not even need to go back to the IRS. It would just disappear. The algorithm determining the percentage to be shaved off could be adjusted as needed to maintain the value of the currency.

Recall that what must be balanced is not the federal budget itself but demand with potential supply in order to prevent price inflation.[545] An FTT could do that automatically. Congress would just vote on a budget and spend the money as it does now, drawing on its account at the central bank, which would create the money on its books. The computer-coded tax would adjust according to the overall price

level in the economy, increasing as prices rose and decreasing
as demand dropped.

Skeptical observers might say that this is the very reason
governments are attempting to eliminate cash—so they can
confiscate a portion of our earnings automatically. But that is
what taxes do; and not only do we have to pay them, we have
to bear our own crosses by sweating through mountains of
paperwork to come up with the numbers. Better to be taxed
at 0.1 percent per trade than at 10 percent for consumer
goods plus an average of 13.5 percent on our incomes. And
under Scott Smith's proposal, the money shaved from trades
would not actually go to the government, so there would
be no opportunity for corrupt bureaucrats to confiscate it.
An FTT would not only massively expand the tax base by
capturing all those speculative trades that currently escape
taxation, but it would be administered painlessly. As Smith
describes the advantages of his system:

> First, it would be highly efficient, since it would eliminate
> the overhead associated with having to aggregate tax rev-
> enues and transfer them to the Treasury. Second, it would
> eliminate the need for and the cost of financing to bridge
> the inevitable gaps between the processes of collecting
> revenue and spending. And third, it would enable the PT
> [Payments Tax] to be utilized as an economic stabilizer. ...
> If the economy slows down, the amount of money being
> removed from the economy by the PT would decline.
> ... Likewise, should the economy heat up, the amount
> of money removed from the economy by the PT would
> increase, serving to cool the economy.

Using the PT in this way would be more effective for
regulating economic activity than the Federal Reserve's
current methodology of moderating interest rates. In fact,
under most economic scenarios we would want the rate
for the payments tax to be set so that it removes less money from the money supply than the Fed creates, because as
an economy grows it requires a larger money supply.[546]

Smith envisions the central bank as both universal
depository and universal lender, with public-service banks
operating as its extensions in the local economy:

> [B]anks would act as financial servicers: originating
> and underwriting loans, servicing loans, foreclosing on
> collateral in the event of default, liquidating foreclosed
> properties, managing lines of credit, and doing essentially
> everything they do now—except that they would be doing
> all of this *as intermediaries for the Federal Reserve.*

. . . If banks served as the interface between the Federal
Reserve and customers, it would obviate the need for imposing lending limits based upon a bank's equity. Instead, banks
would make loans on behalf of the Fed, and a little bank
would have the same lending power as a big bank.[547] The
depositors would be relying for their security not on fragile
bank balance sheets but on the Fed's unlimited ability to
return their money. In that sense, the proposal is similar to
Sovereign Money proposals in which banks would essentially be custodians of government-issued money on behalf of
customers. (See Chapter 13.) The difference would be that
lending would not be dependent on private pools of existing

funds. Loans would simply be drawn from the cloud through the "dumb pipe" of the central bank, and the money would return to the cloud when the loan was repaid.

As noted in Chapter 13, the "creator" of this new money would not actually be the central bank. The central bank would just be the universal ledger keeping track of debits and credits. The money would be created by the borrower, with his local bank serving to validate his credit and guarantee his IOU after applying proper underwriting standards. The borrower's promise would thus be "monetized," turning it into the sort of negotiable instrument that is accepted in the marketplace.

That is actually what bankers do now, but banking regulations and the exigencies of attracting and keeping customers require them to go through a series of complex, opaque and risky maneuvers to conceal the fact that the "money" they are lending is not some pre-existing indestructible commodity like gold that has been acquired from elsewhere and passed to the borrower. Rather, it is just the borrower's own monetized credit. Bankers working in a public system would not need to worry about liquidity or reserves. They would just be public servants applying their underwriting skills to the process of turning their customers' credit into "ready money."

## The End of Interest?

The traditional justification for charging interest on loans is that it is "rent" for using the money of savers who have foregone the money's use for a period of time. But in a public banking system in which loans are simply drawn from the cloud, no savers would be putting their funds at risk. Smith therefore questions the need for interest. He writes:

> Since the Fed is the source of money, it has no cost of funds. Borrowing from a bank would still cost money due to origination and service fees, and of course you would have to pay back the loan, but you would *no longer pay interest on the loan*, so loans would cost substantially less than they do today. ... Interest-free mortgages would cut the monthly cost of homeownership nearly in half.

One problem with eliminating interest, however, is that money borrowed interest-free could too easily go into speculation—buying existing assets on credit and selling them at a higher price—without producing the new goods and services necessary to balance supply with demand and keep prices stable. That is what happened with the Fed's Zero Interest Rate Policy, when banks and their favored clients were able to borrow virtually interest-free. The results were asset bubbles in the stock and real estate markets, destructive stock buybacks by corporate executives, and leveraged buyouts by corporate raiders.

In the case of housing bubbles, Smith's proposed solution is to raise underwriting standards. The US subprime bubble grew because the borrowers were *subprime*. "No-doc, no-down" loans were given to people who had no documented credit history, made no down payment, and had no realistic hope of paying the loans back. The lenders were not worried, because they had discovered they could bundle the loans and sell them as "mortgage-backed securities" to un-suspecting investors, who were blindsided by the opacity of the trades. It was a Ponzi scheme, which collapsed when the Fed raised interest rates and triggered the inevitable cascade of defaults. To avoid that result, credit needs to be limited to qualified applicants who can pay the loans back, who have "skin in the game" in the form of adequate down payments. When a bank qualifies a borrower for a home loan today, it allows up to one-third of the borrower's income to be spent on the mortgage. Smith recommends changing that rule so that perhaps only one-sixth of a buyer's income could be spent on his mortgage.

Another solution that has been proposed for curbing real estate bubbles is to impose a Land Value Tax. Unlike property taxes, a Land Value Tax ignores the value of buildings, personal property and other improvements and instead taxes the unimproved value of the land and its natural resources. The economic efficiency of a Land Value Tax has been known since the 18th century, and many economists have advocated it. The most famous was Henry George, whose most important work, *Progress and Poverty* (1879), sold millions of copies worldwide. He argued that because the supply of land is fixed and the value of its location is created by communities, public works, and Mother Nature, the economic rent of land and its resources is the most logical source of public revenue. He proposed a land value tax that would fund an annual dividend for every citizen.[548]

The land value tax has been implemented in more than 30 countries around the world, including parts of the United States. Its use in several US municipalities dates back to 1913, when the Pennsylvania legislature permitted Pittsburgh and Scranton to tax land values at a higher rate than building values. A 1951 statute gave smaller Pennsylvania cities the same option to enact a two-rate property tax, a variation of the land value tax. About 15 Pennsylvania communities currently use this type of tax program. Hawaii also has experience with two-rate taxation, and Virginia and Connecticut have authorized municipalities to choose a two-rate property tax.[549] A century ago, land value taxes were also successfully applied in Michigan, Ohio, Illinois, and California.[550]

Richard Werner proposes another solution to the problem of asset bubbles. He argues that money creation through banks, whether publicly or privately owned, should be limited to loans for productive purposes. Banking regulation should be aimed not at bank capitalization or asset size but at the purpose of the loans. Credit created for speculation is inflationary because the new money does not create new goods and services but competes for existing assets, driving up prices. But new money will not trigger inflation if it creates new goods and services, since supply will go up with demand, keeping prices stable. Regulation aimed at the purpose for which loans are granted is called "credit guidance" and has been done successfully before. Werner cites the banking policies of post-war Germany and Japan, two war-torn economies that were transformed in a few short decades into world powers. Most homebuyers need to borrow to afford a home, but Werner says this could be the business of nonbank loan funds that lend the existing money of their investors rather than creating it on their books.[551]

The issue of interest, however, remains controversial. As Werner observes, profit margins for nonprofit community banks in Germany are razor thin. They need some interest to cover their costs and stay afloat. Investors in loan funds would also want interest. Credit cards are interest-free the first month, but charging interest thereafter quells the exuberance of consumers who might otherwise spend recklessly and just keep rolling over the loans. With a public option for credit cards, merchant fees could be eliminated, interest could be substantially reduced, and the interest could go back to the government to be put to beneficial public use.

## Other Alternatives for Taming the Speculative Markets

The most direct way to curb derivative and repo trading would be to limit or eliminate their safe harbor status in bankruptcy, and that has been proposed. (See Chapter 6.) Under the current system, the problem with that solution is that it could collapse the banking system that depends on the repo market for liquidity. But a public banking system drawing on the unlimited resources of the central bank would not need the repo market for that purpose; and if the central bank opened its deposit window to everyone, large investors with funds exceeding the FDIC insurance limit would not need the repo market either. Investors large and small would be protected by the central bank's deep pocket and the full faith and credit of the government, while earning a fair interest rate on their deposits. Safe harbor for repo trades could therefore be withdrawn without destabilizing the financial system.

What about derivatives? Some derivatives actually serve useful purposes, such as those protecting farmers from crop failures and the vagaries of the produce market. But the other 95 percent of the derivatives market is primarily for speculation rather than for hedging, and some authorities say this market should be shut down altogether. It could be banned as a forbidden form of casino gambling, which remains illegal in many states. Paul Craig Roberts, former US Treasury Secretary under President Reagan, contends that the whole derivative swaps business could be closed out or netted out, and the chief effect would just be to take $230 trillion of leveraged risk out of the financial system.[552]

To tame the speculative fever driving markets today, however, will take more than just regulation. As *Forbes* financial writer Steve Denning argued in a January 2013 article titled "Big Banks and Derivatives: Why Another Financial Crisis Is Inevitable":

> The financial sector is in effect an extreme example of the shareholder value theory run amok. Pursuit of profit not only undermines the banks themselves but ultimately the global economy as a whole.
>
> Regulation and enforcement will only work if it is accompanied by a paradigm shift in the banking sector that changes the context in which banks operate and the way they are run, so that banks shift their goal from making money to adding value to stakeholders, particularly customers. This would require action from the legislature, the SEC, the stock market and the business schools, as well as of course the banks themselves.[553]

A paradigm shift in the goal of the banking sector from making money to serving stakeholders can best be achieved by transforming banks into public utilities and bankers into salaried public employees, enlisted in the service of the people and the economy.

*Takeaway:* The systemically risky derivative and repo markets could be shrunk, and the burdensome and expensive income tax could be eliminated, by imposing a very small financial transactions tax on every trade. A national public banking system that was backed by the deep pocket of the central bank could replace the repo market as a depository of large investors, and it would reduce the risks that derivatives are supposed to protect investors against. With that system in place, the destabilizing superpriority granted to repos and derivatives in bankruptcy could be eliminated with minimal disruption to markets.

# RE-ENVISIONING MONEY: BANKING THAT EM-POWERS THE PEOPLE

*"Whatever you can do, or dream you can, begin it! Boldness has genius, power, and magic in it."*

—*Goethe*

**We have entered a new millennium,** which needs a new vision and business plan to manifest its true potential. The technological revolution is rapidly changing the face of finance, yet we continue to operate our banking system on a 19th-century model. Today money is created as digits on computer screens; but we still perceive it to be a "thing" like gold that is in limited supply and must be mined, bought or borrowed before it can be lent. Attempting to conform to that model, banks engage in all sorts of sleight of hand to make it appear they are borrowing money they have actually created on their books. The result is an unstable matrix of debt built on debt that has been highly lucrative for the web-spinning financiers but highly risky to the economy, effectively enslaving people by fraud.

The debt-growth model, however, has now reached its inevitable limit. There is no longer real "growth" but just new debt servicing old debt, as the parasite devours its host. Our monetary system needs a radical overhaul to bring it into the 21st century; and to bring that about, we first need to re-conceptualize what money is and how it enters the economy. Today money is just an IOU, a debt or promise to repay, an agreement between parties that can be modified to suit the times. If the people collectively agree that certain work needs to be done, they can issue the money to pay for it, just as the American colonists did through their colonial governments.

The medium of exchange needed to bring workers and materials together does not need to be borrowed before it can be spent. It can be generated on the national credit card and repaid with the productivity it creates, as was success-fully done in the New Deal era in the United States and in many other countries at various times. The government's ability to rebuild the nation's crumbling infrastructure, feed and house the population, provide universal medical care and higher education, and preserve and restore the environment is limited only by the availability of materials and workers (including machines) necessary to get the job done.

Not just the federal government but people individual-ly can become their own bankers, "monetizing" their own future ability to repay. That is actually what we do now when we take out a loan, with the bank acting as guarantor. If the system were publicly owned and operated like a cooperative on mutual credit principles, money could be created and extinguished organically in response to the needs of trade, in a community currency system in which the "community" was the nation itself. The power to create money can also be recaptured by state and local governments, by forming their own publicly owned banks on the model of the state-owned Bank of North Dakota. Reliance on costly private capital for financing public needs has limited municipal growth and reduced public services, while strapping future generations with exponentially growing debt. By eliminating the unnecessary expense of turning public dollars into profits for private middlemen, a public banking system using 21$^{st}$-century software technology can fund the goods, services and infrastructure required to satisfy the needs of the people and the economy without unsustainable debt, taxation or environmental degradation.

## Concrete Steps

It all sounds good in theory, but how can we get there from here? A first step would be to nationalize the Federal Reserve, as Congressman Wright Patman sought to do half a century ago. Nationalizing the Fed does not mean handing over control to the president or a big-lobby-controlled Congress to do with as they will. It means returning the twelve Federal Reserve Banks to public ownership and oversight and transforming the Fed into a public utility like every other public agency, including opening its services to the public. We live in a mixed economy—half private, half public—and banking oversight and control belong in the public sector. Another banking crisis may be required to generate the political will necessary to terminate the central bank's unfettered independence, but with the Fed again raising interest rates into a global debt bubble of unprecedented proportions, that crisis could be imminent.

When the too-big-to-fail banks fail in the next crisis, Congress is unlikely to acquiesce to another bailout, something the Dodd-Frank Act was touted as eliminating. If regulators follow the Dodd-Frank playbook, they will attempt instead to "bail in" creditor funds, including those of large depositors; and in a serious collapse, bail-ins could extend to confiscating the deposits of smaller customers. The likely result will be to generate such outrage among the public that people will never trust banks again. They will be looking for an alternative money system for safe harbor.

Rather than propping up the failed megabanks with either taxpayer or creditor funds, Congress needs to nationalize them, something policymakers considered doing during the last crisis but opted for bailouts instead. To avoid imposing the bill for the banks' nonperforming loans on the taxpayers, the bad loans could simply be moved onto the books of the central bank. Historical precedent shows that the Fed could carry these loans on its books indefinitely without harm to the creditors or the economy. While waiting for the next crisis, Congress should put legislation in place to ensure that the government takes an ownership stake with full voting rights in any financial institution that has to be rescued due to its own profligate activities. The legislation should clearly establish the steps to government ownership and rules for the nationalized bank's governance. (See Chapter 7.)

In a best-case scenario, the Fed would reverse course on its quantitative tightening before another crisis hits and open its deposit and lending windows to the public. Some central bank researchers and Treasury advisors are currently discussing that sort of public option for deposit accounts. The policy change would prevent bank runs, since the central bank's liquidity is unlimited and so there would be no incentive for depositors to panic and run. Opening the Fed's deposit window to all could also eliminate the need for the repo market, with its reliance on risky "rehypothecated" collateral. Large institutional depositors would have a safe place to park their money, and banks would have an unlimited source of liquidity, without resorting to the repo market.

The objection to central banks offering deposit accounts to the public is that it would shrink the deposit base that commercial banks need for liquidity, limiting their ability to make loans. But there would be little need for private bank loans if the central bank were to also open its lending window to the public; and advances in the automation of banking services are making that a feasible alternative today. Services that cannot be automated could be performed by a franchise of local banks operated as public agencies governed by boards representing all stakeholders, similar to the governance structure of the Sparkassen banks and the "platform cooperatives" (e.g. FairCoin). The result would be a network of local public banks drawing on the unlimited liquidity of a central bank mandated to serve the public interest.

Importantly, while the central bank would provide liquidity, it would not actually be the "creator" of new money originated as loans. As in a digital community currency system, money would be created by the borrowers, whether individuals, businesses or governments. The central bank would just maintain the universal ledger, keeping track of debits and credits and clearing transfers between accounts. In that sense it would perform functions similar to a blockchain, but it would not be decentralized, and no energy-intensive "mining" would be needed. There would be no gold-like digital coins, just an accounting system keeping track of transactions denominated in digital US dollars and other national currencies.

A Congress authorized to draw on its Fed account as needed could spend on the infrastructure and social goods expected of government, simply by monetizing the collective credit of the public. As with the Reconstruction Finance Corporation in the 1930s and 1940s, infrastructure loans would be self-funding, repaid with the proceeds of the projects. Other possibilities include a federally funded universal basic income, student debt relief, and federal debt relief. These loans too would be largely self-funded, repaid with the proceeds of the productivity they generated; but to the extent that demand outpaced the availability of workers and materials to create new supply, price inflation could be prevented by drawing excess demand back to the government with taxes, interest or fees.

Overheating of the economy could be avoided by digital software designed to take the temperature of the economy and tax any excess back with an automatically-imposed financial transactions tax when prices rose significantly (and not before). An FTT would be far cheaper for most taxpayers than income and sales taxes and could capture all those financialized transactions that escape taxation now, killing much of the speculative casino that acts as a parasite on the productive economy. The risk of contagion from a derivatives crisis or a run on the shadow banking system could also be curbed by withdrawing their safe harbor status in bankruptcy, eliminating them as attractive investment alternatives. (See Chapters 4 and 17.)

A national public banking system could offer a public credit card with no or very low merchant fees, breaking the monopoly of the giant Wall Street credit card issuers. If this credit were issued through smartphones, as in China and India, merchants would not even need to buy card readers to participate. They could just paste printed barcodes on their walls, allowing the smallest of street merchants to use the system. Credit card applications could be done online on cell phones or computers. For larger loans such as mortgages and business loans, loan officers would still play a role, but they would be public servants on a salary—no bonuses, fees, or commissions; no incentive to speculate or push unwanted financial products on customers. Like the Bank of North Dakota, the public banking system would not be geared to the profit motive. It would be a public utility like water, power, roads and other shared infrastructure.

Although borrowers who defaulted on their loans would be put through bankruptcy proceedings, the loan losses would not need to be imposed on the taxpayers. The debits could just be carried on the central bank's books, leaving the money that was created and not repaid to circulate in the economy. This additional money would actually benefit the economy, by helping to fill the gap between supply and demand and reduce the chronic shortage of funds available to pay down debt and finance productivity. (See Chapter 3.)

In return for accepting the public mantle, local banks would have the security of being relieved of capital requirements and the fear of insolvency, and they would not have to play the risky shell game of pretending deposits were in two places at once. As in a community currency system, they would simply be monetizing the borrowers' own ability to repay. The advantage of a national public credit system over private community currency systems is that the currency would be universally accepted, backed by the full faith and credit of the United States.

Faced with competition from a safe and efficient public central banking system along with other new digital payment systems, even some megabanks might choose to become public utilities, which would have the benefit of allowing them to enlarge their international reach backed by the US government. The trade-off would be that they would need to become nonprofit public servants working for the taxpayers and the economy, with full transparency and accountability to the public.

## Change Is in the Wind

Dismantling the current system will not be easy. Mighty forces are arrayed against changing a system that has decked the financial elite in fantastic wealth. But a new generation is coming of age, with different values from the "me" generation that put profit maximization first, and they are not willing to wait for slow political change. They need a vision and a blueprint to inspire them, and the first step is to come up with a business plan, a roadmap for proceeding that is doable. The political will then needs to be generated to do it, but there are signs that this is happening, with proposals for banking reform and public banking resolutions appearing across the country.[554]

When a viable public banking system is available to replace the private commercial banking dinosaurs, they will no longer be "too big to fail." They can be allowed to fade into extinction or absorbed into the public system, in a natural process of evolution toward a more functional and sustainable monetary scheme. The long-promised age of abundance and leisure beckons on the horizon, made possible by the technological development of a more equitable and efficient system of distribution and exchange.

# THE TRIAL AND ERROR EVOLUTION OF THE AMERICAN MONETARY SYSTEM

Money is a work in progress. Here is a brief history of the evolution of the American monetary system from colonial times to the present:

- **Paper scrip issued by governments.** In 1691, the American colonies began issuing their own paper scrip as an advance against future tax revenues. These "bills of credit" were government IOUs or promises to pay. The colonies flourished as a result, but some colonies wound up overprinting and devaluing their currencies.

- **Government-issued money lent through a government-owned bank.** In the early 1700s, the colony of Pennsylvania refined the new system of government-issued paper money by forming a "land bank," which made loans collateralized by land. The scrip returned to the government on repayment, eliminating the inflation problem when colonial governments issued more scrip than they collected back in taxes. Except for an excise tax on liquor, interest on these loans funded the government without taxes, and without inflation or government debt.[555]

- **Return to foreign coins and "commodity money."** In 1751, King George II banned the issue of paper scrip in the New England colonies and in 1764, King George III banned it in all the colonies. The colonies were reduced to using barter, foreign silver and gold coins ("specie"), and "commodity money"—corn, beaver skins, tobacco, rice, animal skins, livestock, powder and gunshot.[556] Limiting the available currency triggered a major depression.

- **Continental currency.** The colonies rebelled and returned to issuing their own paper money, called the Continental. From 1776 to 1781, they waged and won a war against the world's greatest military power, funded with this homegrown money. But the British responded by massively counterfeiting the Continental and speculating against it; and by the end of the war, it was virtually worthless.[557]

- **Return to silver and gold coins.** Disillusioned with the Continental, in 1789 the delegates to the Constitutional Convention left the power to issue paper money out of the Constitution. A case has been made that "to coin money" in Article I, Sec. 8(5), included "to print money."[558] But if that was the intent, the power was not exercised by the federal government, which continued to recognize only silver and gold coins as official currency.

- **US Bank Notes**. Lacking sufficient gold and silver coins to pay the nation's debts and run an economy, Treasury Secretary Alexander Hamilton resorted to the "fractional reserve" banking system used by the Bank of England. The First US Bank, established in 1791, was 80 percent privately owned; but it was chartered by Congress to perform several central bank functions, including the issuance of paper banknotes ostensibly backed by gold.[559] But they were backed by only a fraction of the necessary reserves, allowing many more notes to be issued than there was gold in the vaults, expanding the money supply.

- **Private banknotes and "free banking."** The First US Bank was followed by the Second US Bank, which was shut down by Andrew Jackson in 1836. Jackson paid off the national debt, but without a national bank issuing a national currency, the money supply shrank, causing a severe recession. The void was filled with banknotes issued privately. Until the Civil War, the country went through a period of "free banking." Commercial banks issued their own banknotes supposedly backed by gold; but again, far more notes were issued than there was gold. The system was unstable and was plagued by bank runs.

- **Greenbacks**. In 1863, President Abraham Lincoln revived the colonial system by issuing 450 million dollars in US Notes (Greenbacks), which were not backed by gold but were 100 percent backed by the government. The Greenbacks not only funded about

40 percent of the Union's effort in the Civil War but helped finance a period of unusual growth, including the construction of the Transcontinental Railroad.

- **National Bank Notes.** In 1863-64, the National Bank Act established the national banking system and created a uniform national currency backed by government bonds. Federally chartered national banks could issue this currency as banknotes bearing their own names. State and local banknotes were eliminated by heavy taxation.

- **Greenbacks stopped; silver demonetized.** After Lincoln was assassinated in 1865, the Greenback program was halted; and in 1876, silver was no longer accepted as legal tender. The result was to radically shrink the money supply, plummeting the country into another depression.

- **Checkbook money.** Blocked from issuing their own banknotes, bankers who were unwilling to join the federal system devised a system of "checkbook money." Rather than printing "banknotes," they created money simply by writing it into their customers' accounts as deposits when the customers took out loans.

- **Federal Reserve Notes.** Following a particularly bad bank panic in 1907, the Federal Reserve was established in 1913 to backstop bank runs with a national gold reserve. Federal Reserve Notes became the official national currency.

- **Gold standard abandoned domestically.** In 1933, Franklin Roosevelt responded to a global banking crisis by taking the dollar off the gold standard domestically. Among other banking reforms, the Glass-Steagall Act was passed, protecting depositors with deposit insurance and preventing bankers from speculating with the deposits.

- **Gold and US dollar as international reserve currency.** In 1944, the Bretton Woods system was agreed to internationally. Gold and US dollars redeemable in gold became the international reserve currency.

- **Gold standard abandoned internationally.** In 1971, Richard Nixon took the dollar off the gold standard internationally, after runs on US gold reserves caused the Treasury to run dangerously low.

- **"Oil-backed" dollar.** In 1974, Henry Kissinger made a secret deal with the OPEC countries to sell oil only in US dollars, effectively "backing" the dollar with oil.[560]

- **Cash replaced by deposits.** Over the course of the 20th century, cash became a smaller and smaller fraction of the money supply used by the public, as bank-money created as deposits skyrocketed. The public traded in this bank money, while banks traded in "reserves" held at the central bank. The public became dependent on banks for their medium of exchange.

- **Shadow bank money; "near money."** In 1999, the Gramm-Leach-Bliley Act effectively repealed a major portion of the Glass-Steagall Act; and in 2005, the Bankruptcy Reform Act gave derivatives and repo "superpriority" in bankruptcy. The result was a massive expansion of the "near-monies" of the shadow banking system, including derivatives and repo (short-term sales and repurchases simulating secured loans).

- **Socialization of bank losses.** In 2008, the shadow banking system collapsed. The US government bailed out the banks with taxpayer money, nullifying the capitalist model by socializing the banks' losses while privatizing their profits.

- **Quantitative easing (QE).** The rules were changed again when, from 2008 to 2014, the central bank pumped $3.7 trillion created with computer keystrokes into the reserve accounts of banks.

- **Bail-ins.** In 2010, the Dodd-Frank Act replaced bailouts with "bail-ins." Insolvent "systemically important" banks were officially authorized to recapitalize themselves by confiscating the money of their creditors, including their depositors.

- **Bail-ins rejected**. After a "successful" trial run in Cyprus, the new rules were tested in 2017 in Italy, where they failed. The Italian government rejected the EU-mandated rule as too onerous on unsuspecting small investors. The government resorted to a bailout of its failed banks instead.[561]

The current system is not working because it is programmed to serve financiers at the expense of people and economies. Our economic hardware is ready for a reboot, with new software programmed to serve the public interest without parasitic drains.

# GLOSSARY

**Algorithm**: a set of instructions for accomplishing a task in a certain number of steps. A simple example is a recipe.

**Asset:** anything that can be sold for value. Loans are bank assets; deposits are liabilities (an obligation that must eventually be paid, and thus a claim on assets). The formula is: bank assets = bank liabilities + bank capital (what is left when all assets have been sold and all liabilities have been paid).

**Austrian School of Economics**: forerunner of unrestrained free market (libertarian) economics, emphasizing complete freedom of association and sovereignty of individual property rights. Other tenets include (1) abolishment of central banks and return to the gold standard, (2) elimination of bank deposit insurance schemes so that bank failures punish bad investments, (3) institution of an information system that makes real-time price data available to everyone, (4) abandonment of mathematical models as too rigid and limited to be of use.[562]

**Bail-in:** an alternative to bank bailouts, in which "investors," including bondholders and depositors, take a loss rather than governments and taxpayers.

**Bailout:** financial assistance given by a government to a failing business or economy to save it from collapse.

**Basel III (the Third Basel Capital Accord):** a comprehensive set of reform measures developed by the *Basel* Committee on Banking Supervision to strengthen the regulation, supervision and risk management of the banking sector. The first version was published in late 2009, giving banks approximately three years to satisfy all requirements. Largely in response to the credit crisis, banks are required to maintain proper leverage ratios and meet certain minimum capital requirements.

**Bitcoin:** a cryptocurrency and payment system in which peer-to-peer transactions take place between users directly, without an intermediary.

**Blockchain**: a public digital ledger shared by many parties, in which transactions are recorded and confirmed anonymously across a network of computers without the need for a central authority. Once information is entered, it cannot be altered.

**Capital market:** a market for buying and selling equity (stocks) and debt instruments (bonds, mortgages, and other assets requiring a fixed payment to the holder).

**Capitalization**: the sum of a corporation's stock, long-term debt and retained earnings. The term also refers to the number of outstanding shares of a company multiplied by their price.

**Check clearing**: the process of transferring the funds promised in a check to the recipient's account.

**Check kiting:** a fraudulent scheme in which checks are issued against funds that a bank has credited into an account for checks that have been deposited but not cleared. In effect, it is an interest-free and unauthorized loan against funds that do not exist. With careful timing of deposits and withdrawals, this loan can be turned into a large sum.

**Clearing house:** an intermediary between buyers and sellers of financial instruments.

**The "cloud"**: internet-based computer storage that provides shared computer processing resources and data.

**Collateral**: a borrower's pledge of specific property to a lender to secure repayment of a loan.

**Collateralization**: the act whereby a borrower pledges an asset as recourse to a lender in the event that the borrower defaults on the initial loan.

**Contingent capital bonds (also known as bail-in bonds, contingent convertible bonds or CoCo bonds):** fixed-income instruments convertible into equity (shares in the company) if a prespecified trigger event occurs (e.g. bankruptcy).

**Counterparty risk**: the risk borne by each party to a contract that the other party or parties will not live up to their contractual obligations.

**Credit default swap**: a derivative designed to transfer the credit exposure of a fixed-income product (e.g. a mortgage with a fixed interest rate) between two or more parties.

**Cromnibus spending bill (2014)**: federal spending legislation combining a long-term omnibus spending bill with shorter-term continuing resolutions (which merely carry forward previous spending levels and don't allow for new programs to start or for new needs to be met).

**Cryptocurrency**: a digital or virtual currency that uses cryptography for security, making it difficult to counterfeit. A cryptocurrency is not issued by any central authority, making it theoretically immune to government interference or manipulation.

**Deleveraging**: decreasing total financial leverage (debt used to acquire additional assets), usually by paying off any existing debt.

**Derivative**: a security with a price that is dependent upon or derived from one or more underlying assets. Derivatives are sold as a form of insurance, but they are basically bets: one side bets the underlying asset will go up, the other bets it will go down.

**Distributed ledger**: a consensually shared database of digital data geographically spread across multiple sites, countries, or institutions, which operates without a central administrator or centralized data storage.

**Dodd-Frank (the Dodd-Frank Wall Street Reform and Consumer Protection Act of 2010)**: a massive piece of financial reform legislation passed by the Obama administration in 2010 in response to the financial crisis of 2008.

**Encrypted signature**: a digital file attached to an email or other electronic document that uses encryption and decryption algorithms to verify the document's origin and contents.

**Equity**: the value of an asset less the value of all liabilities attached to the asset.

**Excess reserves**: capital reserves held by a bank or financial institution in excess of what is required by regulators, creditors or internal controls.

**Federal Deposit Insurance Corporation (FDIC)**: the U.S. corporation insuring deposits in the United States against bank failure. The FDIC insures deposits of up to $250,000 per institution.

**Fed funds market**: excess reserves that commercial banks and other financial institutions deposit at regional Federal Reserve banks; these funds can then be lent to other market participants with insufficient money on hand to meet their lending and reserve needs. The loans are unsecured and are made at a relatively low interest rate, called the **federal funds rate** or overnight rate.

**Fiat**: currency that a government has declared to be legal tender but that is not backed by a physical commodity.

**Fractional reserve banking**: a banking system in which only a fraction of bank deposits are backed by actual cash on hand and available for withdrawal. Under the gold standard, fractional reserve banking referred to issuing more banknotes than the bank had on reserve to cover withdrawals.

**"Free" banking**: a monetary arrangement in which banks are subject to no special regulations beyond those applicable to most enterprises and are free to issue their own paper currency (banknotes).

**Gross domestic product** (GDP): the monetary value of all the finished goods and services produced within a country's borders in a specific time period.

**Glass-Steagall Act**: legislation passed by the US Congress in 1933 as the Banking Act, which prohibited commercial banks from participating in the investment banking business.

**Gold standard**: a monetary system in which a country's currency or paper money has a value directly linked to gold.

**Graham-Leach-Bliley Act (Financial Services Modernization Act of 1999)**: a regulation passed by Congress in 1999, the main effect of which was to repeal the Glass-Steagall Act.

**Hedge funds**: investment funds employing various strategies to earn high return for their investors. Hedge funds face less regulation than mutual funds and other investment vehicles.

**High-frequency trading:** a program trading platform that uses powerful computers to transact a large number of orders at very fast speeds, beating out other contenders.

**Leverage:** an investment strategy involving the use of borrowed money to generate larger returns.

**Liquid assets:** assets that can be converted into cash quickly, with minimal impact on the price received in the market.

**Liquidity:** the degree to which an asset or security can be quickly bought or sold in the market without affecting its price.

**Liquidity trap:** when people and businesses hold on to their money because expected returns from investments are low or they think a recession is beginning. They get trapped in a self-fulfilling prophecy that precipitates a liquidity crisis and recession.

**Mandatory stay:** in US bankruptcy law, an automatic injunction that halts actions by creditors, with certain exceptions, to collect debts from a debtor who has declared bankruptcy.

**Margin call:** a demand by a broker that an investor deposit further cash or securities to cover possible losses.

**Market maker:** one who assumes the risk of holding a certain number of shares of a particular security in order to facilitate the trading of that security. Market makers compete for customer orders by displaying buy and sell quotations for a guaranteed number of shares. The difference between the price at which a market maker is willing to buy a security and the price at which the firm is willing to sell it is called the market maker spread.

**Modern Monetary Theory (MMT):** a macroeconomic theory that describes and analyses modern economies in which the national currency is fiat money, established and created by the government. The key insight of MMT is that a "monetarily sovereign government is the monopoly supplier of its currency and can issue currency of any denomination in physical or nonphysical forms. As such the government has an unlimited capacity to pay for the things it wishes to purchase and to fulfill promised future payments, and has an unlimited ability to provide funds to the other sectors. Thus, insolvency and bankruptcy of this government is not possible. It can always pay."

**Monetize**: to convert an asset or other object into money or legal tender.

**Money center bank:** a very large commercial bank, usually head-quartered in a large gateway city, which earns a substantial portion of its revenue from transactions with governments, big businesses, and other banks.

**Money market**: an organized exchange on which participants can lend and borrow large sums of money for a period of one year or less.

**Naked short selling**: when an investor sells shares short (sell shares he doesn't own) before actually borrowing them or determining if they can be borrowed.

**Nationalization:** the process by which a government takes control of a company or industry, usually without compensation to the company for the loss of the seized assets and potential income.

**Neoclassical economics**: the currently dominant school of economic thought, ostensibly built on the foundation laid by 18th century classical economists. It is "classical" in the sense that it based on the belief that competition leads to an efficient allocation of resources, with regulation of economic activity to establish equilibrium between demand and supply through the operation of market forces. It is "neo" in the sense that it departs sharply from the classical viewpoint in its analytic approach, which places great emphasis on mathematical techniques.

**Netting (of derivatives)**: offsetting the value of multiple positions or payments due between two or more parties. Netting can be used to determine which party is owed remuneration in a multiparty agreement.

**Open market operations**: the buying and selling of government securities in the open market in order to expand or contract the amount of money in the banking system. It is the most common tool the Federal Reserve uses to implement and control monetary policy.

**Open source**: a computer program whose source code is made available for use or modification as users or other developers see fit. Open source software is usually developed as a public collaboration and made freely available.

**Orderly liquidation (versus disorderly liquidation)**: Liquidation is an event that usually occurs when a company is insolvent, meaning it cannot pay its obligations as and when due. In an "orderly liquidation," the company's operations are brought to an end and its assets are divided up among creditors and shareholders according to the priority of their claims. In a "disorderly liquidation," a rush to grab the collateral precipitates defaults and bankruptcies in related companies, with the potential to cause an economic crisis.

**Over-the-counter derivative**: a type of financial derivative that is directly negotiated between two parties rather than through an exchange.

**"Peer-to-peer" lending** (sometimes abbreviated **P2P lending**): the practice of lending money to individuals or businesses through online services that match lenders directly with borrowers.

**Portfolio management**: the process of managing the assets of a mutual fund or other investment vehicle, including choosing and monitoring appropriate investments and allocating funds accordingly.

**Primary dealer**: a firm that buys government securities directly from a government, with the intention of reselling them to others.

**Prime broker**: a broker servicing large, active trading operations such as hedge funds. A prime broker can be thought of as a sort of central broker, facilitating and coordinating extensive, complex trading in a variety of financial instruments. Prime brokerage services are provided by major investment banks such as Merrill Lynch and Goldman Sachs.

**Push-out rule**: a rule requiring certain types of derivatives to be pushed out of the insured arm of a bank into another arm or entity that does not benefit from federal backing.

**Real-time execution**: instantaneous completion.

**Rehypothecation**: the practice by banks and brokers of using, for their own purposes, assets that have been posted as collateral by their clients.

**Repo** (also known as repurchase agreement): a form of short-term borrowing for dealers in government securities. The dealer sells the government securities to investors, usually on an overnight basis, and buys them back the following day.

**Retail banking** (also known as consumer banking): the typical mass-market banking in which individual customers use local banks or branches of larger commercial banks.

**Reverse repo:** the purchase of securities with the agreement to sell them at a higher price at a specific future date.

**Risk-weighted assets**: assets used to determine the minimum amount of capital that must be held by banks and other institutions to reduce the risk of insolvency.

**Safe harbor**: a provision that affords protection from liability or penalty under specified circumstances.

**Savings and loan association**: a federally chartered institution whose purpose is to collect savings deposits and provide residential mortgage loans.

**Security:** an investment instrument (other than an insurance policy or fixed annuity) issued by a corporation, government, or other organization, which offers evidence of debt or equity.

**Securitization**: aggregating similar instruments, such as loans or mortgages, into a negotiable security.

**Shadow banking system:** financial intermediaries not subject to regulatory oversight involved in facilitating the creation of credit across the global financial system. It also refers to unregulated activities by regulated institutions.

**Shell game:** a confidence trick used to perpetrate fraud.

**Smart contract:** a computerized transaction protocol intended to contribute to, verify or implement the negotiation or performance of a contract. Smart contracts allow the performance of trackable, irreversible transactions without third parties. They contain all required information about contract terms, and they execute the envisaged actions automatically.[563]

**Super-priority in bankruptcy**: the right of certain creditors of a bankrupt debtor to receive payment before others who would seem to have superior claims to money or assets.

**Swap**: derivative contracts entered into by companies, banks, financial institutions, and other organizations for the purpose of reducing risk. They include **interest rate swaps**, which can effectively turn fixed-rate debt into floating rate debt or vice versa; and **currency swaps**, which can reduce the chance of a major currency move making it much harder to pay off a debt in another country's currency. If properly structured, swaps can act as a form of insurance that offsets and stabilizes cash flows, assets, and liabilities. The major dangers are **counter-party risk** (failure of the party or parties on the other side of the contract to pay) and overly complex, opaque terms that wind up imposing unanticipated losses on the "insured" (notably local governments).

**Systemic risk**: the possibility that an event at the company level could trigger severe instability or could collapse an entire industry or economy.

**Systemically important financial institution**: any firm so designated by the US Federal Reserve, whose collapse would pose a serious risk to the economy.

**Trading portfolio**: the various financial instruments held by an investor.

**Uncleared derivatives**: derivative trades that take place between two counterparties directly rather than through an exchange.

**Unconditional basic income (also called basic income guarantee or universal basic income)**: a form of social security in which all citizens or residents of a country regularly receive an unconditional sum of money, either from a government or from some other public institution, in addition to any income received from elsewhere.

**Venture capitalist**: an investor who either provides capital to start-up ventures or supports small companies that wish to expand but do not have access to equities (stock) markets.

**Wholesale banking**: the provision of services by banks to large corporate clients, mortgage brokers, real estate developers and investors, international trade finance businesses, institutional customers (such as pension funds and government entities or agencies), and services offered to other banks or other financial institutions.

**Wholesale finance**: financial services conducted between financial service companies and institutions such as banks, insurers, fund managers, and stockbrokers. Modern wholesale banks engage in finance wholesaling, underwriting, market making, consultancy, mergers and acquisitions, and fund management.

**Wholesale funding**: a method used by banks in addition to core demand deposits to finance operations and manage risk. Wholesale funding sources include, among others: federal funds, public funds (those from state and local municipalities), US Federal Home Loan Bank advances, the US Federal Reserve's primary credit program, foreign deposits, and brokered deposits.

**Wildcat banking:** the banking industry in the United States from 1837 to 1865, when banks were chartered by state law without federal oversight. They often issued their own banknotes (promissory notes) without having sufficient gold to back them.

**Zombie banks**: a bank or financial institution with negative net worth, which continues to operate as a result of government backing or bailouts.

## NOTES

1 Paul Buchheit, "Morbid Inequality: Now Just SIX Men Have as Much Wealth as Half the World's Population," *Common Dreams*, 20 February 2017, https://www.commondreams.org/views/2017/02/20/morbid-inequality-now-just-six-men-have-much-wealth-half-worlds-population

2 "The 2008 Housing Crisis Displaced More Americans than the 1930s Dust Bowl," *National Center for Policy Analysis*, 11 May 2015, http://www.ncpa.org/sub/dpd/index.php?Article_ID=25643; Jim Puzzanghera, "Economy Has Recovered 8.7 Million Jobs Lost in Great Recession," *Los Angeles Times*, 6 June 2014, http://www.latimes.com/business/la-fi-jobs-20140607-story.html

3 Quoted in Irving Fisher, *100% Money* (Foreword), Adelphi Co, 1936, reprinted by Pickering and Chatto, Ltd (now Routledge) (full text online at: fisher-100money.blogspot.fr).

4 Patricia Buckley, Rumki Majumdar, "In Whose Interest? Examining the Impact of an Interest Rate Hike," *Deloitte University Press*, June 2016, http://www.businessinsider.com/yellen-speech-at-harvard-may-27z-2016-5

5 Hal Boedeker, "Bernanke: 2008 Crisis Worse than Great Depression," *Orlando Sentinel*, 25 September 2015, http://www.orlandosentinel.com/entertainment/tv/tv-guy/os-bernanke-2008-financial-crisis-was-worst-20150925-post.html; Peter Ryan, Kim Landers, "I Didn't See Subprime Crisis Coming: Greenspan," *ABC News Australia*, 17 September 2007, http://www.abc.net.au/news/2007-09-17/i-didnt-see-subprime-crisis-coming-greenspan/672120

6 "Shadow Banking System," *Investopedia*, https://www.investopedia.com/terms/s/shadow-banking-system.asp

7 "Making Money from Making Money: Seigniorage in the Modern Economy," *New Economics Foundation*, 31 January 2017, http://neweconomics.org/2017/01/making-money-making-money/

8    "Federal Reserve Reform, Tim Canova," *Chapman Business Report*, 31 January 2012, https://www.youtube.com/watch?v=sv-UUjF0tnM

9    "Federal Reserve FAQs: About the Fed," *Federal Reserve*, https://www.federalreserve.gov/faqs/about-the-fed.htm

10   Kimberly Amadeo, "Federal Reserve Board of Governors and Its Members: Who Really Controls the Fed?," *The Balance*, 26 October 2018, https://www.thebalance.com/what-is-the-federal-reserve-board-3305527; "10 Years After: The Financial Crisis and the New York Federal Reserve District," *Center for Popular Democracy*, 8 March 2018, https://populardemocracy.org/news/publications/10-years-after-financial-crisis-and-new-york-federal-reserve-district

11   "10 Years After," op. cit..; "Federal Reserve FAQs: About the Fed," op. cit.

12   "10 Years After," op. cit.

13   Matthew Boesler, "Phillips Curve Doesn't Help Forecast Inflation, Fed Study Finds," *Bloomberg*, 24 August 2017, https://www.bloomberg.com/news/articles/2017-08-24/phillips-curve-doesn-t-help-forecast-inflation-fed-study-finds; Nick Bunker, "Is the Fed Being Misguided by the Phillips Curve?," *Washington Center for Equitable Growth*, 21 June 2017, http://equitablegrowth.org/equitablog/value-added/is-the-fed-being-misguided-by-the-phillips-curve/; "Transcript of Chair Yellen's Press Conference," *FederalReserve.gov*, 14 June 2017, https://www.federalreserve.gov/mediacenter/files/FOMCpresconf20170614.pdf; Rethinking Macroeconomic Policy Conference, *Peterson Institute*, 13 October 2017, https://www.youtube.com/watch?time_continue=6106&v=vLSNp9UOVu0

14   Neel Kashkari, "Why I Dissented Again," *Medium*, 16 June 2017, https://medium.com/@neelkashkari/why-i-dissented-again-b8579ab664b7

15   John C. Williams' Speeches, "The Federal Reserve's Mandate and Best Practice Monetary Policy," *Federal Reserve Board of San Francisco*, 13 February 2012, https://www.frbsf.org/our-district/press/presidents-speeches/williams-speeches/2012/february/williams-federal-reserve-mandate-best-practice-monetary-policy/

16   Frances Coppola, "The Fed's Interest Rate Rise Was A Mistake," *Forbes*, 27 September 2018, https://www.forbes.com/sites/francescoppola/2018/09/27/the-feds-interest-rate-rise-was-a-mistake/#3a300cc92dc8

**17**   J. W. Mason, "What Recovery? The Case for Continued Expansionary Policy at the Fed," *Roosevelt Institute*, 25 July 2017, http://rooseveltinstitute.org/wp-content/uploads/2017/07/Monetary-Policy-Report.pdf

**18**   Manoj Singh, "The 2007-08 Financial Crisis In Review," *Investopedia*, https://www.investopedia.com/articles/economics/09/financial-crisis-review.as

**19**   "How Banks Make Money in Derivatives," *Capital Institute*, 19 December 2010, http://capitalinstitute.org/blog/how-banks-make-money-derivatives/

**20**   Kevin DeMeritt, "$1.14 Quadrillion in Derivatives—What Goes Up ... ," Gold-Eagle.com (June 16, 2008).

**21**   Roger Arnold, "We Can See the End of Growth from the View of 'Peak Debt,'" *The Street*, 23 March 2016, http://realmoney.thestreet.com/articles/03/23/2016/we-can-see-end-growth-view-peak-debt

**22**   John Aidan Byrne, "Next Crash Will Be 'Worse Than the Great Depression': Experts," New York Post, 22 September 2018, https://nypost.com/2018/09/22/next-crash-will-be-worse-than-the-great-depression-experts/; Nomi Prins, "The Next Financial Crisis Will Be Worse Than the Last," NomiPrins.com, 31 December 2017, http://www.nomiprins.com/thoughts/2017/12/31/the-next-financial-crisis-will-be-worse-than-the-last.html

**23**   Robert Barone, "Fed Tightening Has Frighteningly High Correlation To Subsequent Recessions," *Forbes*, 17 March 2017, https://www.forbes.com/sites/greatspeculations/2017/03/17/fed-tightening-has-frighteningly-high-correlation-to-subsequent-recessions/#119481ba4b99

**24**   "Libor's Rise Matters for Trillions of Debt," Liz McCormick, Bloomberg, 13 December 2017, https://www.bloomberg.com/news/articles/2017-12-13/love-it-or-hate-it-libor-s-rise-matters-for-trillions-of-debt

**25**   Ben Eisen and Chelsey Dulaney, "Libor's Rise Accelerates, Squeezing Short-Term Borrowers," *Wall Street Journal*, 27 March 2018, https://www.wsj.com/articles/libors-rise-accelerates-squeezing-short-term-borrowers-1522152000

**26**   "The Debt to the Penny and Who Holds It," *Treasury Direct*, April 2018, https://treasurydirect.gov/govt/reports/pd/debttothepenny.htm

27   Aaron Hankin, "How Will the Fed Reduce its Balance Sheet?", *Investopedia*, 20 September 2017, https://www.investopedia.com/insights/how-will-fed-reduce-balance-sheet/

28   P. Buckley, et al., op. cit.; Jeanne Sahadi, "Interest Payments on US Debt Could Top $1 Trillion," *CNN Money*, 15 March 2018, https://money.cnn.com/2018/03/15/news/economy/interest-on-the-debt/index.html

29   Beardsley Ruml, "Taxes for Revenue Are Obsolete," *American Affairs*, Jan 1946, Winter Number, Vol VIII, No 1, pages 35 ff, http://www.constitution.org/tax/us-ic/cmt/ruml_obsolete.pdf

30   Devin Smith, "MMT and Debunking AMI: Positive Money," *New Economic Perspectives*, 4 February 2017, http://neweconomicperspectives.org/2017/02/mmt-debunking-ami-postive-money.html

31   "Performing Services for the U.S Treasury," *Federal Reserve Bank of Philadelphia*, https://www.philadelphiafed.org/about-the-fed/who-we-are/treasury-services; "Federal Reserve Banks as Depositaries and Fiscal Agents of United States," *Federal Reserve Act*, Sec. 15 (1), https://www.federalreserve.gov/aboutthefed/section15.htm; Cullen Roche, "Modern Monetary Theory (MMT) Critique," *Pragmatic Capitalism*, 7 September 2011, https://www.pragcap.com/modern-monetary-theory-mmt-critique/

32   Kenneth Garbade, "Direct Purchases of U.S. Treasury Securities by Federal Reserve Banks," *New York Federal Reserve*, Staff Report No. 684, August 2014, https://www.newyorkfed.org/medialibrary/media/research/staff_reports/sr684.pdf

33   Marco Cagetti, et al., "Federal Debt in the Financial Accounts of the United States," *FederalReserve.gov*, 8 October 2015, https://www.federalreserve.gov/econresdata/notes/feds-notes/2015/federal-debt-in-the-financial-accounts-of-the-united-states-20151008.html; Institute for Policy Studies, "Borrowing and the Federal Debt," *National Priorities Project*, https://www.nationalpriorities.org/budget-basics/federal-budget-101/borrowing-and-federal-debt/

34   K. Garbade, op. cit., page 9.

35   Richard Kotlarz, "The Iraq War and the Rest of the American Revolution," *EconomicTree.org*, 2 May 2011, http://economictree.org/Iraq_Am_Revolution2.html

36   "An Act To Amend The Federal Reserve Act, And For Other Purposes," Hearing Before the Committee on Banking and Currency, House of Representatives Eightieth Congress First Session, On

H. R. 2233, Superseded by H. R. 2413, March 3-5, 1947, quoted by John Hemington in "Why We Don't Understand Money and Debt—And Why It's Important that We Do," *Public Banking Institute*, 30 September 2015, http://www.publicbankinginstitute.org/why_we_don_t_understand_money_and_debt_and_why_it_s_important_that_we_do

**37**  Jerry Voorhis, *The Strange Case of Richard Milhaus Nixon* (Paul S. Ercksson, Publisher, 1972).

**38**  Matt Clinch, "It''s Time for the World to End Its Debt-Fueled Growth Model: BIS," *CNBC*, 22 June 2016. http://www.cnbc.com/2016/06/22/bis-its-time-for-the-word-to-end-its-debt-fueled-growth-model.html

**39**  Michael Corkery, "Minneapolis Fed Chief Proposes Eliminating Too Big to Fail Banks," *New York Times Deal Book*, 17 November 2016, https://www.nytimes.com/2016/11/17/business/dealbook/minneapolis-fed-chief-proposes-eliminating-too-big-to-fail-banks.html?_r=0

**40**  John Aidan Byrne, op. cit.; Nomi Prins, op. cit.

**41**  David Kupelian, "Bernanke: Federal Reserve Caused Great Depression," *World Net Daily*, 19 March 2008, http://www.wnd.com/2008/03/59405/

**42**  "Then and Now: Fed Policy Actions During the Great Depression and Great Recession," *St. Louis Federal Reserve*," November 2011, https://research.stlouisfed.org/pageone-economics/uploads/newsletter/2011/Lib1111ClassrmEdition.pdf; John Stossel, "It's Time to Put the Federal Reserve Out of Business," *Fox News*, http://www.foxnews.com/opinion/2013/10/30/it-time-to-put-federal-reserve-out-business.html

**43**  Steve Mariotti, "When Owning Gold Was Illegal in America: And Why It Could Be Again," *Huffington Post*, 27 June 2016, https://www.huffingtonpost.com/steve-mariotti/when-owning-gold-was-ille_b_10708196.html

**44**  D. Kupelian, op. cit.

**45**  "Volcker's Announcement of Anti-Inflation Measures," *Federal Reserve History*, https://www.federalreservehistory.org/essays/anti_inflation_measures

**46**  Robert Guttman, *How Credit-money Shapes the Economy* (M.E. Sharpe: New York, 1994), pages 242-244.

**47**    William Black, *The Best Way to Rob a Bank is to Own One* (Austin: University of Texas Press 2005); Kenneth Robinson, "Savings and Loan Crisis," *Federal Reserve History*, 22 November, 2013, http:// www.federalreservehistory.org/Events/DetailView/42;

**48**    "Killer Derivatives, Zombie CDOs and Basel Too?", Institutional Risk Analytics (August 14, 2007); Gary Anderson, "Hoarding the New Gold: Early History about Structured Finance," *Talk Markets*, 27 July 2016, http://www.talkmarkets.com/content/ bonds/hoarding-the-new-gold-early-history-about-structured-finance?post=101531&uid=4798

**49**    Martin Neil Baily, Aaron Klein, "It's Time for Sensible Regulation of Derivatives," Brookings, 23 January 2013,https://www.brookings. edu/opinions/its-time-for-sensible-regulation-of-derivatives/

**50**    "Banks Don't Do Much Banking Anymore—and That's a Serious Problem," *Pacific Standard*, 3 February 2014, https://psmag.com/ banks-don-t-do-much-banking-anymore-and-that-s-a-serious-problem-d9c1fe47d0a8#.coilgjb2n

**51**    Matt Egan, "5,300 Wells Fargo Employees Fired Over 2 Million Phony Accounts," 8 September 2016, http://money.cnn. com/2016/09/08/investing/wells-fargo-created-phony-accounts-bank-fees/

**52**    California Reinvestment Coalition, "Small Business Access to Credit — The Little Engine that Could: If Banks Helped," *calreinvest. org*, December 2013, http://calreinvest.org/system/resources/W1si-ZiIsIjIwMTMvMTIvMjMvMTdfMTNfNTJfOTQzX0NSQ19T-bWFsbF9CdXNpbmVzc19SZXBvcnRfMjAxMy5wZGYiXV0/ CRC%20Small%20Business%20Report%202013.pdf

**53**    Federal Reserve Bank of St. Louis, "Commercial Banks in the U.S. with Average Assets Under $100M," 18 August 2018, https://fred. stlouisfed.org/series/US100NUM

**54**    Carrie Sheffield, "The Little Black Book of Billionaire Secrets: Dodd-Frank Is Killing Community Banks," *Forbes*, 9 February 2015, https://www.forbes.com/sites/carriesheffield/2015/02/09/ dodd-frank-is-killing-community-banks/#174d767973a7; Juan Cole, "Why Rand Paul Was Right to Kill the So-Called Patriot Act: It Was Never About Terrorism," *Truthdig*, 1 June 2015, https:// www.truthdig.com/articles/why-rand-paul-was-right-to-kill-the-so-called-patriot-act-it-was-never-about-terrorism/

**55**    Brewster Kahle, "Bank Secrecy Act = Bank Surveillance Act,"

*Brewster Kahle's Blog*, 18 November 2013, http://brewster.kahle.
org/2013/11/18/bank-secrecy-act-bank-surveillance-act/

**56**  Richard Newman, "9/11 and Patriot Act Changed the Way You
Bank," *App.com (USA Today)*, 8 September 2016,http://www.app.
com/story/money/business/main-street/2016/09/08/911-patriot-
act-banks/90003828/

**57**  Matthew L. Schwartz, Jaime Sneider, "Should Banks Be Criminally
Liable for Not Reporting Fishy Emails?", *American Banker*, 19 April
2017, https://www.americanbanker.com/opinion/should-banks-be-
criminally-liable-for-not-reporting-fishy-emails

**58**  Shea Dittrich, "How Basel III Capital Requirements Hurt Community Banks," *American Banker*, 26 September 2012, https://
www.americanbanker.com/opinion/how-basel-iii-capital-require-
ments-hurt-community-banks

**59**  Charles Levinson, "How Wall Street Captured Washington's Effort
to Rein in Banks," *Reuters*, 9 April 2015, http://www.reuters.com/
investigates/special-report/usa-bankrules-weakening/

**60**  Richard Morris, Monica Reyes Grajales, "The FDIC's New Capital
Rules and Their Expected Impact on Community Banks," *Mondaq*,
6 October 2014, http://www.mondaq.com/unitedstates/x/344612/
Financial+Services/The+FDICs+New+Capital+Rules+And+Their+-
Expected+Impact+On+Community+Banks

**61**  Ryan Smith, "On Its Fifth Anniversary, Hensarling Slams Dodd-
Frank," *MPA Magazine*, 22 July 2015, http://www.mpamag.com/
news/on-its-fifth-anniversary-hensarling-slams-doddfrank-23302.
aspx

**62**  Trump Signs the Biggest Rollback of Bank Rules Since the
Financial Crisis," *CNBC*, 24 May 2018, https://www.cnbc.
com/2018/05/24/trump-signs-bank-bill-rolling-back-some-dodd-
frank-regulations.html

**63**  Satyajit Das, "Opinion: The Bigger Banks Get, the Harder We
Will Fall," *Market Watch*, 10 February 2017 https://www.mar-
ketwatch.com/story/the-bigger-banks-get-the-harder-we-will-
fall-2017-02-10

**64**  Rachel Ensign, "Biggest Three Banks Gobble Up $2.4 Trillion in
New Deposits Since Crisis," *Wall Street Journal*, 22 March 2018,
https://www.wsj.com/articles/biggest-three-banks-gobble-up-2-4-
trillion-in-new-deposits-since-crisis-1521711001

65  "Need a Corporate Loan? Forget Your Bank—Tap the Shadow Banking System Instead," *Sober Look*, 12 November 2013, http://soberlook.com/2013/11/need-corporate-loan-forget-your-bank.html

66  "Big Banks Are Fleeing the Mortgage Market," *Market Watch*, 12 Feb 2016, http://www.marketwatch.com/story/big-banks-are-fleeing-the-mortgage-market-2016-02-12.

67  Marcy Gordon, "Regulator: Shrink Freddie Mac, Fannie Mae," *Associated Press*, 5 March 5, 2013, http://www.usatoday.com/story/money/business/2013/03/05/fannie-freddie-combine/1964227/

68  Gara Afonso, , et al., "Who's Lending in the Fed Funds Market?," *Liberty Street Economics, New York Fed*, 2 December 2013, http://libertystreeteconomics.newyorkfed.org/2013/12/whos-lending-in-the-fed-funds-market.html

69  Stephen Gandel, "By Every Measure, the Big Banks Are Bigger," *Fortune*, 6 November 2015, http://fortune.com/2013/09/13/by-every-measure-the-big-banks-are-bigger/

70  John Cassidy, "What Good Is Wall Street?", *The New Yorker*, 29 November 2010, http://www.newyorker.com/magazine/2010/11/29/what-good-is-wall-street

71  Board of Governors of the Federal Reserve System, "Report to the Congress on the Profitability of Credit Card Operations of Depository Institutions," *FederalReserve.gov*, June 2013, https://www.federalreserve.gov/publications/other-reports/files/ccprofit2013.pdf

72  Fred Williams, "Fed: Credit Card Banking Remains Highly Profitable," *CreditCards.com*, 13 June 2016, http://www.creditcards.com/credit-card-news/card-issuer-bank-profit.php

73  "Average Household Credit Card Balance Tops $16,000 in 2016," *Talk Business & Politics*, 19 December 2016, http://talkbusiness.net/2016/12/money-talk-average-household-credit-card-balance-tops-16000-in-2016/

74  Stacy Mitchell, "Soaring Credit Card Transaction Fees Squeeze Independent Businesses," *Institute for Local Self-Reliance*, 5 May 2009, https://ilsr.org/soaring-credit-card-transaction-fees-squeeze-independent-businesses/; Jennifer Surane and Christopher Cannon, "Why China's Payment Apps Give U.S. Bankers Nightmares," *Bloomberg*, 23 May 2018, https://www.bloomberg.com/graphics/2018-payment-systems-china-usa/

75  Justin Lahart, "Number of the Week: Finance's Share of Economy

Continues to Grow," *Wall Street Journal*, 10 December 2011, https://blogs.wsj.com/economics/2011/12/10/number-of-the-week-finances-share-of-economy-continues-to-grow/

**76**  Ibid.

**77**  "Know the Facts," *Campaign for Postal Banking*, May 2015, http://www.campaignforpostalbanking.org/wp-content/uploads/2015/05/KnowtheFacts.pdf

**78**  "Need a Corporate Loan?", *Sober Look*, op. cit.

**79**  Ianthe Dugan, "As Banks Retreat, Hedge Funds Smell Profit," *Wall Street Journal*, 22 July 2013, http://www.wsj.com/news/articles/SB10001424127887324637504578567383459564510

**80**  Sheila Bair, "Is BlackRock Too Big to Fail?", *Fortune*, 4 December 2013, http://fortune.com/2013/12/04/is-blackrock-too-big-to-fail/

**81**  "Why the 'Living Wills' of Top US Banks Failed the Test," *Wharton*, 18 April 2016, Http://knowledge.wharton.upenn.edu/article/why-the-living-wills-of-top-u-s-banks-failed-the-test/

**82**  Pam Martens and Russ Martens, "The Fed Sends a Frightening Letter to JPMorgan and Corporate Media Yawns," *Wall Street on Parade*, 14 April 2016, http://wallstreetonparade.com/2016/04/the-fed-sends-a-frightening-letter-to-jpmorgan-and-corporate-media-yawns/

**83**  Editorial Board, "Bank Health, Imperiled," *New York Times*, 3 July 2017, https://www.nytimes.com/2017/07/03/opinion/federal-reserve-banks-stress

**84**  Office of the Comptroller of the Currency, "Quarterly Report on Bank Trading and Derivatives Activities," *OCC.gov*, First Quarter 2016, https://www.occ.gov/topics/capital-markets/financial-markets/derivatives/dq116.pdf

**85**  Michael Moore, Elizabeth Dexheimer, "J.P. Morgan to Cut $100 Billion of Deposits to Limit Capital," *Bloomberg*, 24 February 2015, http://www.bloomberg.com/news/articles/2015-02-24/jpmorgan-to-cut-100-billion-of-deposits-to-limit-capital-needs

**86**  "Is It Time to Panic about Deutsche Bank?", *Zero Hedge*, 4 February 2016, http://www.zerohedge.com/news/2016-02-03/it-time-panic-about-deutsche-bank

**87**  "Warren Buffett on Derivatives," excerpts from Berkshire Hathaway annual report for 2002, *FinTools.com*, http://www.fintools.com/docs/Warren%20Buffet%20on%20Derivatives.pdf

**88** Frederick Lantz, "New Challenges for Keeping Public Money Safe," *Governing*, 30 October 2014, http://www.governing.com/gov-institute/voices/col-banks-collateral-insurance-protecting-public-deposits.html

**89** Caitlin Long, "Why Financial Regulators Are Warming to Blockchains—And Rightfully So," *Alt-M*, 26 Apr 2016. http://www.alt-m.org/2016/04/26/why-financial-regulators-are-warming-to-blockchains-and-rightfully-so/

**90** R. Waldman, op. cit.

**91** Michael McLeay, et al, "Money Creation in the Modern Economy, *Bank of England*, Q1 2014, http://www.bankofengland.co.uk/publications/Documents/quarterlybulletin/2014/qb14q1prerelease-moneycreation.pdf; "How Money Is Created," *Deutsche Bundesbank*, 25 April 2017, http://www.bundesbank.de/Redaktion/EN/Topics/2017/2017_04_25_how_money_is_created.html?startpageId=Startseite-EN&startpageAreaId=Teaserbereich&startpageLinkName=2017_04_25_how_money_is_created+397964

**92** McLeay, et al., op. cit.

**93** Zoltan Jakab, Michael Kumhof, "Banks Are Not Intermediaries of Loanable Funds—and Why This Matters," *VOX*, 18 Jun 2015, www.voxeu.org/article/banks-are-not-loanable-funds-intermediaries-macroeconomic-implications

**94** David Graeber, "The Truth Is Out: Money Is Just an IOU, and the Banks Are Rolling in It," *The Guardian*, 18 Mar 2014, www.theguardian.com/commentisfree/2014/mar/18/truth-money-iou-bank-of-england-austerity

**95** "Endogenous Versus Exogenous Money, One More Time," *Unlearning Economics*, 9 September 2012, https://unlearningeconomics.wordpress.com/2012/09/22/endogenous-versus-exogenous-money-one-more-time/

**96** See summary in "Debt: The First 5000 Years," *Wikipedia*, https://en.wikipedia.org/wiki/Debt:_The_First_5000_Years

**97** Perry Mehrling, "Financialization and Its Discontents," *Institute for New Economic Thinking*, 2 August 2016, https://www.ineteconomics.org/perspectives/blog/financialization-and-its-dicontents

**98** William Hummel, "In Defense of Private Banking," *Money: What It Is, How It Works*, 2 March 2016, http://wfhummel.net/private-banking.html; Scott Fullwiler, James Leach, "Krugman's Flashing

Neon Sign," *New Economic Perspectives*, 1 April 2012, www.neweconomicperspectives.org/2012/04/krugmans-flashing-neon-sign.html

**99**   Tim Worstall, "The Financial Transactions Tax Will Just Kill the Banking Economy,"*Forbes*, 8 May 2013, www.forbes.com/sites/timworstall/2013/05/08/the-financial-transaction-tax-will-just-kill-the-banking-economy/

**100**   Richard Werner, "How Do Banks Create Money, and Why Can Other Firms Not Do the Same? An Explanation for the Coexistence of Lending and Deposit-Taking," *International Review of Financial Analysis* 36:71-77, December 2014, http://www.sciencedirect.com/science/article/pii/s1057521914001434; Richard Werner, "Can Banks Individually Create Money Out of Nothing?—The Theories and Empirical Evidence,"15 July 2014, *ScienceDirect*, www.sciencedirect.com/science/article/pii/S1057521914001070

**101**   Adam Levitin, "Safe Banking: Finance and Democracy," *University of Chicago Law Review* 83(1):357-455, December 2016, https://www.researchgate.net/publication/301584705_Safe_Banking_Finance_and_Democracy

**102**   R. Werner, "Can Banks Individually Create Money Out of Nothing?", op. cit.

**103**   Bernard Lietaer, "Beyond Greed and Scarcity," *Yes! Magazine*, 30 June 1997, http://www.yesmagazine.org/issues/money-print-your-own/beyond-greed-and-scarcity (paragraphs transposed).

**104**   Tax Justice Network 2012, "Revealed: Global Super-Rich Has at Least $21 Trillion Hidden in Secret Tax Havens," *Taxjustice*, 19 Jul 2012, http://www.taxjustice.net/cms/upload/pdf/The_Price_of_Offshore_Revisited_Presser_120722.pdf

**105**   Mary Mellor, *The Future of Money: From Financial Crisis to Public Resource* (London: Pluto Press 2010), https://www.amazon.com/Future-Money-Financial-Crisis-Resource/dp/0745329942/ref=sr_1_1

**106**   Derryl Hermanutz, The Road to Debt Bondage: How Banks Create Unpayable Debt (CreateSpace, August 2018).

**107**   Michael Hudson, *And Forgive Them Their Debts: Lending, Foreclosure and Redemption — From Bronze Age Finance to the Jubilee Year* (ISLET-Verlag Dresden, 2018), https://michael-hudson.com/2018/08/and-forgive-them-their-debts/

**108**   Paul Sheard, "Repeat After Me: Banks Cannot and Do Not 'Lend Out' Reserves," *Standard & Poor's*, 14 August 2013, https://www.

kreditopferhilfe.net/docs/S_and_P__Repeat_After_Me_8_14_13. pdf

**109** Joseph Huber, "Split-Circuit Reserve Banking—Functioning, Dysfunctions and Future Perspectives," *Real-World Economics Review*, issue no. 80, 26 June 2017, pp. 63-84, http://www.paecon.net/ PAEReview/issue80/Huber80.pdf

**110** Jamie Merchant, "We Don't Need to Break Up The Big Banks. We Need to Put Them Under Democratic Control," *In These Times*, 2 February 2016, http://inthesetimes.com/article/18816/big-banks-too-big-to-fail-nationalize-democratize-finance

**111** Financial Deepening Without Financial Excesses," Speech by Hervé Hannoun, BIS 43rd SEACEN Governors' Conference, Jakarta, 21 March 2008, http://www.bis.org/speeches/sp080403.pdf

**112** Melanie Fein, "The Shadow Banking Charade," *Social Science Research Network*, 15 February 2013, http://papers.ssrn.com/sol3/ papers.cfm?abstract_id=2218812

**113** Gillian Tett, "Web of Shadow Banking Must Be Unravelled," *Financial Times*, 12 August 2010, https://www.ft.com/content/112ff210-a62b-11df-9cb9-00144feabdc0

**114** "Desperately Seeking $11.2 Trillion in Collateral, or How 'Modern Money' Really Works," *Zero Hedge*, 1 May 2013, http://www.zero-hedge.com/news/2013-05-01/desperately-seeking-112-trillion-collateral-or-how-modern-money-really-works

**115** Manmohan Singh, "Collateral Flows and Balance Sheet(s) Space," Federal Reserve Board of Atlanta, 15 July 2016, https://www.frbatlanta.org/-/media/Documents/news/conferences/2016/1201-impact-of-extraordinary-monetary-policy-on-the-financial-sector/ papers/singh-collateral-flows-and-balance-sheets-space.pdf

**116** "Re-use of Collateral Is Major Tool for Leveraged Finance," *RepoWatch*, 1 August 2010, https://repowatch.org/2010/08/01/re-use-of-collateral-is-major-tool-for-leveraged-financing/

**117** Mary Fricker, "About Repo," *Repowatch.org*, 7 April 2011, updated 4 March 2017, https://repowatch.org/about-repo/.

**118** Gary Gorton, "Questions and Answers about the Financial Crisis," *National Bureau of Economic Research*, February 2010, http://www. nber.org/papers/w15787

**119** Enrico Perotti, "The Roots of Shadow Banking," *Voxeu.org*, December 2013, http://voxeu.org/sites/default/files/file/PolicyInsight69.pdf

**120** "Did JPM's CIO Intentionally Start the Margin Call Avalanche that Crushed Lehman?," 3March 2013, *Zero Hedge* http://www.zero-hedge.com/news/2013-03-03/did-jpms-cio-intentionally-and-mali-ciously-start-margin-call-avalanche-crushed-lehma

**121** M. Fricker, op. cit., citations omitted.

**122** M. Fricker, op. cit.

**123** Dominic Elliott, "Regional Banks Grab Hold of Repo Grenade," *Reuters*, 10 November 2015, https://www.breakingviews.com/con-sidered-view/regional-banks-grab-hold-of-repo-grenade/; Robert M. Smith, "L'exception Française: Why French Banks Dominate US Repo Trading," *Risk.net*, 1 September 2016, https://www.risk.net/derivatives/2469133/lexception-francaise-why-french-banks-domi-nate-us-repo-trading

**124** William Hummel, "The Money Market," *Money: What It Is, How It Works*, 15 October 1999, http://wfhummel.net/moneymarket.html

**125** George Blackburne, "Commercial Loans and Money Center Banks," *Loans.com*, 18 Jan 2016, http://info.c-loans.com/commercial-loans-and-money-center-banks

**126** W. Hummel, op. cit.

**127** G. Gorton, op. cit.

**128** M. Fricker, op. cit.

**129** Ibid.

**130** Ibid.

**131** Jo Michell, "Do Shadow Banks Create Money? 'Financialisation' and the Monetary Circuit," *PKSG*, March 2016, https://www.post-keynesian.net/downloads/working-papers/PKWP1605.pdf

**132** Manmohan Singh, James Aitken, "The (Sizable) Role of Rehypoth-ecation in the Shadow Banking System," *IMF.org*, July 2010, http://www.imf.org/external/pubs/ft/wp/2010/wp10172.pdf

**133** Bryan Noeth, Rajdeep Sengupta, "Is Shadow Banking Really Bank-ing?," *St. Louis Federal Reserve*, October 2011, https://www.stlouis-fed.org/~/media/files/pdfs/publications/pub_assets/pdf/re/2011/d/shadow_banking.pdf

**134** Margaret Elliott, "Repo's Gone Global and Hip," *Derivatives Strat-egy*, February 1997, http://www.derivativesstrategy.com/magazine/archive/1997/0297fea1.asp

**135** Peter Cohan, "Big Risk: $1.2 Quadrillion Derivatives Market Dwarfs World GDP," *AOL.com*, 9 June 2010, http://www.aol. com/article/2010/06/09/risk-quadrillion-derivatives-market-gd-p/19509184/?gen=1

**136** Jim Rickards, "Derivatives Should Be Banned from Financial Markets," *US News*, 16 July 2012, http://www.usnews. com/opinion/blogs/economic-intelligence/2012/07/16/deriva-tives-should-be-banned-from-financial-markets

**137** Pam Martens, Russ Martens, "Bailed Out Citigroup Is Going Full Throttle into Derivatives that Blew Up AIG," *Wall Street on Parade*, 4 August 2016, http://wallstreetonparade.com/2016/08/bailed-out-citigroup-is-going-full-throttle-into-derivatives-that-blew-up-aig/

**138** M. Fricker, op. cit., citing Viral Acharya, et al., *Regulating Wall Street: The Dodd-Frank Act and the New Architecture of Global Finance* (Wiley, November 2010).

**139** P. Martens, et al., "Bailed Out Citigroup Is Going Full Throttle … ," op. cit.

**140** Ibid.

**141** David Malone, "Plan B—How to Loot Nations and Their Banks Legally," *Information Clearing House*, 17 December 2011, Http:// www.informationclearinghouse.info/article30016.htm

**142** Robert Teitelman, "The Case Against Favored Treatment of Derivatives," *The Deal*, 10 May 2011, http://www.law.harvard.edu/pro-grams/corp_gov/MediaMentions/05-10-11_Deal.pdf

**143** E. Perotti, op. cit.

**144** D. Malone, op. cit.

**145** Ibid.

**146** See Ellen Brown, "Why the US Need Not Fear a Sovereign Debt Crisis: Unlike Greece, It Is Actually Sovereign," *WebofDebt.com*, 22 July 2010, Http://www.webofdebt.com/articles/greece_skids.php

**147** Graham Summers, "The $555 Trillion Derivatives Debt Implosion Is About to Begin," *Zero Hedge*, 25 June 2016, http://www.zero-hedge.com/news/2016-06-25/555-trillion-derivatives-debt-implo-sion-about-begin

**148** Glenn Greenwald, "Top Senate Democrat: Bankers 'Own' the U.S. Congress," Salon, 30 April 2009, http://www.salon.com/2009/04/30/ownership/

**149** "Deflation: Making Sure 'It' Doesn't Happen Here," Remarks by
Governor Ben S. Bernanke before the National Economists Club,
Washington, D.C., *Federal Reserve*, 21 November 2002, https://
www.federalreserve.gov/boarddocs/speeches/2002/20021121/

**150** "Quantitative Easing," *Wikipedia*, https://en.wikipedia.org/wiki/
Quantitative_easing#cite_note-49

**151** M. Ray Perryman, op. cit.

**152** Mish Shedlock, "Steve Keen to Mish — Why banks can't lend reserves," *Mike Norman Economics*, 13 July 2012, http://mikenorman-
economics.blogspot.com/2012/07/steven-keen-to-mish-why-banks-
cant-lend.html

**153** Catherine Austin Fitts, "Quantitative Easing," https://solari.com/
articles/quantitative_easing/ [page no longer available].

**154** Ben Bernanke, Donald Kohn, "The Fed's Interest Payments to
Banks," *Brookings*, 16 February 2016, https://www.brookings.
edu/blog/ben-bernanke/2016/02/16/the-feds-interest-pay-
ments-to-banksWilliam Gavin, "Monetary Policy Regimes and the
Real Interest Rate," *St. Louis Federal Reserve*, 16 April 2018, https://
files.stlouisfed.org/files/htdocs/publications/review/2018/04/16/
monetary-policy-regimes-and-the-real-interest-rate.pdf

"Why Have ZIRP and QE Failed?," *ADividedWorld.com*, 17 September
2015, http://www.adividedworld.com/economic-ideas/why-has-
zirp-and-qe-failed/

Ben Bernanke, Donald Kohn, "The Fed's Interest Payments to Banks,"
*Brookings*, 16 February 2016, https://www.brookings.edu/blog/
ben-bernanke/2016/02/16/the/

**155** Izabella Kaminska, "The All You Can Eat Collateral Buf-
fet," *FT Alphaville*, 23 September 2013, https://ftalphaville.
ft.com/2013/09/03/1620872/the-all-you-can-eat-collateral-buffet/;
"From LIBOR to Fed Funds: 5 Facts About the Interbank Lending
Market in the US," *Sober Look*, 2 December 2013, http://soberlook.
com/2013/12/5-facts-about-interbank-lending-in-us.html; http://
soberlook.com/2013/12/banks-outperform-market-with-regional.
html.

**156** Jeffrey Snider, "A Monetary Ghost Town Called Federal Funds
— or Raising a Rate That No One Pays," *David Stockman's Contra
Corner*, 18 November 2015, http://davidstockmanscontracorner.
com/a-monetary-ghost-town-called-federal-funds-or-raising-

a-rate-that-no-one-pays/; David Moon, "Fed Rate Increase Irrelevant," *Knoxville News Sentinel*, 11 December 2016, http://www.knoxnews.com/story/money/business/2016/12/11/david-moon-fed-rate-increase-irrelevant/95103316/

**157**  Scott E.D. Skyrm, "Fed Funds and Repo," *Treasury.nl*, 27 May 2014, http://www.treasury.nl/blog/fed-funds-and-repo/

**158**  Alyssa Anderson, John Kandrac, "Monetary Policy Implementation and Financial Vulnerability: Evidence from the Overnight Reverse Repurchase Facility," *Review of Financial Studies*, 18 December 2017, https://academic.oup.com/rfs/advance-article-abstract/doi/10.1093/rfs/hhx141/4756472?redirectedFrom=fulltext

**159**  Barry Ritholtz, "Fed: Who Is Holding All the Excess Reserves?," *Ritholtz.com*, 23 November 2015, http://ritholtz.com/2015/11/fed-who-is-holding-all-the-excess-reserves/

**160**  William Gavin, "Monetary Policy Regimes and the Real Interest Rate," *St. Louis Federal Reserve*, 16 April 2018, https://files.stlouisfed.org/files/htdocs/publications/review/2018/04/16/monetary-policy-regimes-and-the-real-interest-rate.pdf

**161**  "Why Have ZIRP and QE Failed?," *ADividedWorld.com*, 17 September 2015, http://www.adividedworld.com/economic-ideas/why-has-zirp-and-qe-failed/

**162**  Dean Baker, "Wall Street's Greatest Heist: The Tarp," *The Guardian*, 20 September 2010, https://www.theguardian.com/commentisfree/cifamerica/2010/sep/20/tarp-bailout-banks-wall-street

**163**  M. Fricker, "About Repo," op. cit.

**164**  Hester Peirce, "Derivatives Clearinghouses: Clearing the Way to Failure," *Cleveland State Law Review*, June 2016, https://www.mercatus.org/publication/derivatives-clearinghouses-clearing-way-failure

**165**  "Volcker Rule," *Investopedia*, 2018, https://www.investopedia.com/terms/v/volcker-rule.asp

**166**  Erika Eichelberger, "Citigroup Wrote the Wall Street Giveaway the House Just Approved," *Mother Jones*, November 2014, http://www.motherjones.com/politics/2014/12/spending-bill-992-derivatives-citigroup-lobbyists

**167**  P. Martens, et al., "Bailed Out Citigroup Is Going Full Throttle ... ," op. cit.

**168**  John Butler, "Someone Has to Pay—Will It Be You?," *Financial Sense*, 4 April 2013. http://www.financialsense.com/print/contributors/john-butler/someone-has-got-to-pay-will-it-be-you

**169**  Jianping Zhou, et. al, "From Bail-out to Bail-in: Mandatory Debt Restructuring of Systemic Financial Institutions," *International Monetary Fund*, 24 April 2012, https://www.imf.org/external/pubs/ft/sdn/2012/sdn1203.pdf

**170**  "Burning Sensation," *The Economist*, 21 July 2012, http://www.economist.com/node/21559344

**171**  Jack Ewing, "As Cyprus Recovers from Banking Crisis, Deep Scars Remain," *New York Times*, 16 March 2015, http://www.nytimes.com/2015/03/17/business/international/as-cyprus-recovers-from-banking-crisis-deep-scars-remain.html

**172**  Teo Kermeliotis, "All You Need to Know About Cyprus Presidential Election," *Al Jazeera*, 29 January 2018, https://www.aljazeera.com/news/2018/01/cyprus-presidential-election-180126223607469.html

**173**  See Ellen Brown, "Bail-Out Is Out, Bail-In Is In," *EllenBrown.com*, 29 April 2013, https://ellenbrown.com/2013/04/29/bail-out-is-out-bail-in-is-in-another-argument-for-publicly-owned-banks/

**174**  Huw Jones, "G 20 Proposes Buffer to End Too Big to Fail Banks," *Reuters*, 10 November 2014, http://uk.reuters.com/article/g20-banks-regulations-idUKL6N0SY0PW20141110

**175**  Avinash Persaud, "Why Bail-In Securities Are Fool's Gold," *Peterson Institute for International Economics*, November 2014, https://piie.com/publications/pb/pb14-23.pdf

**176**  "OTC Derivatives and CCP," *Fimarkets.com*, 13 March 2013, http://www.fimarkets.com/pagesen/OTC_derivatives_CCP.php

**177**  David Unkovic, "Reasons to Be Concerned About Act 72 Pledges," *FindLaw*, 21 June 2017, http://corporate.findlaw.com/business-operations/reasons-to-be-concerned-about-act-72-pledges.html

**178**  Nathan Lewis, "The Cyprus Bank 'Bail-In' Is Another Crony Bankster Scam," *Forbes*, 3 May 2013, https://www.forbes.com/sites/nathanlewis/2013/05/03/the-cyprus-bank-bail-in-is-another-crony-bankster-scam/#2bb917bf2685

**179**  "Deposit Insurance Fund Trends Fourth Quarter 2017," FDIC, https://www.fdic.gov/bank/analytical/qbp/2017dec/qbpdep.html

**180**  Darrell Delamaide, "Can FDIC Handle the Failure of a Megabank?", *USA Today*, 30 May 2013, http://www.usatoday.com/story/money/business/2013/05/28/delamaide-fdic-megabank-failure/2365955/

181 Secular Investor, "Stunning: Italy Says NO to Bail-In Scenarios," *Zero Hedge*, 1 June 2017, http://www.zerohedge.com/news/2017-06-01/stunning-italy-says-no-bail-scenario%E2%80%99s

182 "Warren Investigation Finds Taxpayers Could Be on the Hook for $10 Trillion in Risky Derivatives," *Real News Network*, 16 November 2015, http://therealnews.com/t2/index.php?option=com_content&task=view&id=31&Itemid=74&jumival=15097

183 Tyler Durden, "Guest Post: Some More Thoughts on FDIC and the 'Systemic Risk Exception' Clause," *Naked Capitalism*, 21 March 2009, https://www.nakedcapitalism.com/2009/03/guest-post-some-more-thoughts-on-fdic.html

184 Yves Smith, "When You Weren't Looking, Democrat Bank Stooges Launch Bills to Permit Bailouts, Deregulate Derivatives," *Naked Capitalism*, 19 March 2013,http://www.nakedcapitalism.com/2013/03/when-you-werent-looking-democrat-bank-stooges-launch-bills-to-permit-bailouts-deregulate-derivatives.html

185 Ruchir Sharma, "How the Next Downturn Will Surprise Us," *New York Times*, 18 September 2018, https://www.nytimes.com/2018/09/18/opinion/economy-debt-markets-crash.html

186 Yalman Onaran, "Can We Survive the Next Financial Crisis?," *Bloomberg*, September 10, 2018, https://www.bloomberg.com/graphics/2018-lehman-anniversary/

187 Ibid.

188 Philip van Doorn, "Big Bank Phobia: Glass-Steagall Would Be Folly," *The Street*, 20 May 2013, https://www.thestreet.com/story/11926787/1/big-bank-phobia-glass-steagall-would-be-folly.html

189 Ibid.

190 Alex Pollock, "Glass-Steagall Never Saved Our Financial System, So Why Revive It?," *The Hill*, 11 June 2017, http://thehill.com/blogs/pundits-blog/finance/337289-glass-steagall-never-saved-our-financial-system-so-why-revive-it

191 Melanie Fein, "The Shadow Banking Charade," *SEC.gov*, 15 February 2013, https://www.sec.gov/comments/s7-04-09/s70409-95.pdf

192 A. Pollock, op. cit.

**193** Speech by Adair Turner, Chairman, British Bankers' Association annual conference, *FSA*, 30 June 2009, http://www.fsa.gov.uk/pages/Library/Communication/Speeches/2009/0630_at.shtml

**194** Gerard Comizio and Nathan Brownback, "Glass-Steagall Revival Could Have Profound Impact," *Law360*, 26 May 2017, https://www.law360.com/articles/928515/glass-steagall-revival-could-have-profound-impact

**195** Dan Freed, "Fed's Kashkari Unveils Plan to Tackle 'Too Big to Fail' Banks and Funds," *Reuters*, 16 November 2016, http://www.reuters.com/article/us-usa-fed-kashkari-idUSKBN13B1LD

**196** Ibid.

**197** Philip van Doorn, "Big Bank Phobia: Liquidity, Stupid, Not Just Capital," *The Street*, 17 May 2013. Https://www.thestreet.com/story/11926054/1/big-bank-phobia-liquidity-stupid-not-just-capital.html

**198** Philip van Doorn, "Big Bank Phobia: Not Too Big To Fail," *The Street*, 16 May 2013. Https://www.thestreet.com/story/11925187/1/big-bank-phobia-not-too-big-to-fail.html

**199** Stephen Keen, "Defending Bankruptcy Exemptions for Repos and Sec Lending," *Derivatives & Repo Report*, 30 January 2017, https://www.derivativesandreporeport.com/2017/01/defending-bankruptcy-exemptions-for-repos-and-sec-lending/

**200** Samantha Regan, "'Safe Harbor' for Financial Contracts: The Fed's Final Rule to Enhance Financial Stability," *Accenture*, 27 October 2017, https://financeandriskblog.accenture.com/regulatory-insights/regulatory-alert/safe-harbor-for-financial-contracts-the-feds-final-rule-to-enhance-financial-stability

**201** "Collateral, UCITS and the Re-use of Assets," *Deloitte*, 2016, https://www2.deloitte.com/content/dam/Deloitte/lu/Documents/financial-services/IM/lu_wp_collateral-ucits-assets_12012015.pdf

**202** Joe McHale, "Say Hello to SFTR, the New Regulatory Challenge Faced by Firms in the EU," *Bloomberg*, 3 October 2018, https://www.bloomberg.com/professional/blog/say-hello-sftr-new-regulatory-challenge-faced-firms-eu/

**203** Thomas Murray, "The Collateral Question and the Role of Repo," *Tabb Forum*, 17 June 2015, http://tabbforum.com/opinions/the-collateral-question-and-the-role-of-repo

**204** Katy Burne, "Pressure in Repo Market Spreads," *Wall Street Journal*,

2 April 2015, http://www.wsj.com/articles/pressure-in-repo-market-spreads-1428013415

**205** Gary Gorton, "Questions and Answers about the Financial Crisis," *National Bureau of Economic Research*, February 2010, http://www.nber.org/papers/w15787

**206** Cardiff Garcia, "Misunderstanding Financial Crises," a Q&A with Gary Gorton, *FT Alphaville*, 25 October 2012, https://ftalphaville.ft.com/2012/10/25/1223861/misunderstanding-financial-crises-a-qa-with-gary-gorton/

**207** Frank Sorrentino, "Restoring Glass-Steagall Won't Solve Anything," *American Banker*, 24 August 2016, https://www.americanbanker.com/opinion/restoring-glass-steagall-wont-solve-anything

**208** Jamie Merchant, "We Don't Need to Break Up The Big Banks. We Need to Put Them Under Democratic Control," *In These Times*, 2 February 2016, http://inthesetimes.com/article/18816/big-banks-too-big-to-fail-nationalize-democratize-finance

**209** Nassim Taleb, "Time to Nationalize US Banking System?", *FORA.tv*, 12 February 2009, https://www.youtube.com/watch?v=v05lV-JzeQDQ&feature=related

**210** Matt Taibbi, "Everything Is Rigged: The Biggest Price-Fixing Scandal Ever," *Rolling Stone*, 25 April 2013, https://www.rollingstone.com/politics/politics-news/everything-is-rigged-the-biggest-price-fixing-scandal-ever-82255/

**211** David Sanger, "Nationalization Gets A New, Serious Look", *New York Times*, 1 January 2009, http://www.nytimes.com/2009/01/26/business/economy/26banks.html?_r=3

**212** Matthew Rothschild, "Nationalize the Banks," *The Progressive*, 2 February 2009, http://www.progressive.org/mag/wx021109.html

**213** Christine Schewen, "Ignoring FDIC, ABC's Stark Says Bank Nationalization Happens 'In Socialist Countries' and Is 'Not Supposed to Happen' in the U.S.," *Media Matters*, 24 February 2009, http://mediamatters.org/research/2009/02/24/ignoring-fdic-abcs-stark-says-bank-nationalizat/147710

**214** Renee Haltom, "Failure of Continental Illinois," Federal Reserve Bank of Richmond, *Federal Reserve History*, May 1984, http://www.federalreservehistory.org/Events/DetailView/47

**215** Thomas Hanna, "The Crisis Next Time: Planning for Public Ownership as an Alternative to Corporate Bank Bailouts," *The*

*Next System*, 2 July 2018, https://thenextsystem.org/learn/stories/
crisis-next-time-planning-public-ownership-alternative-corpo-
rate-bank-bailouts

**216** Willem Buiter, "The End Of American Capitalism As We Knew
It," *Financial Times*, 17 September 2008, http://blogs.ft.com/ma-
verecon/2008/09/the-end-of-american-capitalism-as-we-knew-
it/#axzz4JPltzEAz

**217** Gar Alperovitz, "Wall Street Is Too Big to Regulate," *The New York
Times*, 23 July 2012, http://www.nytimes.com/2012/07/23/opinion/
banks-that-are-too-big-to-regulate-should-be-nationalized.html.
See Louis Jacobson, "Bernie Sanders Says Six Bank Companies
Have Assets Equaling 60 Percent of U.S. GDP," *Politifact*, 6 October
2011, https://www.politifact.com/truth-o-meter/statements/2011/
oct/06/bernie-s/bernie-sanders-says-six-bank-companies-have-as-
sets/

**218** Nouriel Roubini, "Nationalize Insolvent Banks," *Forbes*, 12 Feb.
2009, http://www.forbes.com/2009/02/11/geithner-banks-national-
ization-opinions-columnists_0212_nouriel_roubini.html

**219** Michael Hudson, "Orwellian Doublethink: 'Nationalize the
Banks,' 'Free Markets,'" *Global Research*, 23 February 2009,
http://www.globalresearch.ca/orwellian-doublethink-national-
ize-the-banks-free-markets/12418

**220** Rick Newman, "Why Bank Nationalization Is So Scary," *US News*,
22 February 2009, http://money.usnews.com/money/blogs/flow-
chart/2009/02/22/why-bank-nationalization-is-so-scary

**221** Richard Werner, "How to End the European Financial Crisis—at
No Further Cost and Without the Need for Political Changes,"
*University of Southampton*, CBFSD Policy Discussion Paper 2-12, 31
July 2012, https://eprints.soton.ac.uk/341650/

**222** Karan Kaul, et al., "Declining Agency MBS Liquidity Is Not All
about Financial Regulation," *Urban Institute*, November 2015, http://
www.urban.org/sites/default/files/publication/72621/2000503-De-
clining-Agency-MBS-Liquidity-Is-Not-All-about-Financial-Regu-
lation.pdf; Norbert Michel, "Quantitative Easing, The Fed's Balance
Sheet, and Central Bank Insolvency," *Heritage Foundation*, August
14, 2014, http://www.heritage.org/monetary-policy/report/quantita-
tive-easing-the-feds-balance-sheet-and-central-bank-insolvency

**223** T. Hanna, op. cit.

**224** Jesus Gonzalez-Garcia, et al., "State-Owned Banks and Fiscal Discipline," *IMF.org*, 2013, https://www.imf.org/external/pubs/ft/wp/2013/wp13206.pdf

**225** Alejandro Micco, et al., "Public Banks in Latin America," *Inter-American Development Bank*, 25 February 2005, http://www6.iadb.org/WMSFiles/products/research/files/pubS-490.pdf

**226** James Galbraith, *The Predator State: How Conservatives Abandoned the Free Market and Why Liberals Should Too* (Free Press 2008), page 112.

**227** Robert Hockett, "Finance Without Financiers," in Fred Block & Robert Hockett, *Real Utopias: Democratizing Finance* (Erik Olin Wright, ed., 2018) (forthcoming), https://ssc.wisc.edu/~wright/929-utopias-2018/wp-content/uploads/2018/01/Hockett-Finance-without-Financiers-17-June-2017.pdf

**228** Alvin Rabushka, "Representation without Taxation: The Colonial Roots of American Taxation, 1700-1754," *Policy Review*, December 2003, https://www.questia.com/library/journal/1G1-112022644/representation-without-taxation-the-colonial-roots. See also Alvin Rabushka, "The Colonial Roots of American Taxation, 1607-1700," *Hoover Institution Policy Review*, 1 August 2002, https://www.hoover.org/research/colonial-roots-american-taxation-1607-1700

**229** Aaron Fernando, "A Movement for Public Banking Gains Momentum," *The Progressive*, 11 June 2018, https://progressive.org/dispatches/public-banking-gains-momentum-180611/; "Public Bank," *Wikipedia*, https://en.wikipedia.org/wiki/Public_bank. See also http://PublicBankingInstitute.org.

**230** Chester Dawson, "Shale Boom Helps North Dakota Bank Earn Returns Goldman Would Envy," *Wall Street Journal*, 16 November 2014, https://www.wsj.com/articles/shale-boom-helps-north-dakota-bank-earn-returns-goldman-would-envy-1416180862

**231** Lou Raguse, "From Boom to Bust, Big Changes in ND Oil," *KARE*, 28 April 2016, http://www.kare11.com/news/from-boom-to-bust-big-changes-in-nd-oil/156422333

**232** "2015 Annual Report," *Bank of North Dakota*, 20 April 2016, https://bnd.nd.gov/2015-annual-report/

**233** "Bank of North Dakota Releases 2017 Annual Report," *Bank of North Dakota*, 17 April 2018, https://bnd.nd.gov/bank-of-north-dakota-releases-2017-annual-report/

**234** Amy Dalrymple, "UPDATE: Reaction to ND governor's budget plan with more big cuts," *Inforum*, 7 December 2016, http://www. inforum.com/news/4174959-update-reaction-nd-governors-budget-plan-more-big-cuts

**235** J. Harkinson, op. cit.; Nick Smith, "Bank of N.D. Profits Could Be Included in Budget Shortfall Fix," *Bismarck Tribune*, 26 July 2016, http://bismarcktribune.com/news/local/govt-and-politics/bank-of-n-d-profits-could-be-included-in-budget/article_d3117a91-85c9-575f-8499-0b0464052fdb.html; Amy Dalrymple, "Reaction to ND Governor's Budget Plan with More Big Cuts," *InForum*, 7 Dec whoember 2016, http://www.inforum.com/news/4174959-update-reaction-nd-governors-budget-plan-more-big-cuts

**236** Josh Harkinson, op. cit.

**237** Jason Judd and Heather McGee, "Banking on America: How Main Street Partnership Banks Can Improve Local Economies," *Demos*, http://www.demos.org/sites/default/files/publications/Demos_NationalBankPaper.pdf

**238** "Public Banks: Bank Of North Dakota," *Institute for Local Self-Reliance*, 2 July 2015, https://ilsr.org/rule/bank-of-north-dakota-2/

**239** Josh Harkinson, "How the Nation's Only State-Owned Bank Became the Envy of Wall Street," *Mother Jones*, 28 March 2009, http://www.motherjones.com/politics/2009/03/how-nations-only-state-owned-bank-became-envy-wall-street/

**240** Marc Armstrong, "Public Banks Could Break the Impasse Over Marijuana Money," *Truthout*, 24 August 2016, http://www.truth-out.org/news/item/37343-public-banks-could-break-the-impasse-over-marijuana-money

**241** See Ratings Direct, "Bank of North Dakota," page 5, *Standard & Poor's*, 2 October 2014, https://bnd.nd.gov/pdf/sp_report_2014.pdf; Ratings Direct, "Bank of North Dakota," page 4, *Standard & Poor's*, 7 November 2017, https://bnd.nd.gov/credit-rating/;

**242** "Flex PACE Program," *Bank of North Dakota*, 2017, https://bnd.nd.gov/business/flex-pace-program/

**243** BND Opens Second Application Period for BND Infrastructure Loan Fund," *BND.nd.gov*, 12 February 2016, https://bnd.nd.gov/bnd-opens-second-application-period-for-bnd-infrastructure-loan-fund/

**244** Justin Marlowe, "Municipal Bonds and Infrastructure Development—Past, Present, and Future," *ICMA.org*, 2015 white paper, http://icma.org/en/icma/knowledge_network/documents/kn/Document/307554/Municipal_Bonds_and_Infrastructure_Development__Past_Present_and_Future

**245** Bank of North Dakota, "2017 BND Annual Report", pages 18-20, https://bnd.nd.gov/annual-report/

**246** "California Proposition 68, Parks, Environment, and Water Bond (June 2018)," *Ballotpedia*, https://ballotpedia.org/California_Proposition_68,_Parks,_Environment,_and_Water_Bond_(June_2018)

**247** Paul Rogers, "Delta Tunnels Plan's True Price Tag: As Much as $67 Billion", San Jose Mercury News, http://www.mercurynews.com/ci_24795356/delta-tunnels-plans-true-price-tag-much-67

**248** Stan Hazelroth (interview), "The Bank Not Built: The California Infrastructure Bank," *PBS.org*, 19 May 2009, http://www.pbs.org/wnet/blueprintamerica/reports/by-topic/growth-development/a-national-infrastructure-bank-the-state-i-bank/554/

**249** See Sean Watterson, "Can Public Banking Save the World?", *Non-profit Quarterly*, 9 July 2018, https://nonprofitquarterly.org/2018/07/09/can-public-banking-save-the-world/; and many other articles posted on the Public Banking Institute blog, http://www.publicbankinginstitute.org/blog

**250** Kurt Mettenheim and Olivier Butzbach, "Alternative Banking and Recovery from Crisis," *Progressive Economy Forum* (Brussels), 5-7 March 2014, http://www.progressiveeconomy.eu/sites/default/files/papers/Kurt%20Von%20Mettenheim%20Alternative%20Banking%20and%20Recovery%20from%20Crisis.pdf

**251** Sparkassenstiftung für Internationale Kooperation e.V., "International Cooperation, Projects and Partners Annual Report," January 2015, *www.sparkassenstiftung.de*, http://www.sparkassenstiftung.de/fileadmin/user_upload/pdf/Jahresberichte/JB_2015_E.pdf

**252** Geoff Riley, "EU Economics: Germany Leads Euro Zone Revival," *Tutor2u*, 25 February 2011, https://www.tutor2u.net/economics/blog/resilient-german-economy-leads-euro-zone-revival

**253** Peter Dorman, "What Is Public Capital?," *EconoSpeak*, 16 July 2011, http://econospeak.blogspot.com/2011/07/what-is-public-capital.html

**254** Lucas Guilkey, "Renewable Energy, Cannabis Industries Lead the Charge for an Oakland Public Bank," *Oakland North*, 26 September

2017, citing Sparkassen economist Wolfram Morales, https://oak-landnorth.net/2017/09/26/renewable-energy-cannabis-industries-lead-the-charge-for-an-oakland-public-bank/

**255** "2013 Global Forum on Financial Inclusion for Development," *Universal Postal Union*, http://www.upu.int/en/activities/financial-inclusion/2013-forum-on-financial-inclusion.html

**256** Mark Scher, "Postal Savings and the Provision of Financial Services," *UN.org*, December 2001, http://www.un.org/esa/esa01dp22.pdf

**257** "United States Postal Savings System," *Wikipedia*, https://en.wikipedia.org/wiki/United_States_Postal_Savings_System

**258** Christopher W. Shaw, "'Banks of the People': The Life and Death of the U.S. Postal Savings System," *Journal of Social History*, 9 September 2017, https://doi.org/10.1093/jsh/shx036

**259** Jennifer Calfas, "The 6 Biggest Employers in the U.S. Right Now," *Time*, 27 April 2017, http://time.com/money/4754123/biggest-us-companies/; "Fiscal Year 2018 Annual Report to Congress," *USPS.com*, http://about.usps.com/who-we-are/financials/annual-reports/fy2018.pdf

**260** "Postal Service Modernization Bills Introduced," *Bernie Sanders*, 13 February 2013, https://www.sanders.senate.gov/newsroom/press-releases/postal-service-modernization-bills-introduced-saturday-mail-preserved

**261** "Providing Non-Bank Financial Services for the Underserved," *USPS Office of Inspector General*, 27 January 2014, http://op.bna.com.s3.amazonaws.com/der.nsf/r%3FOpen%3dtbay-9lnpd6

**262** "2015 FDIC National Survey of Unbanked and Underbanked Households ," *FDIC*, https://www.fdic.gov/householdsurvey/

**263** Daniel Marans, "Kirsten Gillibrand Unveils A Public Option For Banking," *HuffPost*, 25 April 2018, https://www.huffingtonpost.com/entry/kirsten-gillibrand-postal-banking-bill_us_5ae07f-9fe4b07be4d4c6feae

**264** Jordan Haedtler, et al., "Making the Federal Reserve Fully Public: Why and How," *PopularDemocracy.org*, August 2016, https://populardemocracy.org/sites/default/files/A-Public-Fed-Why-and-How.pdf

**265** See Chapter 1.

**266** See Bill Platt, "Andrew Levin on Why the Fed Is in Need of Reform," *Dartmouth News*, 20 September 2016, https://news. dartmouth.edu/news/2016/09/andrew-levin-why-fed-need-reform; Danielle DiMartino Booth, "Rebuild the Fed from the Bottom Up," *NewsMax*, 9 January 2017, http://www.newsmax.com/Finance/ DanielleDiMartinoBooth/trump-fed-yellen-trump/2017/01/06/ id/767154/; "Bernanke's Former Advisor: 'People Would Be Stunned to Know the Extent to Which the Fed Is Privately Owned,'" *Zero Hedge*, 11 April 2016, http://www.zerohedge.com/ news/2016-04-11/bernankes-former-advisor-people-would-be-stunned-know-extent-which-fed-privately-own.

**267** "Press Release," Board of Governors of the Federal Reserve System, 11 January 2016, https://www.federalreserve.gov/newsevents/press/ other/20160111a.htm.

**268** WSJ Staff, "Transcript of President Trump's Interview with the Wall Street Journal: President Discusses U.S.-Saudi Relations, the Federal Reserve, the Economy, Trade and More," *Wall Street Journal*, 24 October 2018, https://www.wsj.com/articles/transcript-of-president-trumps-interview-with-the-wall-street-journal-1540388205; Barney Jopson, et al., "Republican Attack on Fed Casts Doubt over Global Bank Rules," *Financial Times*, 3 February 2017, https://www.ft.com/ content/8cc3c248-e9f5-11e6-893c-082c54a7f539.

**269** J. Haedtler, et al., op. cit.

**270** Morgan Ricks, John Crawford, Lev Menand, "Central Banking for All: A Public Option for Bank Accounts," *Great Democracy Initiative*, June 2018, https://greatdemocracyinitiative.org/wp-content/ uploads/2018/06/FedAccountsGDI.pdf

**271** Robert Hackett, "Why Big Business Is Racing to Build Blockchains," *Fortune*, 22 August 2017, http://fortune.com/2017/08/22/ bitcoin-ethereum-blockchain-cryptocurrency/

**272** Timothy May, "The Crypto Anarchist Manifesto," *activism.net*, 22 November 1992, https://www.activism.net/cypherpunk/crypto-anarchy.html?utm_content=bufferc924a

**273** Jamie Bartlett, "Forget Far-Right Populism—Crypto-Anarchists Are The New Masters," *The Guardian*, 4 June 2017, https://www. theguardian.com/technology/2017/jun/04/forget-far-right-populism-crypto-anarchists-are-the-new-masters-internet-politics

**274** Etienne Brodu, "Blockchain, Degeneration of an Ideal," *Ouishare Magazine*, 7 November 2017, http://magazine.ouishare.

net/2017/11/blockchain-degeneration-of-an-ideal/

**275** Olga Kharif, "The Bitcoin Whales: 1,000 People Who Own 40 Percent of the Market," *Bloomberg*, 8 December 2017, https://www.bloomberg.com/news/articles/2017-12-08/the-bitcoin-whales-1-000-people-who-own-40-percent-of-the-market

**276** Bert Ely, "Bitcoin Is a Ponzi Scheme, and It Will Collapse Like One," *The Hill*, 11 December 2017, https://thehill.com/opinion/finance/364306-bitcoin-is-a-ponzi-scheme-and-it-will-collapse-like-one

**277** Satoshi Nakamoto, "Bitcoin Open Source Implementation of P2P Currency," *P2P Foundation*, 11 February 2009http://p2pfoundation.ning.com/forum/topics/Bitcoin-open-source

**278** Joshua Davis, "The Crypto-Currency," *The New Yorker*, 10 October 2011, http://www.newyorker.com/magazine/2011/10/10/the-crypto-currency

**279** Colin Thompson, "How Does the Blockchain Work?", *Blockchain Review*, 2 October 2016, updated 22 July 2017, https://medium.com/blockchain-review/how-does-the-blockchain-work-for-dummies-explained-simply-9f94d386e093

**280** Martin Hiesboeck, "Block Chain Is the Most Disruptive Invention Since the Internet Itself," *Digital Doughnut*, 6 April 2016, https://www.digitaldoughnut.com/articles/2016/april/blockchain-is-the-most-disruptive-invention-since

**281** Teeka Tiwarn, Blockchain webinar, *Palm Beach Research Group*, 17 April 2017, https://pros.palmbeachgroup.com/p/1704PBOCRYPTOPOST/MPBOT427/Full

**282** Simon Black, "200 Lines of Code Will Disrupt This Multi-Trillion Dollar Industry," *Sovereign Man*, 10 April 2017, https://www.sovereignman.com/trends/200-lines-of-code-will-disrupt-this-multi-trillion-dollar-industry-21252/

**283** Ryan Vlastelica, "Why Bitcoin Won't Displace Visa or Mastercard Soon," MarketWatch, 18 December 2017, https://www.marketwatch.com/story/why-bitcoin-wont-displace-visa-or-mastercard-soon-2017-12-15

**284** Kyle Croman, et al., "On Scaling Decentralized Blockchains," International Conference on Financial Cryptography and Data Security, *Financial Cryptography and Data Security*, pp 106-125, 31 August 2016, http://www.comp.nus.edu.sg/~prateeks/papers/Bitcoin-scaling.pdf

**285** "Cryptocurrency Market Capitalizations," *CoinMarketCap*, https://coinmarketcap.com/ ; "Bitcoin," historical chart, *Coindesk*, http://www.coindesk.com/price/

**286** "Bitcoin Help: Introduction," *BitcoinWiki*, 21 August 2015, https://en.Bitcoin.it/wiki/Help:Introduction; "Bitcoin Anonymity -- Is Bitcoin Anonymous?", https://www.buybitcoinworldwide.com/anonymity

**287** Michael Baxter, "The End of Banking As We Know It?", *Fresh Business Thinking*, 24 July 2016, http://www.freshbusinessthinking.com/the-end-of-banking-as-we-know-it/

**288** M. Hiesboeck, op. cit.

**289** Cody Brown, "How to Lose $8k Worth of Bitcoin In 15 Minutes with Verizon and Coinbase.com," *Medium*, 31 May 2017, https://medium.com/@CodyBrown/how-to-lose-8k-worth-of-bitcoin-in-15-minutes-with-verizon-and-coinbase-com-ba75fb8d0bac

**290** Shaun Waterman, "Top DOJ Official Calls for Regulation of Crypto-Currencies," *Fedscoop*, 29 June 2016, https://www.fedscoop.com/top-doj-official-calls-for-regulation-of-crypto-currencies/

**291** "Cryptocurrencies: Looking Beyond the Hype," *BIS Annual Economic Report*, 17 June 2018, https://www.bis.org/publ/arpdf/ar2018e5.htm; Bitcoin Is an 'Environmental Disaster' And 'Could Bring the Internet to a Halt', Study Says," *South China Morning Post*, 18 June 2018, https://www.scmp.com/business/money/money-news/article/2151205/bitcoin-environmental-disaster-and-could-bring-internet

**292** Anatoliy Zhdanov, "Big Transaction Fees Are a Problem for Bitcoin," *CNBC.com*, 20 April 2018, https://www.cnbc.com/2017/12/19/big-transactions-fees-are-a-problem-for-bitcoin.html; Nafis Alam, "Can Cryptocurrencies Like Bitcoin Survive Scrutiny from Central Banks?," *The Conversation*, 19 September 19 2017, https://theconversation.com/can-cryptocurrencies-like-bitcoin-survive-scrutiny-from-central-banks-84137

**293** David Scutt, "Here's How Much Currency Is Traded Every Day," *Business Insider Australia*, 2 September 2016, http://www.businessinsider.com/heres-how-much-currency-is-traded-every-day-2016-9

**294** "USD Exchange Trade Volume," *Blockchain* , 20 April 2018, https://blockchain.info/charts/trade-volume

**295** Izabella Kaminska, "But, But... I Thought Bitcoin Was Supposed to Be Cheap?", *FT Alphaville*, 17 March 2017, https://ftalphaville. ft.com/2017/03/17/2186161/but-but-i-thought-bitcoin-was-sup-posed-to-be-cheap/

**296** A. Zhdanov, op. cit.

**297** Ofir Beigel, "7 Bitcoin Debit Cards Compared and Reviewed (2017)," *99Bitcoins*, 9 December 2016, https://99bitcoins.com/bit-coin-debit-card-compared-reviewed/

**298** Christopher Malmo, "Bitcoin Is Unsustainable," *Motherboard*, 29 June 2015, https://motherboard.vice.com/en_us/article/ae3p7e/bit-coin-is-unsustainable

**299** Sue Chang, "Morgan Stanley Thinks Bitcoin Is Nothing More Than a Poster Child for Speculation," *MarketWatch*, 12 July 2017, http://www.marketwatch.com/story/morgan-stanley-thinks-bitcoin-is-nothing-more-than-a-poster-child-for-speculation-2017-07-12

**300** Alex Hern, "Senior Bitcoin Developer Says Currency 'Failed Exper-iment'," *The Guardian*, 15 January 2016, https://www.theguardian.com/technology/2016/jan/15/mike-hearn-senior-bitcoin-develop-er-says-currency-failed-experiment

**301** Stan Schroeder, "Bitcoin's Secretive Creator Could Become the World's First Trillionaire," mashable.comm 12 December 2017, https://mashable.com/2017/12/12/bitcoin-satoshi-trillion-aire/#She6pj_osZqj

**302** Laurie Law, et al., "How To Make a Mint: The Cryptography of Anonymous Electronic Cash," National Security Agency Office of Information, Security Research and Technology, Cryptology Divi-sion, 18 June 1996, http://groups.csail.mit.edu/mac/classes/6.805/articles/money/nsamint/nsamint.htm

**303** Ben Tarnoff, "How the Internet Was Invented," *The Guardian*, 15 July 2016, https://www.theguardian.com/technology/2016/jul/15/how-the-internet-was-invented-1976-arpa-kahn-cerf

**304** Matthew Sparkes, "Who Is the Reclusive Billionaire Creator of Bitcoin?," *Telegraph*, 4 March 2014, https://www.telegraph.co.uk/technology/10673546/Who-is-the-reclusive-billionaire-creator-of-Bitcoin.html

**305** "What is Ethereum. Guide for Beginners," *Cointelegraph.com*, 7 February 2018, https://cointelegraph.com/ethereum-for-beginners/what-is-ethereum#people-to-follow

**306** Andrew Tar, "Smart Contracts, Explained," *Cointelegraph*, 31 October 2017, https://cointelegraph.com/explained/smart-contracts-explained

**307** Ibid.; Jimmy Song, Bitcoin entrepreneur, "The Truth about Smart Contracts," *Medium*, 11 June 2018, https://medium.com/@jimmysong/the-truth-about-smart-contracts-ae825271811f

**308** A. Zhdanov, op. cit.; Oscar Jonsson, "Why Cryptocurrencies Could Push the Dollar from World Reserve Currency Status," *Forbes*, 7 November 2017, https://www.forbes.com/sites/laurashin/2017/11/07/why-cryptocurrencies-could-push-the-dollar-from-world-reserve-currency-status/

**309** "Nexus Crypto Currency Simplified—A Guide for Everyone," *Steemit.com*, 23 September 2016, https://steemit.com/bitcoin/@gjsteele71/nexus-crypto-currency-simplified-a-guide-for-everyone

**310** Amanda Johnson, "BitShares 101: Basics of the World's 4th Most Popular Cryptocurrency", *Cointelegraph*, 21 April 2015, https://cointelegraph.com/news/bitshares-101-basics-of-the-worlds-4th-most-popular-cryptocurrency

**311** "What Is EOS?", *WeUseCoins.com*, https://www.weusecoins.com/what-is-eos/

**312** Yaoqi Jia, "Demystifying Hashgraph: Benefits and Challenges," *Hackernoon*, 8 November 2017, https://hackernoon.com/demystifying-hashgraph-benefits-and-challenges-d605e5c0cee5; Lansana, "Why Hashgraph Will Never Replace Blockchain," *Medium*, 26 December 2017, https://medium.com/@Lansana/i-was-wrong-hashgraph-is-actually-very-bad-bf7d9b2e8d99; "Frequently Asked Questions," *Hedera Hashgraph*, https://www.hederahashgraph.com/faq#what-is-the-hedera-hashgraph-council-what-is-the-role-of-this-governing-body

**313** See e.g. Jonald Fyookball, "Lightning Network Centralization Leads to Economic Censorship," *Bitcoin.com*, 9 October 2017, https://news.bitcoin.com/lightning-network-centralization-leads-economic-censorship/; Jonald Fyookball, Mathematical Proof That the Lightning Network Cannot Be a Decentralized Bitcoin Scaling Solution, *Medium.com*, 26 June 2017, https://medium.com/@jonaldfyookball/mathematical-proof-that-the-lightning-network-cannot-be-a-decentralized-bitcoin-scaling-solution-1b8147650800; Egor Homakov, "Why Lightning and Raiden Networks Will Not Work," *Medium.com*, 16 December 2017, https://medium.com/failsafe/why-lightning-and-raiden-networks-will-not-work-d1880e4bc294

**314** "Basic Income + Blockchain," *Grantcoin*, http://www.grantcoin.org/; EquaCoin, https://equacoin.com/

**315** "SolarCoin," https://solarcoin.org/wp-content/uploads/2017/07/SolarCoin-Onepager-2017.pdf

**316** "We, the People, Are the Butterflies," *PayServices.com*, 2017, https://www.payservices.com/error.php?

**317** "Initial Coin Offering," *Wikipedia*, https://en.wikipedia.org/wiki/Initial_coin_offering

**318** Kristin Houser, "Let's Have a Heart to Heart: Are Blockchain Tokens Really Nothing More Than 'A Scheme?'", *Future Society*, 18 September 2017, https://futurism.com/lets-have-a-heart-to-heart-are-blockchain-tokens-really-nothing-more-than-a-scheme/

**319** Ibid.; "What is An Initial Coin Offering? Raising Millions In Seconds," *Blockgeeks*, 2017, https://blockgeeks.com/guides/initial-coin-offering/

**320** Penny Crosman, "Spinoff Rumors or Not, JPM's Blockchain Unit Is Evolving," American Banker, 23 April 2018, https://www.americanbanker.com/news/spinoff-rumors-or-not-jpmorgan-chases-blockchain-unit-is-evolving

**321** Devon Allaby, "The Trust Trade-Off: Permissioned vs Permissionless Blockchains," *Fjordnet.com*, 27 October 2016, https://www.fjordnet.com/conversations/the-trust-trade-off-permissioned-vs-permissionless-blockchains/

**322** Izabella Kaminska, "Taking the Block Out of Blockchain...," *Financial Times*, 22 November 2017, https://ftalphaville.ft.com/2017/11/22/2196054/taking-the-block-out-of-blockchain/

**323** David Floyd, "Banks Claim They're Building Blockchains. They're Not," *Investopedia*, 28 September 2017, updated 23 February 2018, https://www.investopedia.com/news/banks-building-blockchains-distributed-ledger-permission/

**324** Izabella Kaminska, "Truth and Fiction in Blockchain's Brave New World," *Financial Times*, 2 January 2018. https://www.ft.com/content/1858c8a0-efa7-11e7-ac08-07c3086a2625

**325** Daniel Jeffries, "What Will Bitcoin Look Like in Twenty Years?," *Hacker Noon*, 31 October 2017, https://hackernoon.com/what-will-bitcoin-look-like-in-twenty-years-7e75481a798c

**326** Kai Stinchcombe, "Ten Years in, Nobody Has Come Up With a Use for Blockchain," *Hackernoon.com*, 22 December 2017, https://hackernoon.com/ten-years-in-nobody-has-come-up-with-a-use-case-for-blockchain-ee98c180100

**327** Perry Mehrling, "Can Bitcoin Replace the Dollar?", *Institute for New Economic Thinking*, 14 October 2017, https://www.ineteconomics.org/perspectives/blog/can-bitcoin-replace-the-dollar

**328** P. Mehrling, "Can Bitcoin Replace the Dollar?", op. cit. [paragraphs transposed].

**329** Perry Mehrling, "Financialization and Its Discontents," *Institute for New Economic Thinking*, 2 August 2016, https://www.ineteconomics.org/perspectives/blog/financialization-and-its-dicontents

**330** Jeffrey Tucker, "The Austrian Influences on Bitcoin," *Austrian Center*, http://www.austriancenter.com/the-austrian-influences-on-bitcoin/

**331** "Why Was 21 Million Picked As the Number of Bitcoins to Be Created?", *Stack Exchange*, https://bitcoin.stackexchange.com/questions/8439/why-was-21-million-picked-as-the-number-of-bitcoins-to-be-created

**332** Antal Fekete, "Detractors of Adam Smith's Real Bills Doctrine," *Safehaven.com*, 13 July 2005, https://safehaven.com/article/3409/detractors-of-adam-smiths-real-bills-doctrine

**333** Yokei Yamaguchi, Kaoru Yamaguchi, "Peer-to-Peer Public Money System," *Muratopia*, 2017, http://www.muratopia.org/Yamaguchi/doc/P2P-PM-System.pdf

**334** Paraphrased from "Local Exchange Trading System," *Wikipedia*, https://en.wikipedia.org/wiki/Local_exchange_trading_system

**335** Katie Gilbert, "Why Local Currencies Could Be on the Rise in the U.S. -- and Why It Matters," *Forbes*, 22 September 2014, https://www.forbes.com/sites/katiegilbert/2014/09/22/why-local-currencies-could-be-on-the-rise-in-the-u-s-and-why-it-matters/2/#25a214f67259

**336** See Ellen Brown, "The Crime of Alleviating Poverty: A Local Community Currency Battles the Central Bank of Kenya," 28 June 2013, *Truthdig*, http://www.truthdig.com/report/item/the_crime_of_alleviating_poverty_a_local_community_currency_20130628

**337** "Local Exchange Trading System," op. cit.; *CommunityForge.Net*, http://communityforge.net/

**338** Community Exchange System, *Wikipedia*, https://en.wikipedia.org/wiki/Community_Exchange_System; "Conversion Rates," *Community Exchange System*, https://www.community-exchange.org/home/how-it-works/conversion-rates/

**339** "Interledger," https://Interledger.org

**340** Arthur Brock, "National Currencies Aren't as Centralized, and Bitcoin Isn't as Decentralized, as You Think," *Holo*, 2 June 2016, https://medium.com/holochain/national-currencies-arent-as-centralized-and-bitcoin-isn-t-as-decentralized-as-you-think-fa2afa022a2b

**341** Tristan Roberts, "What Could Come After Blockchain Technology? The What and Why of Holochain", *Medium*, 27 February 2018, https://cryptoinsider.21mil.com/after-blockchain-technology-holochain/

**342** Morgen Peck, "Ripple Credit System Could Help or Harm Bitcoin," *Spectrum*, 14 January 2013, https://spectrum.ieee.org/telecom/internet/ripple-credit-system-could-help-or-harm-bitcoin

**343** Qbix, "What Is Money?", *Qbix*, 3 September 2017, https://qbix.com/blog/index.php/2017/09/what-is-money/

**344** A. Brock, op. cit.

**345** Daniel Roberts, "More Than 75 Banks Are Now on Ripple's Blockchain Network," *Yahoo Finance*, 26 April 2017, https://finance.yahoo.com/news/75-banks-now-ripples-blockchain-network-162939601.html; Qbix, op. cit.

**346** Qbix, op. cit.

**347** "People Powered Money," *Trustlines Network*, https://trustlines.network/

**348** "Our Own Story," Fair-coin.org, https://fair-coin.org/en/our-own-story

**349** Maro, "FairCoin Activates the First 100% Cooperative Blockchain," *FairCoop*, 18 July 2017, https://2017.fair.coop/faircoin-activates-the-first-100-cooperative-blockchain/

**350** Alex Pazaitis, "FairCoin Activates the First Cooperative Blockchain," *P2P Foundation*, 20 July 2017, https://blog.p2pfoundation.net/faircoin-activates-first-cooperative-blockchain/2017/07/20

**351** Joe Blankenship, "FairCoin -- People, Cooperation, Challenges," *TheJoeBlankenship.com*, 20 August 2017, https://thejoeblankenship.com/blogs/faircoin/faircoin.html

**352** "Bitcoin: the Crypto Reserve Currency," https://steemit.com/bit-coin/@maneco64/bitcoin-the-crypto-reserve-currency

**353** Andreas Antonopoulos, *The Internet of Money* (Merkle Bloom LLC, 1st edition, September 5, 2016).

**354** "Digital Token Project Raises Big Money in Initial Coin Offering," *Reuters*, 12 June 2017, http://fortune.com/2017/06/12/digital-to-ken-project-bancor-initial-coin-offering/

**355** "Bernard Lietaer -- Best Summary on Bancor Protocol (Blockchain) vs. the False-flag Bitcoin," *Exopolitics Hungary*, 8 August 2017, <https://www.youtube.com/watch?v>=

**356** Eyal Hertzog, "Response to 'Bancor is Flawed'", *The Bancor Protocol*, 20 June 2017, https://blog.bancor.network/this-analysis-of-bancor-is-flawed-18ab8a000d43

**357** Olga Kharif, "One of the Most High-Profile Initial Coin Offerings Has Crashed 50%," *Bloomberg*, 1 November 2017, https://www.bloomberg.com/news/articles/2017-11-01/shining-star-of-initial-coin-offerings-crashing-back-to-earth

**358** "Bancor Bounce Back? ICO Is Winning Adoption," *Coin Desk*, 20 February 2018, https://www.coindesk.com/bancor-bounce-back-doubted-ico-winning-adoption/; "Bancor," *CoinMarketCap.com*, 22 June 2018, https://coinmarketcap.com/exchanges/bancor-network/

**359** "Bancor to Launch First Blockchain-Based Community Currencies in Kenya," *Business Wire*, 21 June 2018, https://www.businesswire.com/news/home/20180621005727/en/Bancor-Launch-Block-chain-Based-Community-Currencies-Kenya

**360** Vivek Wadhwa, "What the U.S. Can Learn from India's Move Toward a Cashless Society," *Washington Post*, 23 January 2017, https://www.washingtonpost.com/news/innovations/wp/2017/01/23/what-the-u-s-can-learn-from-indias-move-toward-a-cashless-society/

**361** "Tunisia to Replace eDinar with Blockchain-Based Currency," *EconoTimes*, 11 January 2016, http://www.econotimes.com/Tuni-sia-To-Replace-eDinar-With-Blockchain-Based-Currency-140836

**362** "Genesys Fund—Explores the Growing Government Interest in Cryptocurrencies," *Digital Journal,* 22 May 2018, http://www.digi-taljournal.com/pr/3785501#ixzz5HdY9Vm95

**363** Fiona Graham, "M-Pesa: Kenya's Mobile Wallet Revolution," *BBC News*, 22 November 2010, http://www.bbc.com/news/busi-ness-11793290

**364** V. Srinivas, "The Revolution in Banking Sector Technology," *Government of India Press Information Bureau*, 11 August 2017, http://pib.nic.in/newsite/printrelease.aspx?relid=169873

**365** "Poverty in India," *Wikipedia*.

**366** "Bengal Famine of 1943," *Wikipedia*.

**367** Jayati Ghosh, "Bank Nationalisation: The Record," *Macroscan*, 21 July 2005, http://www.macroscan.org/cur/jul05/cur210705Bank_Nationalisation.htm.

**368** Abhijit Banerjee, et al., "Banking Reform in India," *MIT*, June 2005, http://economics.mit.edu/files/779

**369** J. Ghosh, op. cit.

**370** "Nationalised Banks in India," *I Love India*, 5 June 2012, http://www.iloveindia.com/finance/bank/nationalised-banks/index.html.

**371** R. Gandhi, "Consolidation among Public Sector Banks," *Bank for International Settlements*, 22 April 2016.http://www.bis.org/review/r160426d.htm

**372** Balaji Viswanathan, "How Is It Possible That Only 3% Of Indians Pay Income Tax?", *Quora*, 6 March 2016, https://www.quora.com/How-is-it-possible-that-only-3-of-Indians-pay-income-tax

**373** "The Government Is the New Startup in India," *Innovation Is Everywhere*, 27 March 2017, https://www.innovationiseverywhere.com/government-startup-in-india/

**374** Martin George, "11 Myths About Iris Recognition," *Electronic Design*, 19 October 2017, https://www.electronicdesign.com/industrial-automation/11-myths-about-iris-recognition

**375** V. Wadhwa, op. cit.

**376** B. Viswanathan, op. cit.

**377** V. Wadhwa, op. cit.

**378** Sasi Desai, Nipun Jasuja, "The Bedrock of a Digital India: An Overview Of The India Stack And Its Disruptive Potential," *Wharton Fintech*, 27 October 2016, https://medium.com/wharton-fintech/the-bedrock-of-a-digital-india-3e96240b3718

**379** William Davenport, "Bank Credit Cards and the Uniform Commercial Code," *Valparaiso University Law Review*, Spring 1967, http://scholar.valpo.edu/cgi/viewcontent.cgi?article=1035&context=vulr

**380** Personal communication to the author, January 2014.

**381** Nilanjan Banik and Milind Shrikant Padalka, "India's Demonetization: Time for a Digital Economy," *The Diplomat*, 1 December 2016, http://thediplomat.com/2016/12/indias-demonetization-time-for-a-digital-economy/

**382** Bhaskar Chakravorti, "Early Lessons from India's Demonetization Experiment," *Harvard Business Review*, 14 March 2017, https://hbr.org/2017/03/early-lessons-from-indias-demonetization-experiment

**383** See e.g. Makia Freeman, "Cashless Agenda: Who's Behind It in India?," Tools for Freedom, 5 January 2017, http://freedom-articles.toolsforfreedom.com/cashless-agenda-accelerates-india/; Michael Snyder, "Moving Toward a One World Government, a One World Economy and a One World Religion," *Economic Collapse Blog*, http://theeconomiccollapseblog.com/archives/moving-toward-a-one-world-government-a-one-world-economy-and-a-one-world-religion

**384** B. Chakravorti, op. cit.

**385** Milan Vaishnav, Saksham Khosla, "The Indian Administrative Service Meets Big Data," *Carnegie Endowment*, 1 September 2016, http://carnegieendowment.org/2016/09/01/indian-administrative-service-meets-big-data-pub-64457

**386** V. Srinivas, op. cit.

**387** Jennifer Surane and Christopher Cannon, "Why China's Payment Apps Give U.S. Bankers Nightmares," *Bloomberg*, 23 May 2018, https://www.bloomberg.com/graphics/2018-payment-systems-china-usa/

**388** Ibid.

**389** John Engen, "Lessons from a Mobile Payments Revolution," *American Banker*, 23 May 2018, https://www.americanbanker.com/news/why-chinas-mobile-payments-revolution-matters-for-us-bankers

**390** Kevin Wack, "How Amazon Is Shaking Up Financial Services," *American Banker*, 18 March 2018, https://www.americanbanker.com/slideshow/how-amazon-is-shaking-up-financial-services

**391** Andy O'Sullivan, "The Future of Banks Is Probably Not Banks," *Medium*, 15 October 2017, https://startupsventurecapital.com/the-future-of-banks-is-probably-not-banks-5f54a3e81237

**392** Dennis Lehane, "Amazon's Business Practices Are Scorched-Earth

Capitalism," *Social Justice Books* (2018), https://socialjusticebooks. org/about/why-boycott-amazon/

**393** Aleksander Berentsen, Fabian Schar, "The Case for Central Bank Electronic Money and the Non-case for Central Bank Cryptocurrencies," *St. Louis Federal Reserve*, 2 February 2018, https://research. stlouisfed.org/publications/review/2018/02/13/the-case-for-central-bank-electronic-money-and-the-non-case-for-central-bank-cryptocurrencies

**394** Genesys Fund, op. cit.; Jane Wild, "Central Banks Explore Blockchain to Create Digital Currencies," *Financial Times*, 1 November 2016, https://www.ft.com/content/f15d3ab6-750d-11e6-bf48-b372cdb1043a; Frances Coppola, "Central Banks are Considering Their Own Digital Currencies for Global Payments," *AmericanExpress.com*, 2018, https://www.americanexpress.com/us/foreign-exchange/articles/digital-currencies-by-central-banks-for-global-payments/

**395** "Russia's Central Bank to Develop National Cryptocurrency," *Tass*, 2 June 2017, http://tass.com/economy/949263

**396** A. Berensten, et al., op. cit.

**397** "Russia Is Considering An Official Cryptocurrency Called the 'CryptoRuble,'" *Business Insider*, 19 October 2017, http://www.businessinsider.com/russia-is-considering-an-official-cryptocurrency-2017-10

**398** Laura Shin, "Why Cryptocurrencies Could Push the Dollar from World Reserve Currency Status," *Forbes,* 7 November 2017, https://www.forbes.com/sites/laurashin/2017/11/07/why-cryptocurrencies-could-push-the-dollar-from-world-reserve-currency-status/#4ba46b4d6a9e

**399** F. Coppola, op. cit.

**400** Caitlin Long, "Central Banks Can't Ignore Blockchain's Obvious Lure," *American Banker*, 10 June 2016, http://www.americanbanker.com/bankthink/central-banks-cant-ignore-blockchains-obvious-lure-1081428-1.html

**401** Ben Broadbent, "Central Banks and Digital Currencies," Speech given at London School of Economics, *Bank of England*, 2 March 2016, http://www.bankofengland.co.uk/publications/Pages/speeches/2016/886.aspx

**402** Frank Van Lerven, "Setting the Record Straight: Sovereign Money

Is Not Full-Reserve Banking," *Positive Money*, 27 April 2017, http://positivemoney.org/2017/04/sovereign-money-is-not-full-reserve-banking/

**403** M. Baxter, op. cit.

**404** See "Sovereign Money: An Introduction," *Positive Money*, http://positivemoney.org/our-proposals/sovereign-money-introduction/

**405** "Iceland Looks at Ending Boom and Bust with Radical Money Plan," *UK Telegraph*, 31 March 2015, http://www.telegraph.co.uk/finance/economics/11507810/Iceland-looks-at-ending-boom-and-bust-with-radical-money-plan.html; John Miller, "Swiss Group Says It Has Signatures for 'Sovereign Money' Vote," *Reuters*, 31 October 2015, http://uk.reuters.com/article/uk-swiss-sovereign-money-ey-idUKKCN0SP0FW20151031

**406** A. Berentsen, et al., op. cit.

**407** Ibid.

**408** Lucy Meakin, "Cash Isn't Going Down Without a Fight in Digital U.K.," *Bloomberg*, 19 March 2018, https://www.bloomberg.com/news/articles/2018-03-20/cash-isn-t-going-down-without-a-fight-in-digital-u-k

**409** "India Scraps 500 and 1,000 Rupee Bank Notes Overnight," *BBC News*, 9 November 2016, http://www.bbc.com/news/business-37906742

**410** "FDR Takes United States Off Gold Standard," *History*, https://www.history.com/this-day-in-history/fdr-takes-united-states-off-gold-standard

**411** Izabella Kaminska, "Time to Reevaluate Blockchain Hype," *Financial Times*, 3 August 2016, https://ftalphaville.ft.com/2016/08/03/2171799/time-to-reevaluate-blockchain-hype/

**412** David Dawkins, "Bitcoin Price Warning: BTC Will Drop to '$100' After Being 'Regulated into Oblivion'," *UK Express*, 9 July 2018, https://www.express.co.uk/finance/city/985964/Bitcoin-price-ripple-cryptocurrency-ethereum-BTC-to-USD-XRP-Joseph-Stiglitz

**413** Piotr Wojtuszko, Adam Bujnowski, "Central Bank Digital Currency and Its Impact on the Banking System," *Banking Hub*, 22 August 2018, https://www.bankinghub.eu/innovation-digital/central-bank-digital-currency

**414** Barry Ritholtz, "Fed: Who Is Holding All the Excess Reserves?",

*Ritholtz.com*, 23 November 2015, http://ritholtz.com/2015/11/fed-who-is-holding-all-the-excess-reserves/

**415** A. Berentsen, et al., op. cit.

**416** "M2 for China," *FRED*, October 2018, https://fred.stlouisfed.org/series/MYAGM2CNM189N

**417** "China Inflation Rate," *Trading Economics*, December 2018, https://tradingeconomics.com/china/inflation-cpi

**418** "Gross Domestic Product for China," *FRED*, 18 September 2018, https://fred.stlouisfed.org/series/MKTGDPCNA646NWDB

**419** M. Ricks, et al., op. cit.

**420** Ibid., references omitted.

**421** Ibid.

**422** John Barrdear and Michael Kumhof, "The Macroeconomics of Central Bank Issued Digital Currencies," *Bank of England*, July 2016, http://www.bankofengland.co.uk/research/Documents/workingpapers/2016/swp605.pdf

**423** "On Banking: A Reply to Positive Money," *Tax Research UK*, 5 June 2015, http://www.taxresearch.org.uk/Blog/2015/06/05/on-banking-a-reply-to-positive-money/

**424** See Chapter 8.

**425** See Ellen Brown, *The Public Bank Solution*, Third Millennium Press, 2012.

**426** David Fettig, "Lender of More Than Last Resort," *Federal Reserve Bank of Minneapolis*, 1 Dec 2002, https://www.minneapolisfed.org/publications/the-region/lender-of-more-than-last-resort

**427** Ibid.

**428** Timothy Canova, "The Bottom-Up Recovery: A New Deal in Banking and Public Finance (Chapter 3)," Nova Southeastern University Shepard Broad Law Center Research Paper No. 14-004, 27 Oct 2014, in *When Government Helped: Learning from the Successes and Failures of the New Deal*, Oxford University Press, 2014, pp. 51-85, http://papers.ssrn.com/sol3/papers.cfm?abstract_id=2511408

**429** F. Coppola, op. cit.

**430** M. Ricks, et al., op. cit.

**431** Wright Patman in *Congressional Record of the House of Representatives*, Volume 87, Part 7, pp. 7582-7583, September 29, 1941.

**432** Ray Perryman, "The End of Quantitative Easing", *Perryman-Group*, 7 November 2014, http://perrymangroup.com/2014/11/07/the-end-of-quantitative-easing/; Greg Robb, "Here's When Fed Officials Say They Will Hit 2% Inflation Target," *Market Watch*, 15 March 2017, http://www.marketwatch.com/story/heres-when-fed-officials-say-they-will-hit-2-inflation-target-2017-03-15

**433** See e.g. Daniel Amerman, "The ABCs of Popping a Third Asset Bubble," *Seeking Alpha*, 26 March 2018, https://seekingalpha.com/article/4158916-abcs-popping-third-asset-bubble

**434** Jim Puzzanghera, "Federal Reserve Sends Record $97.7-Billion Profit to Treasury," *L.A. Times*, 11 January 2016, http://www.latimes.com/business/la-fi-federal-reserve-profit-20160111-story.html

**435** Veronique de Rugy, "Projected Interest Payments on Federal Debt Balloon", *Mercatus Center*, George Mason University, 1 October 2010, http://mercatus.org/publication/projected-interest-payments-federal-debt-balloon

**436** Patrice Hill, "Bernanke Delivers Blunt Warning on U.S. Debt", *The Washington Times*, 25 February 2010, http://www.washingtontimes.com/news/2010/feb/25/bernanke-delivers-warning-on-us-debt/?page=all

**437** Bill Bonner, "No Cutting Back: The Bernanke Money Printing Story", *Daily Reckoning*, 3 November 2010, http://dailyreckoning.com/no-cutting-back-the-bernanke-money-printing-story/

**438** Jim Puzzanghera, "Federal Reserve Sends Record $97.7-Billion Profit to Treasury," *L.A. Times*, 11 January 2016, http://www.latimes.com/business/la-fi-federal-reserve-profit-20160111-story.html

**439** Ray Perryman, op. cit.

**440** "M2 Update: First Decline after 16 Consecutive Increases", *Zerohedge*, 4 November 2010. http://www.zerohedge.com/article/m2-update-first-decline-after-16-consecutive-increases

**441** Dean Baker, "Deficit Commission Co-Chairs Ignore Economic Reality", *Truthout*, 11 November 2010, www.truth-out.org/archive/component/k2/item/92817:dean-baker--deficit-commission-co-chairs-ignore-economic-reality

**442** Stephen Gandel, "Debt Ceiling: Could Ron Paul's Plan Save Us from Disaster, Twice?", *Time*, 2 July 2012, http://business.time.com/2011/07/05/debt-ceiling-could-ron-pauls-plan-save-us-from-disaster-twice/

**443** Alan Grayson, "Ending the Debt Limit Crisis: Dear Ben Bernanke", *Reuters*, 9 Oct 2013, http://blogs.reuters.com/great-debate/2013/10/09/ending-the-debt-limit-crisis-dear-ben-bernanke/

**444** Warren Mosler, John Carney, "Only Thing We Have to Fear From the Taper Is Fear of the Taper Itself," *CNBC.com*, 18 September 2013, http://www.cnbc.com/2013/09/17/only-thing-we-have-to-fear-from-the-taper-is-fear-of-the-taper-itself.html

**445** Richard Murphy, "The Battle for Money Has Begun," *Tax Research UK*, 6 June 2018, https://www.taxresearch.org.uk/Blog/2018/06/06/the-battle-for-money-has-begun/

**446** Richard Murphy, "Why Governments Need to Issue Bonds Despite Modern Monetary Theory," *Tax Research UK*, 9 November 2018, https://www.taxresearch.org.uk/Blog/2018/11/09/why-governments-need-to-issue-bonds-despite-modern-monetary-theory/

**447** John Carney, "This Is the Biggest Mistake People Are Making About QE Now," *CNBC.com*, 13 Dec 2013, https://www.cnbc.com/2013/12/13/this-is-the-biggest-mistake-people-are-making-about-qe-now.html

**448** "Written Evidence Submitted by Positive Money on the Effectiveness and Impact of Post-2008 UK Monetary Policy," *Positive Money*, 3 March 2017, http://data.parliament.uk/writtenevidence/committeeevidence.svc/evidencedocument/treasury-committee/effectiveness-and-impact-of-post2008-uk-monetary-policy/written/48269.html

**449** "Letter to the Chancellor," *Positive Money*, http://positivemoney.org/lettertochancellor/

**450** Robin Harding, "Abenomics a 'Success,' Declares IMF," *Financial Times*, 19 June 2017, https://www.ft.com/content/56f75512-54c6-11e7-9fed-c19e2700005f

**451** Pascal-Emmanuel Gobry, "The Magic of Abenomics," *The Week*, 24 October 2017, http://theweek.com/articles/732541/magic-abenomics.

**452** Noah Smith, "Japan Goes with Another Round of Abenomics," *Bloomberg*, 25 October 2017, https://www.bloomberg.com/view/articles/2017-10-25/japan-goes-with-another-round-of-abenomics

**453** Eric Lonergan, "Has the Bank of Japan Solved the 'Piketty Problem'? Japan's Unlikely Re-distribution," *EpisodeBlog.com*, 20 February 2017, https://www.episodeblog.com/2017/02/20/bank-japan-solved-piketty-problem-japans-unlikely-re-distribution/

**454** Robin Harding, "Tightening Labour Market Yet to Push Up Wages or Consumer Prices," *Bloomberg*, 27 April 2017, https://www.ft.com/content/3829dda0-2bbb-11e7-9ec8-168383da43b7?mhq5j=e1

**455** "Japan's Unemployment Rate Falls to 22-Year Low of 2.8% in February," *Japan Times*, 31 March 2017, http://www.japantimes.co.jp/news/2017/03/31/business/economy-business/joblessness-falls-22-year-low-2-8-february/#.WV-E04TyvIV; Elena Holodny, "The Japanese Yen Just Spiked to Its Highest Level Since November," *Business Insider*, 11 April 2017, http://uk.businessinsider.com/japanese-yen-currency-update-april-11-2017-2017-4?r=US&IR=T

**456** Kevin Drum, "The Enduring Mystery of Japan's Economy," *Mother Jones*, 27 February 2017, http://www.motherjones.com/kevin-drum/2017/02/enduring-mystery-japans-economy/

**457** Joseph Stiglitz, "Japan Is a Model, Not a Cautionary Tale," *New York Times*, 9 June 2013, https://opinionator.blogs.nytimes.com/2013/06/09/japan-is-a-model-not-a-cautionary-tale]

**458** "Plight of Irregular Workers," Japan Times, 1 May 2016, http://www.japantimes.co.jp/opinion/2016/01/05/editorials/plight-of-irregular-workers/#.WV-HS4TyvIV

**459** Connor Cislo, "Scandal Threatens to Derail Abe's Economic Agenda," *Bloomberg*, 13 March 2018, https://www.bloomberg.com/news/articles/2018-03-13/scandal-threatens-to-throw-abe-s-economic-agenda-off-course

**460** "Bank of Japan Is Not Undertaking Fed-Like Tapering, Says Governor," *Reuters*, 23 November 2018, https://economictimes.indiatimes.com/markets/stocks/news/bank-of-japan-is-not-undertaking-fed-like-tapering-says-governor/articleshow/66760334.cms

**461** Ambrose Evans-Pritchard, "Why Paul Krugman Is Wrong," *The Telegraph*, 15 December 2015, http://www.telegraph.co.uk/finance/economics/11294510/Ambrose-Evans-Pritchard-Why-Paul-Krugman-is-wrong.html

**462** Tejvan Pettinger, "Keynesian Economics," *Economics Help*, 5 February 2017, https://www.economicshelp.org/blog/6801/economics/keynesian-economics/

**463** For an extensive discussion, see Ellen Brown, *The Public Bank Solution* (Baton Rouge: Third Millennium Press, 2013).

**464** Joyce Nelson, Bypassing Dystopia: Hope-Filled Challenges to Corporate Rule (Comox, Canada: Watershed Sentinel Books, 2018).

**465** China Real Time Report, "How China's Trying to Boost Its Economy: 'Qualitative Easing'", *Wall Street Journal*, 11 August 2014, https://blogs.wsj.com/chinarealtime/2014/08/11/how-chinas-trying-to-boost-its-economy-qualitative-easing/

**466** "In China, Focus of Monetary Easing Turns to Surgical Strikes," *Bloomberg*, 1 May 2015, http://www.scmp.com/business/global-economy/article/1782787/china-focus-monetary-easing-turns-surgical-strikes

**467** Shelly Sigo, "Trumps Plan a Recipe for Failure, Former Infrastructure Advisor Says," *Council of Development Finance Agencies*, 29 January 2018, https://www.cdfa.net/cdfa/cdfaweb.nsf/pages/35425/$file/Trump%E2%80%99s%20plan%20a%20recipe%20for%20failure%2C%20former%20infrastructure%20advisor%20says.pdf

**468** Donald Cohen, "Trump's Infrastructure Plan: Fiction? Scam? Actually, Both," *American Prospect*, 14 February 2018, http://prospect.org/article/trumps-infrastructure-plan-fiction-scam-actually-both

**469** John Faso, "We Need an Infrastructure Bank," *Washington Examiner*, 23 January 2018, https://www.washingtonexaminer.com/we-need-an-infrastructure-bank

**470** "Private Equity Returns Far Exceed Declining Market Returns On Multiple Time Horizons," *American Investment Council*, 12 April 2016, https://www.investmentcouncil.org/private-equity-returns-far-exceed-declining-market-returns-on-multiple-time-horizons/

**471** "Government Pays More in Contracts, Study Finds," *The New York Times*, 12 September 2011, https://www.nytimes.com/2011/09/13/us/13contractor.html

**472** Eduardo Engel, et al., "Public-Private Partnerships to Revamp U.S. Infrastructure," *Brookings*, 25 February 2011, https://www.brookings.edu/research/public-private-partnerships-to-revamp-u-s-infrastructure/

**473** David Hall, "Why Public-Private Partnerships Don't Work: The Many Advantages of the Public Alternative," *PSIRU*, February 2015, http://www.world-psi.org/sites/default/files/rapport_eng_56pages_a4_lr.pdf

**474** Liz Essley, "Debt Raises Doubt About Virginia Buying Dulles Greenway Toll Road," *Washington Examiner*, 27 January 2013, https://www.washingtonexaminer.com/debt-raises-doubt-about-virginia-buying-dulles-greenway-toll-road/article/2519749?rel=author

**475** William Mallett, "Indiana Toll Road Bankruptcy Chills Climate for Public-Private Partnerships," *National Council for Public-Private Partnerships*, 29 September 2014, http://www.ncppp.org/wp-content/uploads/2013/02/CRS-Insights-Indiana-Toll-Road-Bankruptcy-Chills-Climate-for-P3s.pdf

**476** Will Freeman and Arthur Kroeber, "China's Fast Track to Development," *Wall Street Journal*, 2 June 2010, https://www.wsj.com/articles/SB10001424052748704025304575283953879199386

**477** Douglas J. Elliott, Kai Yan, "The Chinese Financial System," *Brookings*, July 2013, https://www.brookings.edu/wp-content/uploads/2016/06/chinese-financial-system-elliott-yan.pdf

**478** Chen Zhao, "China: A Bullish Case," *Asia Center, Harvard*, 16 April 2017, https://asiacenter.harvard.edu/news/event-recap-%E2%80%93-china-bullish-case

**479** Robert Skidelsky, "Helicopter Money Is Back in the Air," *The Guardian*, 22 September 2016, https://www.theguardian.com/business/2016/sep/22/helicopter-money-back-in-the-air

**480** Chen Zhao, "Stop Worrying about Chinese Debt," *Financial Times*, 4 December 2017, https://www.ft.com/content/0ca50290-d82c-11e7-9504-59efdb70e12f

**481** Joseph Grundfest, et al., "Getting More Bang for the Fed's Buck," *New York Times*, 23 October 2012, http://www.nytimes.com/2012/10/24/opinion/why-the-fed-should-buy-munis-not-mortgages.html

**482** Laura Bliss, "Be Wary of a Trump-Led Infrastructure Bank," *City Lab*, 22 November 2016, https://www.citylab.com/equity/2016/11/be-wary-of-a-trump-led-infrastructure-bank/508388/

**483** Timothy Canova, Betty Williams, "The Public Option," *New America Foundation*, June 2011, https://www.newamerica.org/economic-growth/policy-papers/the-public-option/; discussed in Penelope Lemov, "The Case for a State-Owned Bank," *Governing*, 12 April 2012, http://www.governing.com/columns/public-finance/col-case-state-owned-bank-north-dakota.html

**484** "Japan Post's Murky Privatization," *Japan Times*, 30 October 2015, https://www.japantimes.co.jp/opinion/2015/10/30/editorials/japan-posts-murky-privatization/

**485** Peter Alford, "Japan's Post Bank Takes Up Bonds Slack," The Australian, 8 April 2010, http://www.theaustralian.com.au/business/japans-post-bank-takes-up-bonds-slack/news-story/d323c-4b34008a13b05332f3113c2731d

**486** Frederic Rolando, "Delivering a National Infrastructure Bank ... through the Post Office," *NALC.org*, July 2013, https://www.nalc.org/news/the-postal-record/2013/july-2013/document/07-2013-president.pdf

**487** James Butkiewicz, "Reconstruction Finance Corporation," *Economic History Association*, 19 July 2002, https://eh.net/encyclopedia/reconstruction-finance-corporation/; "Reconstruction Finance Corporation (RFC)," Encyclopedia of the Great Depression, *Encyclopedia.com*, http://www.encyclopedia.com/economics/encyclopedias-almanacs-transcripts-and-maps/reconstruction-finance-corporation-rfc

**488** Michael Gou, et al., "Banking Acts of 1932," *Federal Reserve History*, 22 November 2013, http://www.federalreservehistory.org/Events/DetailView/12.; Office of the Secretary of the Treasury, *Final Report on the Reconstruction Finance Corporation* (Washington, D.C.: Government Printing Office, 1959), https://fraser.stlouisfed.org/files/docs/publications/rcf/rfc_19590506_finalreport.pdf.

**489** Office of the Secretary of the Treasury, Final Report on the Reconstruction Finance Corporation, ibid.

**490** For a fuller discussion of these and other successful precedents, see Ellen Brown, *The Public Bank Solution*, 2013.

**491** Richard Anderson, "Some Tables of Historical U.S. Currency and Monetary Aggregates Data," *St. Louis Fed Working Paper Series*, April 2003, http://research.stlouisfed.org/wp/2003/2003-006.pdf

**492** Clyde Prestowitz, *The Betrayal of American Prosperity: Free Market Delusions, America's Decline, and How We Must Compete in the Post-Dollar Era* (Simon and Schuster May, 2010), pages 55-56, https://books.google.com/books?id=q_vCY4f7qSkC&dq=lincoln+%26+gdp+doubled&source=gbs_navlinks_s.

**493** Maury Klein, "The Joining of the Rails: Financing the Transcontinental Railroad," *The Gilder Lehrman Institute of American History*, undated, https://www.gilderlehrman.org/history-by-era/development-west/essays/financing-transcontinental-railroad

**494** Irwin Unger, *The Greenback Era* (Princeton University Press, 1964).

**495** J. G. Randall, *The Civil War and Reconstruction* (Boston: Heath & Co., 1937, 2d edition 1961), pages 3-11.

**496** Milton Friedman and Anna Jacobson Schwartz, *A Monetary History*

*of the United States, 1867-1960* (Princeton University Press, 1963), pages 6-7, 26-27.

**497** Richard Murphy, Colin Hines, "Green Quantitative Easing: Paying for the Economy We Need," *Finance for the Future*, December 2010, http://www.financeforthefuture.com/GreenQuEasing.pdf

**498** "The Green New Deal," *Jill2016.com*, https://www.jill2016.com/greennewdeal

**499** Stephanie Kelton, et al., "We Can Pay For A Green New Deal," *Huffpost*, 30 November 2018, https://www.huffingtonpost.com/entry/opinion-green-new-deal-cost_us_5c0042b2e4b027f1097bda5b

**500** David Roberts, "Alexandria Ocasio-Cortez Is Already Pressuring Nancy Pelosi on Climate Change," *Vox.com*, 15 November 2018, https://www.vox.com/energy-and-environment/2018/11/14/18094452/alexandria-ocasio-cortez-nancy-pelosi-protest-climate-change-2020; "What Is the Green New Deal?", *SunriseMovement.Org*, https://www.sunrisemovement.org/gnd-strategy

**501** See Ellen Brown, "The Trillion Dollar Coin: A Debt Solution for the People," *Yes Magazine*, 17 January 2013, https://www.yesmagazine.org/new-economy/trillion-dollar-coin

**502** "How Much Currency Is in Circulation?", *Federal Reserve*, http://www.federalreserve.gov/faqs/currency_12773.htm

**503** Cullen Roche, "Philip Diehl, Former Head of the US Mint Addresses Confusion Over the Platinum Coin Idea," *Pragmatic Capitalism*, 8 January 2013, https://www.pragcap.com/philip-diehl-former-head-of-the-us-mint-addresses-confusion-over-the-platinum-coin-idea/

**504** Geoff Crocker, "The Economic Necessity of Basic Income", *Centre for Welfare Reform*, 2014, http://www.centreforwelfarereform.org/library/by-az/the-economic-necessity-of-basic-income.html

**505** George Zarkadakis, "Will a Robot Replace You?," *Huffington Post*, 8 November 2016, http://www.huffingtonpost.com/george-zarkadakis/will-a-robot-replace-you_b_8506324.html

**506** Katja Grace, et al., "When Will AI Exceed Human Performance? Evidence from AI Experts," *Cornell University Library*, 30 May 2017, http://www.scottlondon.com/reviews/ostrom.html. See also Colin Lewis, "Study Indicates Robots Could Replace 80% of Jobs," *Robotenomics*, 16 April 2014, https://robotenomics.com/2014/04/16/study-indicates-robots-could-replace-80-of-jobs/

**507** Jim Pugh, "Why Switzerland's Universal Basic Income Referendum Matters, Even Though It Failed," *Quartz*, 5 June 2016, https://qz.com/699739/why-switzerlands-universal-basic-income-referendum-matters-even-though-failed/; Rebecca Fortin, "Canada Is Betting on a Universal Basic Income to Help Cities Gutted by Manufacturing Job Loss," *Quartz*, 20 February 2017, https://qz.com/914247/canada-is-betting-on-a-universal-basic-income-to-help-cities-gutted-by-manufacturing-job-loss/; Karl Widerquist, "Brazil: Basic Income in Quatinga Velho Celebrates 3-Years of Operation," *Basic Income*, 7 June 2012, http://basicincome.org/news/2012/06/brazil-basic-income-in-quatinga-velho-celebrates-3-years-of-operation/

**508** S. Copland, op. cit.

**509** Guy Standing, "India's Experiment in Basic Income Grants," *Global Dialogue*, November 2013, http://isa-global-dialogue.net/indias-great-experiment-the-transformative-potential-of-basic-income-grants/

**510** Jim Brunsden, "ECB Urged to Lavish 'Helicopter Money' on Consumers," *Financial Times*, 16 June 2016, https://www.ft.com/content/c5d08c5c-339c-11e6-bda0-04585c31b153

**511** Ben Dyson, Graham Hodgson, "Digital Cash: Why Central Banks Should Start Issuing Electronic Money," *Positive Money*, January 2016, http://positivemoney.org/wp-content/uploads/2016/01/Digital_Cash_WebPrintReady_20160113.pdf

**512** J. Brunsden, op. cit.; *Unconditional Basic Income Europe*, https://basicincome-europe.org/ubie/

**513** Mark Blyth and Eric Lonergan, "Print Less but Transfer More: Why Central Banks Should Give Money Directly to the People", *Foreign Affairs*, September/October 2014, https://www.foreignaffairs.com/articles/united-states/2014-08-11/print-less-transfer-more

**514** G. Crocker, op. cit.

**515** S. Copland, op. cit.; Josh Mitteldorf, "How Much Labor do We Need?", *Daily Inspiration*, 4 September 2017, https://dailyinspirationblog.wordpress.com/2017/09/04/ubi/

**516** John McChesney, "GI Bill's Impact Slipping in Recent Years," *National Public Radio*, 26 September 2007, http://www.npr.org/templates/story/story.php?storyId=14715263

**517** Chuck Leddy, "A Critical Look at the GI Bill's Impact," *Boston Globe*, 10 September 2009, http://archive.boston.com/ae/books/articles/2009/09/10/a_critical_look_at_the_gi_bills_impact/

**518** Jared Lyon, "The GI Bill's Impact on the Past, Present and Future," *IVMF, Syracuse University*, https://ivmf.syracuse.edu/2013/06/21/the-gi-bills-impact-on-the-past-present-and-future/

**519** "Student Debt Apocalypse," *Mybudget360,* http://www.mybudget360.com/student-debt-apocalypse-median-wages-versus-median-student-debt-college-loan-growth/

**520** "" Zack Friedman, "Student Loan Debt Statistics in 2018: A $1.5 Trillion Crisis," *Forbes*, 13 June 2018, https://www.forbes.com/sites/zackfriedman/2018/06/13/student-loan-debt-statistics-2018/#205465af7310

**521** Preston Mueller, "The Non-dischargeability of Private Student Loans: A Looming Financial Crisis?", *Emory Law*, http://law.emory.edu/ebdj/content/volume-32/issue-1/comments/non-dischargeability-private-student-loans-looming-crisis.html

**522** Tim Worstall, "Meet the Economics 'Genius' behind Jeremy Corbyn," *The Register (UK)*, 16 Aug. 2015, http://www.theregister.co.uk/2015/08/16/richard_murphy_corbyn_economics/

**523** J. W. Mason, "What Recovery? The Case for Continued Expansionary Policy at the Fed," *Roosevelt Institute*, 25 July 2017, http://rooseveltinstitute.org/wp-content/uploads/2017/07/Monetary-Policy-Report.pdf

**524** D. Hermanutz, op. cit.

**525** Kimberly Amadeo, "What Is the Real Unemployment Rate?," *The Balance*, 1 June 2018, https://www.thebalance.com/what-is-the-real-unemployment-rate-3306198

**526** John Williams, "Alternate Unemployment Charts," *ShadowStats.com*, 1 June 2018, http://www.shadowstats.com/alternate_data/unemployment-charts

**527** Joseph Stiglitz, "Austerity Has Strangled Britain. Only Labour Will Consign It to History," *The Guardian*, 7 June 2017, https://www.theguardian.com/commentisfree/2017/jun/07/austerity-britain-labour-neoliberalism-reagan-thatcher

**528** Dom Galeon, "New Report Claims UBI Would Grow the U.S. Economy by $2.5 Trillion," *Futurism*, 1 September 2017, https://futurism.com/new-report-claims-ubi-would-grow-the-u-s-economy-by-2-5-trillion/

**529** "2017 Index of Economic Freedom," *Heritage Foundation*, 2017, http://www.heritage.org/index/explore?view=by-variables.

**530** Lucas Kawa, "STUDY: Every $1 if Infrastructure Spending Boosts the Economy by $2," *Business Insider*, 30 November 2012, http://www.businessinsider.com/infrastructure-economic-multiplier-2012-11

**531** Michael Hudson, "Financial Predators v. Labor, Industry and Democracy", *Michael-Hudson*, 2 Aug 2012, http://michael-hudson.com/2012/08/financial-predators-v-labor-industry-and-democracy/

**532** Paul Buchheit, "Morbid Inequality: Now Just SIX Men Have as Much Wealth as Half the World's Population," *Common Dreams*, 20 February 2017, https://www.commondreams.org/views/2017/02/20/morbid-inequality-now-just-six-men-have-much-wealth-half-worlds-population

**533** "Statistical Release: OTC Derivatives Statistics at End June 2017," *BIS.org*, 2 November 2017, https://www.bis.org/publ/otc_hy1711.pdf

**534** Marilyne Tolle, "Central Bank Digital Currency: The End of Monetary Policy As We Know It?", *Bankunderground.co.uk*, 25 July 2016, https://bankunderground.co.uk/2016/07/25/central-bank-digital-currency-the-end-of-monetary-policy-as-we-know-it/

**535** Scott Smith, The Economist Tale: How Technology Enables a National's Income, the End of Income Taxes, and a Balanced Budget (2017), pages 51-52, www.EconomistsTale.com.

**536** Wikipedia, "Financial Transaction Tax," https://en.wikipedia.org/wiki/Financial_transaction_tax

**537** Joe Kirwin, "EU Financial Transactions Tax Talks Kicked to End 2017," *Bloomberg*, 10 July 2017, https://www.bna.com/eu-financial-transactions-n73014461368/

**538** Joe Kirwin, "EU to Restart Financial Transactions Tax Negotiations," *Bloomberg*, 1 May 2018, https://www.bna.com/eu-restart-financial-n57982091709/

**539** Izabella Kaminska, "How to Kill The European Repo Market in 10 Easy Steps," *Alphaville FT*, 7 May 2013, https://ftalphaville.ft.com/2013/05/07/1489382/how-to-kill-the-european-repo-market-in-10-easy-steps/

**540** "Desperately Seeking $11.2 Trillion in Collateral, Or How 'Modern Money' Really Works," *Zero Hedge*, 1 May 2013, http://www.zerohedge.com/news/2013-05-01/desperately-seeking-112-trillion-collateral-or-how-modern-money-really-works

**541** John Carney, "The Size of the Bank Bailout: $29 Trillion," *CNBC.com*, 14 December 2011, https://www.cnbc.com/id/45674390

**542** Ryan Tracy, "Banks Retreat from Market That Keeps Cash Flowing," *Wall Street Journal*, 13 August 2014, http://www.wsj.com/articles/banks-retreat-from-market-that-keeps-cash-flowing-1407890157

**543** Yves Smith, "Banks Withdrawing from Repo Market," *Naked Capitalism*, 13 August 2014, http://www.nakedcapitalism.com/2014/08/banks-withdrawing-repo-market.html

**544** Ibid.

**545** Devin Smith, "MMT and Debunking AMI: Positive Money," *New Economic Perspectives*, 4 February 2017, http://neweconomicperspectives.org/2017/02/mmt-debunking-ami-postive-money.html

**546** Scott Smith, op. cit., pages 51-52.

**547** Ibid., pages 78-83.

**548** Jason Hickel, "Basic Income Isn't Just a Nice Idea. It's a Birthright," *The Guardian*, 4 March 2017, https://www.theguardian.com/global-development-professionals-network/2017/mar/04/basic-income-birthright-eliminating-poverty

**549** Richard Dye and Richard England, "Assessing the Theory and Practice of Land Value Taxation," *Lincoln Institute of Land Policy*, February 2010, https://www.lincolninst.edu/publications/policy-focus-reports/assessing-theory-practice-land-value-taxation

**550** Mason Gaffney, The Mason Gaffney Reader—Essays on Solving the "Unsolvable" (The Henry George Institute, 2013).

**551** "Richard Werner: Banking & The Economy," *The Free Lunch*, 30 March 2011, https://www.youtube.com/watch?v=wDHSUgA29Ls

**552** Paul Craig Roberts, "Collapse at Hand," *PaulCraigRoberts.org*, 5 June 2012, http://www.paulcraigroberts.org/2012/06/05/collapse-at-hand/

**553** Steve Denning, "Big Banks and Derivatives: Why Another Financial Crisis Is Inevitable," *Forbes*, 8 January 2013, https://www.forbes.com/sites/stevedenning/2013/01/08/five-years-after-the-financial-meltdown-the-water-is-still-full-of-big-sharks/

**554** Sean Watterson, "Can Public Banking Save the World?," *Nonprofit Quarterly*, 9 July 2018, https://nonprofitquarterly.org/2018/07/09/

can-public-banking-save-the-world/

**555** Alvin Rabushka, "Representation without Taxation: The Colonial
Roots of American Taxation, 1700-1754," *Questia*, 2003, https://
www.questia.com/library/journal/1G1-112022644/representa-
tion-without-taxation-the-colonial-roots

**556** "History of Colonial Money," *Boston Federal Reserve* [undated],
https://www.bostonfed.org/-/media/Documents/education/pubs/
historyo.pdf

**557** Karl Rhodes, "The Counterfeiting Weapon," *Richmond Federal
Reserve*, 2012 (first quarter), https://www.richmondfed.org/~/media/
richmondfedorg/publications/research/region_focus/2012/q1/pdf/
economic_history.pdf

**558** Robert Natelson, "Paper Money and the Original Understanding of
the Coinage Clause," *Harvard Journal of Law & Public Policy*, Vol.
31, no. 3, pages 1017-81.

**559** "The First Bank of the United States, 1791–1811," *Federal Reserve
History*, 4 December 2015, https://www.federalreservehistory.org/
essays/first_bank_of_the_us

**560** "1973 Oil Crisis," *Wikipedia*, 27 May 2017, https://en.wikipedia.org/
wiki/1973_oil_crisis

**561** Secular Investor, "Stunning: Italy Says NO to Bail-In Scenarios,"
*Zero Hedge*, 1 June 2017, http://www.zerohedge.com/news/2017-06-
01/stunning-italy-says-no-bail-scenario%E2%80%99s

**562** Austrian School of Economics," *Business Dictionary*, http://www.
businessdictionary.com/definition/Austrian-School-of-Economics.
html

**563** Andrew Tar, "Smart Contracts, Explained," *Cointelegraph*, 31 October 2017, https://cointelegraph.com/explained/smart-contracts-ex-
plained

# INDEX

## A

dot.com bubble 18

Abe, Shinzo, 272

Abenomics, 272, 274, 401

American International Group (AIG), 19, 42, 78-79, 82-83, 108, 129, 255, 374

Alaska, 151

Allaby, Devon, 182

Alibaba, 225-226

AliPay 225-227

Alperovitz, Gar, 128

Amazon, 170, 196, 225-229, 396

American Bankers Association, 156

American Revolution, 131

Anglo Irish Bank, 127

Antonopoulos, Andreas, 206

Arizona, 151

Arnold, Roger, 21

asset-backed securities, 65, 75, 116, 306

ATM fees, 40

Austrian economics, 304

Automated Clearing House, 145, 203

automation, 182, 300, 337, 395

## B

bail-in, 96-102, 148, 223, 235, 245, 259, 336, 348, 351-352, 377-378, 411

Baker, Dean, 265, 376, 400

Bancor, 206-209, 394

Bangla-Pesa, 194, 208

Bank of America, 33, 37, 39, 71, 95, 101-102, 108, 112, 126, 128, 148

Bank of Canada, 278

Bank of Canada Act, 278

Bank of England, 48, 127, 131, 235-236, 252, 316, 345, 370, 397, 399

Bank of Japan, 132, 272, 275, 401, 402

Bank of North Dakota (BND), 142-143, 149, 162, 258, 334, 339, 382-384

Bank of the Commons, 205

Bank for International Settlements, 20, 26, 35, 171-172, 178, 318, 395

Bank Panic of 1907, 155

banks as intermediaries, 53

Bank Secrecy Act, 35, 249, 366-367

Banking Act of 1935, 24

Bankruptcy, 68, 79-83, 85, 90, 96-97, 100-101, 114, 256, 282, 306, 330, 332, 338-339, 348, 352, 355-356, 359; orderly resolution, 96; safe harbor, 79-83, 114, 125, 330, 336, 338, 358, 379

Bankruptcy Fairness Act of 2016, 114

Bankruptcy Reform Act of 2005, 306

Barrdear, John, 252, 359, 399

Bartlett, Jamie, 164, 386

Basel III, 35, 113, 351, 366-367

Bear Stearns, 82, 108, 113, 255

Bernanke, Ben, 11, 29, 88-90, 263-264, 303, 361, 365, 375, 386, 400-401

bills of credit, 139-141, 190, 202, 343

Bitcoin, 7, 134, 163-185, 187, 189,

## ABOUT THE AUTHOR

Ellen Brown is an attorney, founder and chairman of the Public Banking Institute, and the author of 13 books and over 350 articles. In the best-selling *Web of Debt*, she shows how a private banking cartel has usurped the power to create money from the people themselves, and how we the people can get it back. In its 2013 sequel The Public Bank Solution, she traces the evolution of two banking models that have competed historically, public and private; and explores contemporary public banking systems globally. She also co-hosts a radio program on PRN.FM called "It's Our Money with Ellen Brown." She has degrees from UC Berkeley and UCLA School of Law, and is a Fellow at The Democracy Collaborative. Her blog articles are posted at EllenBrown.com.

## ABOUT THE DEMOCRACY COLLABORATIVE

The Democracy Collaborative is a research and development lab for the democratic economy.

Learn more at democracycollaborative.org.

CPSIA information can be obtained
at www.ICGtesting.com
Printed in the USA
BVHW092118290519
549636BV00004B/7/P